FAITH AND THE PLAY OF IMAGINATION

On the Role of Imagination in Religion

by

D A V I D   J.   B R Y A N T

MERCER

ISBN 0-86554-319-4 [casebound]
ISBN 0-86554-349-6 [paperback]

Faith and the Play of Imagination
copyright © 1989
Mercer University Press, Macon GA 31207
All rights reserved
Printed in the United States of America

The paper used in this publication meets
the minimum requirements of American National Standard
for Information Sciences—Permanence of Paper
for Printed Library Materials, ANSI Z39.48-1984

Library of Congress Cataloging-in-Publication Data
Bryant, David J.
Faith and the play of imagination / by David J. Bryant.
xiii + 217 pages 15 x 23 cm. 6 x 9—(Studies in American biblical
hermeneutics : 5)
Includes index
ISBN 0-86554-319-4 [casebound] (alk. paper)
ISBN 0-86554-349-6 [paperback] (alk. paper)
1. Imagination—Religious aspects—Christianity. 2. Theology—
Methodology. I. Title. II. Series.
BR115.I6B79 1989   88-37108
230'.01—dc19   CIP

•CONTENTS•

Dedicated to
MARY ANN TRUJILLO

·EDITOR'S PREFACE·

In this book David Bryant explores the necessary prelude for a new North American theology of liberation—a project that occupies many of us in various ways. Indeed, Bryant draws our attention to the concept of imagination as the central component of such a theology. Moreover, if the Studies in American Biblical Hermeneutics series has achieved its own liberation from the "tyranny of the disciplines" and found a genuine interdisciplinary focus in its theological orientation, then no book in the series has a greater claim for standing at its spiritual center. How often do American biblical theologians draw extensive intellectual nourishment from the philosophy of Emmanuel Kant? Bryant does, and is convincing in the way that he does it (cf. the chapter "Kant on the Imagination"). Many of us who went through the ranks of biblical study were told now and again that the science in which we were engaged had little or nothing to do with philosophy. In fact, philosophy seemed in general to have a bad name in our program of study, vaguely implying intellectual domination and/or dogmatism. Our teachers were wrong about it, and Bryant shows us precisely how and why they were wrong. The philosophy was always there; it is only that we were not encouraged to look at it carefully and critically.

Indeed, philosophy has everything to do with biblical study—so do theology and literary criticism, as well as the great works of literature. And that is only the beginning of a truly public reading of the Bible. Study of the Bible is contextual, and those of us who still read it would be well advised to take this contextual component as seriously as does Bryant. We can no longer claim to read the Bible in a categorically different way than we read everything else. In that sense, the democratizing forces unleashed with such force in the eighteenth century have truly created one world. We are all (religionist and nonreligionist) in the same boat now, like it or not. Typically, it seems to me that Americans instinctively know that, yet old habits are not easily forgotten. *Faith and the Play of Imagination* helps us better understand how the loss of precritical biblical sacramentality can represent a great gain in terms of human nourishment. Bryant does this by exploring the relationship between faith, imagination, and theological method in what is a very imaginative way in its own right.

Bryant draws out his argument in conversation with the American theologian Gordon Kaufman. Kaufman's stress on the linguisticality and historicity of human life eliminated the category of revelation. It was replaced somewhat imprecisely with the concept of imagination. From this starting point, Bryant moves to refine our understanding of the nature of imagination itself in order to unveil other paths of illumination for our faith and theological method. Bryant seizes Kaufman's rightful emphasis on the imagination and makes even more of it than Kaufman thought possible. I sensed something of the central importance of this concept in the first book of the series, *Reimagining America,* but in an immensely less sophisticated and self-conscious way than is evidenced in this book. The point in my mind then, as well as now, is simply that what we "know" is only known in a particular historical and cultural context. In conjunction with Bryant's hermeneutics of the imagination, two conclusions result: first, that our experience of the world is mediated by means of imaginative constructions, and second, that the critique of those constructions can also only come about through employing imaginative categories. Thus, in the work of hermeneutics, we find imagination coming in at the initial stages and imagination going out at the final ones. Imagination itself is the constant. In terms of this series, it is the one avenue that bridges the chronological and cultural gap between the Bible and American culture. Small wonder that it is important to glean what insights we can from Kant and whoever else might throw light upon this dimly perceived road!

Bryant's concluding words are most instructive in light of this discussion: "Like fictional texts, the biblical text appeals to the imagination by proposing a possible world in which we could live and realize our inherent possibilities." Our aim is to build a theoretical framework that places the biblical heritage in the mainstream intellectual arena of our cultural debate. Contrary to popular belief among scholars, this task does not simply imply a *deconstruction* (to use an image that may be overworked in our day) of the Bible. Rather, what also begs for our reconsideration is the way that we go about reading the Bible within the context of the community in which we live. The Bible itself cannot liberate us; liberation depends upon reading the Bible with the incipient tools of liberation that our culture provides us. The theological struggle is to engage the Bible in such a way that those tools can be identified and maximized to the fullest extent possible.

Despite the rather extensive discussion of Kant's views on the imagination and certain key hermeneutical turns taken by Hans-Georg Gadamer, the roots of this book run deep into the specific ground of the American theological experience. Kaufman is the central figure in this regard, but Kaufman himself stands in a line of American biblical interpreters that includes, among others, Amos Wilder, Ray Hart, David Tracy, Sallie McFague, and Julian Hartt. In addition, Bryant gives significant place to the work of Paul Ricoeur, who perhaps more than any other hermeneutical thinker bridges the gap between the Continent and America. Doubtlessly, it is this American heritage that enables Bryant to accentuate the role of praxis in the authentic expression of the Christian faith.

As indicated above, however, the real payoff is that this book makes considerable strides in articulating a theological position that is not bound simply to the church, but reaches beyond it to include the American public in general. This position, it seems to me, has been the American tendency from the beginning, the deeper meaning behind the doctrine of separation of church and state. In this regard, perhaps Bryant's position is best summarized in his own words:

> We do not have direct access to the meaning of the biblical text—its meaning emerges only through our conversation with it—so that we cannot presume to have an ahistorical and timeless grasp of its meaning. Consequently, it is only through the interplay of text and present situation, in the context of the effective history of the text, that the meaning of the biblical witness emerges.

This is an eloquent testimony to the rationale for the Studies in American Biblical Hermeneutics series as a whole. The theological meaning of the series, in other words, is *fundamentally* to liberate the Bible from the categories of timelessness in which we have wrapped it. By "fundamentally" I mean the full application of our intellectual powers and insights at every level of the interpretive process, involving both the text as object to be read and reader as text to be studied. No more exegesis in a bottle! To break the logjam of contemporary scholarship that conquers by dividing into the narrow divisions of our specialties, it will be necessary to call upon the intellectual resources of us all. Whatever insight from whatever quarter that helps us to unlock the liberating spirit of the Bible in our particular time and place is game for American biblical hermeneutics, regardless of its point of origin or nationality.

—*Charles Mabee*
Marshall University

• A C K N O W L E D G M E N T S •

During the time this book was taking shape, a number of people were of valuable assistance. I am grateful to each of them. Daniel L. Migliore helped me to form the idea for this project and contributed to its completion through many insightful critiques and suggestions. Mark Kline Taylor proved to be a stimulating and encouraging conversation partner at several crucial points. And Gibson Winter's insights helped to inspire and shape much that is in this work. Finally, I owe an incalculable debt of gratitude to my companion, friend, and wife, Mary Ann Trujillo. She has been a constant source of encouragement and has helped in more ways than I could possibly number. Naturally, any infelicities are my responsibility alone.

·INTRODUCTION·

"Before the message there must be the vision, before the sermon the hymn, before the prose the poem." These words of Amos Wilder suggest that imagination is not a peripheral element of faith but rather is an essential dimension. That Wilder does not mean to treat religious faith as a product of fantasy, and therefore as an interesting but ultimately nonessential part of human life, is evident from his insistence that "human nature and human societies are more deeply motivated by images and fabulations than by ideas. This is where power lies and the future is shaped."[1] That is to say, the shape of our lives and the goals toward which we extend ourselves are rooted in an imaginative interpretation of the world and of our place in it.

Wilder's appreciation of the imaginative dimension of faith finds echoes in many other places. Paul Ricoeur argues that "any ethic that addresses the will in order to demand a decision must be subject to a poetry that opens up new dimensions for the imagination."[2] Taking his start from Ricoeur's formulation, Frederick Herzog maintains that the difference between liberation theology and some of its critics is a difference in the basic shape of the imagination. In this light, he states, "We are struggling to find a new creative imagination to undergird Christian discipleship. . . . The opening up

---

[1]Amos Niven Wilder, *Theopoetic: Theology and the Religious Imagination* (Philadelphia: Fortress Press, 1976) 2.

[2]Paul Ricoeur and Eberhard Jüngel, *Metapher: Zur Hermeneutik religiöser Sprache* (Munich, 1974) 70, as quoted by Frederick Herzog, *Justice Church: The New Function of the Church in North American Christianity* (Maryknoll NY: Orbis Books, 1980) 87.

of new dimensions for the imagination is the foremost challenge of systematic theology as liberation theology in North America."[3] The determinative role of imagination is also affirmed by the observation of George Stroup, at the end of an article on revelation, that "revelation always entails the interpretation and appropriation" of revelatory events, "and the imagination plays an essential role in this process of interpretation."[4] He further notes that contemporary theology has not yet adequately addressed the question of the nature of the imagination and its role in interpreting and appropriating the Christian revelation.

The accuracy of Stroup's observation becomes apparent when one examines some of the major theological works that make use of the term *imagination*. The word tends to be used without any effort to define it or to lay out its significance explicitly for theology. For example, in his recent work, Gordon Kaufman speaks of theology as an imaginative activity of the human subject. Indeed, he has published a book entitled *The Theological Imagination*. However, as one reads this and one of his earlier works that makes much of the imaginative nature of theology, *An Essay on Theological Method*, it becomes clear that we must try to extrapolate what he means by imagination from the general tenor of his proposals, for he gives no explicit definition of it. His discussion reveals a tendency to regard the imagination as the free activity of the human subject, who constructs and reconstructs images or concepts of the world and God in order to create an environment in which we can live humanly and humanely. In other words, Kaufman apparently defines imagination as the power or activity by which the human subject projects meaning, using whatever tools and materials the past may make available.

Another prominent American theologian, David Tracy, has written a book called *The Analogical Imagination*. In spite of using such a title, however, he nowhere explicitly develops what he means by imagination, analogical or otherwise. At certain points, he refers approvingly to some writings of Paul Ricoeur, without fully clarifying his understanding of the term.

Ray Hart's *Unfinished Man and the Imagination* does spend some time dealing with the imagination. In fact, Hart has some insightful things to say about it. However, he focuses on the dissolving and reconstructive

---

[3]Herzog, *Justice Church*, 87.

[4]George Stroup, "Revelation," in *Christian Theology: An Introduction to Its Traditions and Tasks*, ed. Peter C. Hodgson and Robert H. King (Philadelphia: Fortress Press, 1982) 111.

power of the imagination in a way that does not adequately address the issue that is the primary concern of Stroup's observation and of this book. Moreover, he views the imagination as an organon of the will, an understanding that fails to account sufficiently for the degree to which the will itself is shaped by the work of imagination. I will argue that Ricoeur is right to claim that an appeal to the will must be preceded by the opening up of new dimensions for the imagination.

Others have also made use of the notion of imagination without indicating what they mean by the term or how precisely it comes into play in theology. In her recent book *Metaphorical Theology*, Sallie McFague has hinted at the relationship between metaphor and imagination but does not develop the idea at any length. George Lindbeck, too, in his *Nature of Doctrine*, speaks of a place for imagination in theology, without engaging in an examination of imagination, even as it relates to faith and theology. Julian Hartt has written *Theological Method and Imagination*, without saying anything directly about the subject. And Ronald F. Thiemann has written an article entitled "Revelation and Imaginative Construction," in which he critiques Kaufman's tendency to oppose the notions of revelation and imagination and offers his own proposal of how revelation relates to imagination. Yet Thiemann never deals with the nature of the imagination.[5]

This lack becomes especially problematic in light of the sort of arguments raised by Kaufman. His proposal for theological method assumes that a recognition of the imaginative nature of faith entails the conclusion that the viewpoint of faith is an essentially human construction. In this light, he denies that revelation can serve as a methodological foundation for theology and replaces it with human construction, that is, the imagination. Furthermore, since the language of faith is a human construct that has come into being for human purposes, it should be constructed and reconstructed to achieve ends we deem important. In particular, it must serve the ends of relativization and, above all, humanization. Such a proposal raises immediately the question of whether the idea of God should be treated as a tool for making life more human and humane. Does this approach do justice to the origin and meaning of the symbol of God? Or even to the nature of human language in general? Does this method assume a greater autonomy for the human subject than is really the case? What are the implications of the imaginative nature of human life for the-

---

[5]Ronald F. Thiemann, "Revelation and Imaginative Construction," *Journal of Religion* 61 (1981): 242-63.

ology's relationship to the category of revelation? What is the relationship between faith and theology? What sources and criteria should be operative for theology? And how should they come into play? Such questions, arising from Kaufman's program, provide the focus for this book.

Clearly, the issue at the heart of these questions is the nature of the imagination. Given Kaufman's implied definition of the imagination, it must necessarily replace revelation once one recognizes the imaginative character of faith. However, this understanding of the imagination is not without its problems, since, in spite of Kaufman's own historicist stance, it does not sufficiently appreciate the historically determined nature of the imagination's operation. My purpose here is to articulate a different and more adequate view of the imagination, to examine the relationship between faith and imagination, and to explore the implications of this relationship for theological method.

The conclusions that I reach about the imagination do not constitute a claim about the a priori, transcendental foundation for human life, so that imagination could then be taken as the epistemological ground for human knowledge. Rather, the approach to the imagination adopted here treats it as a dimension of the historicity of human life. In line with this approach, I attempt not to treat imagination as a faculty of either the transcendental or empirical self but to focus on certain functions or powers in human life that share a common characteristic that we call the work of imagination. The procedure I have adopted presupposes that an understanding of the operation of the imagination in human life in general will provide some basic insights into the nature of faith as an imaginative venture.

The methodological underpinning for this approach is a method of correlation. That is, my procedure is based on the conviction that there is a correlation between Christian faith and human life, with its questions and responses, that makes it possible to move fruitfully from an exploration of a feature of human life—namely, its generally imaginative character—to an examination of its implications for Christian faith. Christian faith, in other words, does not remove us from our human situation. Consequently, we can expect the latter to have implications for the former. The method of correlation informing my work does not, however, try to find, at some point prior to the actual language and experience of Christian faith itself, some dimension of human life that requires or somehow calls for religious faith. In view of the historicity and linguisticality of human life, I seriously doubt that one can really isolate and demonstrate the existence of such a dimension without a presupposition that already predisposes one to think in such terms. Given such a presupposition, it is indeed possible to point to this dimension of faith and argue for its coherence and adequacy to human experience. But this is a very different move than a transcendental analysis that hopes to provide an abstract description of life at its a priori foundations, an analysis with which all reasonable people must agree.

Since I pursue questions raised by Kaufman's work, I begin in chapter 1 with the development of Kaufman's thought, concentrating on the major parameters of his recent work. Kaufman has always stressed the historicity of human life. Yet, although this insight once provided a basis for a claim that revelation is the necessary starting point for Christian faith and theology, he now combines the concept of historicity with the notion of imagination in such a way as to deny a fundamental position for the category of revelation. He replaces this time-honored, and in his view time-worn, doctrine with the concept of imagination, understood as an essentially constructive power. We construct and reconstruct concepts of the world, the human, and God in order to make possible a human and humane life. The central question I raise is whether imagination should replace revelation in this way. Pivotal to this question is the issue of whether the imagination is both constructive and receptive.

I argue in chapters 2 and 3 that the imagination is indeed constructive and receptive. Its receptivity takes the form of being shaped by the past in a way that attunes it to the interplay between life and world. This understanding of the imagination emerges from a journey that begins with Kant's treatment of the productive, or "transcendental," imagination. His insight into the imagination's powers of synthesis, generalization, and subsumption provides a clue that guides Mary Warnock's description of imagination as the power of "seeing as." She offers a bridge that I use to move from Kant to Paul Ricoeur's treatment of imagination in terms of metaphors and metaphoric process. However, I find that Ricoeur's discussion of the imagination does too little in the way of placing it in its historically determinative context and of describing its intersubjective nature. For this aspect I turn to Hans-Georg Gadamer's models of play and the fusion of horizons. My own understanding of the imagination brings these various elements together by describing it as the power of taking something as something by means of meaningful forms, which are rooted in our history and have the power to disclose truths about life in the world. Creative imagination arises out of the openness of these forms both to new experiences and to new and illuminating combinations of forms.

Chapter 4 then moves to a consideration of how faith is imaginative and what, in light of my description of the imagination, this conclusion means for faith, especially for faith's relationship to the Bible and to the rest of Christian tradition. Kaufman is clearly right to insist that faith is imaginative and that the work of the imagination in faith entails the construal of realities we never encounter within our world. The imagination, therefore, both takes the whole as having a certain meaning by using certain finite realities as analogues of the whole and then takes everything in the world in terms of this construal of the whole. For Christian faith this movement of the imagination is decisively shaped by the biblical testimony to the trace of God in history. The various genres within the Bible have the productive power of redescribing reality in a way that can engage and lead our imaginations. Because Christian faith is thus dependent on the biblical witness, the Bible acts as an authority for the Christian community. Its authority is given stronger grounding by the fact that the Bible functions this way in the context of a community of faith.

I also argue that the Bible comes to us through a lengthy history that shapes our horizon and can productively contribute to our understanding of the meaning of the biblical witness. The Christian imagination, then, is shaped by the biblical witness as it is mediated through Christian traditions. Moreover, since understanding takes the form of a fusion of horizons, I argue that the wider human culture and its history make an important contribution to even the Christian imagination. Because understanding emerges through the play of conversation, the Christian imagination and hence Christian faith are shaped through a dialectical interplay between the Bible, its effective-history in Christian traditions, and the many other dimensions of life contributing to our horizon. Within this conversation, however, the Bible does have a special weight in that the subject matter of the conversation is that to which the Bible gives testimony in a unique and irreplaceable way.

Chapter 5 then draws out the implications of my discussion of imagination and faith for the work of theology. Theology is seen as a second-order conceptual and critical activity that reflects on and critically examines what emerges in the life of faith. The nature of its sources is disclosed through considering the implications of articulating understanding through the model of a fusion of horizons. I argue for a number of sources for theology. The fusion of horizons also helps to inform the discussion of theology's material norm and its criteria of relative adequacy to the situation. In discussing criteria of relative adequacy, I return to Kaufman's criteria to suggest how they might still have a role to play in this approach to theology. Finally, the truth question is considered in light of the concept of disclosure and of the historical claims embedded in the Christian faith.

My intention is not to prove, against Kaufman, that faith and theology are actually in touch with a God who transcends human life. Rather,

I hope to show the inadequacy of Kaufman's understanding of imagination and faith, and therefore of theology, and to develop a possible approach that treats these matters more adequately. I intend to show, in other words, that the Christian theologian can follow the lead of a faith grounded in and shaped by the biblical witness and still be a reasonable person even by contemporary standards. Indeed, there is reason to believe and hope that faith and theology actually have to do with One who has come, comes, and will come to transform our lives and our world.

THEOLOGY AS IMAGINATIVE CONSTRUCTION

The idea that theology is a human enterprise is not new. Even before the modern turn to the subject, theologians were aware that theirs was a human, sometimes all too human, task constantly in need of scrutiny and revision. Nevertheless, theologians in the past have also generally assumed that, although pronouncements of a theological system were to some degree dependent on the work of the human mind, its starting point was divine and therefore beyond question. Thus, Thomas Aquinas was aware that his system was shaped by his own ability to engage in reasoning processes that were heavily indebted to other finite humans, especially Aristotle.[1] Yet he also argued that, unlike other fields of human knowledge, theology is based on first principles given by divine revelation and therefore has the surest foundation of any form of human science.[2] More recently, Karl Barth has insisted, with an impressive show of certainty and consistency, that the origin of Christian faith and theology lies in the fact that "God has spoken"—that is, in the unshakable reality of God's revelation through Jesus Christ.[3] Although Barth's position is not simply a variation on the Thomistic notion of theology as the highest form of science, a similarity remains: even though theology is a human enter-

---

[1]Aquinas, however, exhibited no sense of the historically conditioned nature of Aristotle's thought.

[2]*Summa theologiae*, I, q. 1, arts. 1-10, especially art. 8.

[3]Karl Barth, *Church Dogmatics*, vol. 1, pt. 1, *The Doctrine of the Word of God*, trans. G. W. Bromiley (Edinburgh: T. & T. Clark, 1975) especially 143-62.

prise, its starting point is rooted in divine revelation, a disclosure from beyond ourselves.

This starting point has become problematic for many in our time, including a number of theologians. Gordon D. Kaufman is such a theologian. In 1975 he published an essay that tried to find a grounding for theology that would not take revelation as its basis, that would, as far as theological method is concerned, leave revelation behind as an archaic concept whose usefulness has long since been lost.[4] This is a startling development for a theologian who had, in one of his earliest published articles, strongly argued that the revelation mediated through the biblical witness must be the foundation for Christian life and thought and had developed this point at length in a systematic theology twelve years later.[5] However, even in his early writings one finds themes whose development helped to bring about this dramatic shift. This chapter concerns itself primarily with Kaufman's more recent proposals in order to highlight the issues that they raise.

To help focus these proposals, I explore here Kaufman's earlier work as a prelude to his current work. As appropriate, I also make brief forays into some of the philosophical and theological background to his thought. But the primary purpose throughout the chapter is not to examine Kaufman's thought for its own sake but to clarify the significant issues it brings to the fore. For, even if one does not wish to follow his lead, he has posed some questions that no one who wishes to do theology in our time can afford to ignore.

Kaufman's work merits exposition and analysis for a number of reasons. In the first place, Kaufman is a significant figure in contemporary American theology. Furthermore, his work represents an important example of the continuing influence of neo-Kantian thought on theology today. In particular, his stress on the regulative function of the idea of God is Kantian, though the way in which he anchors and develops his concept of God differs considerably from Kant's approach.[6] Furthermore, Kauf-

---

[4]Gordon D. Kaufman, *An Essay on Theological Method* (Missoula MT: Scholars Press, 1975).

[5]Kaufman, "The Ground of Biblical Authority: Six Theses," *Journal of Bible and Religion* 24 (1956): 25-30; and idem, *Systematic Theology: A Historicist Perspective* (New York: Charles Scribner's Sons, 1968).

[6]For a discussion of the similarities and differences between Kant and Kaufman, see Ronald F. Thiemann, *Revelation and Theology: The Gospel as Narrated Promise* (Notre Dame IN: University of Notre Dame Press, 1985) 49-56.

man's work is strongly influenced by the American pragmatic tradition. Even though he rarely makes explicit use of pragmatic philosophers, his conception of the purpose of theology and of the manner in which one is to judge the adequacy and truth of theological concepts is very close to the pragmatic notion of truth.[7] He thus represents a stream of thought that has had wide influence in American theology.

One fascinating result of the pragmatic strain in Kaufman's thought is that it makes his approach formally similar to the approaches of a number of theologians who differ from him in other important ways. For example, Kaufman's pragmatism closely aligns him, at a formal level, with theologians who understand Christian faith primarily in terms of its function in human life.[8] A number of theologians who take this approach do not share Kaufman's willingness to reject traditional notions of God's reality. On the other hand, functionalist approaches in themselves have few resources to resist the reductionist tendency to assume that faith has to do with nothing beyond human efforts to organize life.[9] Thus, Kaufman has effectively raised a question that grows out of the widely influential functionalist approach, namely, the question of whether theological concepts have to do with a reality transcending human life and the world in which people must find their way, or whether they are articulations of an "intramental" reality. A closely related issue raised by Kaufman is the question of the role of Scripture and tradition in Christian life and thought. For, if theology's purpose and concepts are created by and for humans, why depend on notions formulated in the archaic past?

In a word, Kaufman has served contemporary theology by raising a few of the central questions arising out of the demise of the neo-orthodox consensus. He has done so by adopting a number of perspectives widely shared in American theology today and pursuing them in directions that

---

[7]Kaufman's understanding of the purpose of theological concepts and of the manner in which one assesses their adequacy and truth is developed in detail later in this chapter. As will become apparent, he is not entirely consistent in his pragmatism, yet it does constitute his general approach.

[8]Prominent representatives of this functionalist approach include George Lindbeck, Charles M. Wood, and Paul Holmer.

[9]This is not to say, of course, that theologians in this camp have not tried to overcome this difficulty. See, e.g., George A. Lindbeck's discussion of the truth of Christian faith in *The Nature of Doctrine: Religion and Theology in a Postliberal Age* (Philadelphia: Westminster Press, 1984) 63-69. However, the functionalist approach in itself provides few if any resources for dealing effectively with this issue.

others have eschewed yet that seem to be suggested by the perspectives themselves.

Since Kaufman's thought has consistently come to a focus on issues related to the limitations and possibilities of human life in the world, the analysis of his early work will arrange itself accordingly. Also, since there is a fairly evident break between the publication of *God the Problem* and *An Essay on Theological Method*, the latter work and those following it will be taken as representative of his present position, and all earlier works will be treated as expressions of his earlier thought.[10] This arrangement requires qualification on at least two counts, however. In the first place, Kaufman's treatments of human limitations and possibilities are intimately intertwined, so that focusing on one side alone threatens to distort by failing to see that intrinsic connection. Still, it should be possible to examine each side in a way that brings out its full dimensions without losing sight of its relations to the other side. In the second place, although *Essay on Theological Method* does signal an important shift in Kaufman's position, one can already find some indications in *God the Problem* that the shift is coming, or perhaps has already begun.[11]

---

[10]Naturally, there are also some important continuities between Kaufman's earlier and later thought. Furthermore, his thought has continued to develop after the shift that is the primary focus of this discussion. The warrant for the scheme I am suggesting is the fundamental significance of Kaufman's change of mind about the role of the concepts of revelation and imagination.

[11]See especially "God as Symbol," in *God the Problem* (Cambridge MA: Harvard University Press, 1972) 82-115. There are indications within *God the Problem* that the shift has not yet fully taken place, particularly in the fact that revelation remains a primary methodological principle. See, for example, the chapter "Revelation and Cultural History," 148-70, which was a part of the Andrew C. Zenos Lectures at McCormick Theological Seminary in November 1970 (as was the essay "God as Symbol"). Note also that in his preface Kaufman states that the change of focus between his *Systematic Theology* and *God the Problem* "should not be interpreted as meaning I am retracting the claims of the earlier volume" (p. xii). An indication that revelation remained methodologically important for Kaufman at this time is his article "What Shall We Do with the Bible?" *Interpretation* 25 (1971): 95-112, which appeared just before the publication of *God the Problem*. There he argues that the Bible remains important for Christian faith because it is the primary source document for recovering the revelatory events that are the basis for Christian faith and theology.

It should be noted that the essays in *God the Problem* cover a wide range of time. I could not determine the exact date of the last essay, "The Secular Utility of God-

Following the proposed structure, then, this chapter first discusses Kaufman's early works in order to bring out what they say about the limits to human life and about the nature of the human project within these limits. It then examines how his thought underwent a transformation that was in many ways still continuous with what went before. This comparison will furnish a basis for a closer examination of his understanding and use of imagination. Through this exploration of Kaufman's thought, some questions that go to the heart of the theological enterprise will emerge, as will some critical questions about Kaufman's work.

• Kaufman's Early Work •

The Limits of Human Life

Although Kaufman recognizes several forms of limitation in human life (for example, biological and temporal), the kind of limitation that interests him from the beginning is epistemological. That is, the limits of human life that he stresses again and again are all grounded in the boundaries to what we can know. Such concern arises from the conviction that what we know—at least what we think that we know, about humans and the world in which they live—fundamentally orients our lives.[12] At the same time, Kaufman senses a problem here, in even his earliest writings, because what we "know" about ourselves and our world is actually something we have imaginatively projected rather than something of which we have a clear and certain perception. At its root, the reason for this is that we have no direct perception of reality, whether the object of inquiry is the world or ourselves (32-33).

The view that there is an indirect relationship between our cognitive faculties and that which they cognize is, of course, not new. The work of

---

Talk," but it was written in its present form sometime after 1966 (cf. 258 n. 1). The other essays can be dated as follows: "The Problem of God," 1966 (at least its central substance was published at that time); "Christian Theology and the Scientific Study of Religion," 1970 (Zenos Lectures); "Transcendence without Mythology," 1966 (*Harvard Theological Review*); "Two Models of Transcendence," 1965 (*The Heritage of Christian Thought*); "God as Symbol," 1970 (Zenos Lectures); "On the Meaning of 'Act of God,' " 1968 (*Harvard Theological Review*); "Revelation and Cultural History," 1970 (Zenos Lectures); "God and Evil," 1970 (Zenos Lectures); "Secular, Religious, and Theistic World-Views," 1968 (see 203); and "The Foundations of Belief," 1970 (Zenos Lectures).

[12]See, e.g., Kaufman, *Relativism, Knowledge, and Faith* (Chicago: University of Chicago Press, 1960) 95-103, 114. Subsequent citations are noted in the text and refer to this edition.

Hume and Kant had already firmly established it, as far as many philosophers and theologians of our time are concerned. And, indeed, Kaufman makes several references to Kant as the ultimate source of his own understanding of the limits of human knowledge.[13] In his first book, however, the major foundation for his view of the boundaries imposed on our knowledge does not appear to be Kant's philosophy but the sociology of knowledge, especially as represented by Karl Mannheim (4-5). This fact should not be surprising, since the basic concern of the book is a complex of problems surrounding the claim (well grounded, in Kaufman's view) that all our knowledge is relative. In this context, the realization of limits to our knowledge comes not from the abstract reasoning of logic—which can lead only to the self-contradictory theoretical assertion that we can know no truth—but from the subjective experience of the internal coherence and compelling nature of a variety of points of view that cannot be reconciled with one another. This experience of seeing things from different points of view, without being able to appeal to a logic that transcends them all in order to arrive at a determination of which viewpoint is the right one, leads one to realize that our knowledge is intimately affected by our historicocultural context. Our affirmations about our world and ourselves, then, are not the result of the operations of pure logic working with a direct perception of objects (13-23, 32-33, 47-52).

If this experience is in fact the source of a self-consistent relativism, a type of relativism that Kaufman calls "internal relativism" (13-23),[14] the real foundation for our insight into the limits of knowledge is not the abstract reasoning of philosophy but the operations of the kind of historical consciousness analyzed by Wilhelm Dilthey and R. G. Collingwood. For it is this type of understanding (*Verstehen*), an understanding that penetrates a text in order to reach the original experience of its author and thereby relive or reexperience (*nacherleben*) the author's experience, that makes possible our subjective realization of the cogency of different worldviews (16-17). And Dilthey was able to describe and analyze this kind of understanding better than all others. Thus, work such as his is the real basis of modern relativism, rather than the work of those concerned to analyze perception. "Contemporary relativism is rooted in historical studies rather than in the analysis of perception, and the analysis of per-

---

[13]Kaufman, "Transcendence without Mythology," in *God the Problem*, 55 n. 13, 59 n. 16; idem, "On the Meaning of 'Act of God,' " in ibid., 122.

[14]Here Kaufman echoes H. R. Niebuhr's discussion of "external history" and "internal history" in Niebuhr's *Meaning of Revelation*.

ception which develops follows, rather than precedes, the fundamental insight into the relativistic character of knowledge" (17).

Since Dilthey recognized the historicocultural roots of our knowledge, his analysis of consciousness, in Kaufman's view, helps us to understand the dynamics involved here. Thus, Kaufman's description of the structure of consciousness is largely indebted to Dilthey's work. This description is of interest because the concept of imagination, which becomes increasingly important for Kaufman's thought, emerges here in a significant way. It does so because consciousness, as noted above, is not simply an immediate perception of objects by an already-given self. On the contrary, the emergence of consciousness depends on what happens at a more fundamental, preconscious level of existence (30). At this primordial level there is no awareness of a distinction between subject and object; rather, there are spontaneous drives within the self that encounter resistance from outside forces. The experience of this resistance leads one to the awareness that one is a self in a world of objects. Now if this is an accurate analysis of the foundation and rise of human consciousness, we can see that "the subject-object polarity is in fact an abstraction" (33). And, if an abstraction, it is a construction as well.

Kaufman analyzes the nature of our construction of the subject-object polarity by using the concepts of attention, memory, and imagination. Memory comes into play as that which makes possible a realization that our drives have encountered resistance. For such a realization can occur only when we remember what we desired and see the disparity between that and the circumstances that have actually resulted from our activity (31-32). This, however, is only the most basic level of consciousness. There are other levels as well; and at each, memory plays an essential role, for it makes possible thought about our experiences and therefore the increasingly complex development of our view of the world through comparison, selection of the data we deem important, and arrangement of our experiences of objects into ever more comprehensive wholes. Such cognitive activity results in the development of several "levels" of consciousness. Kaufman lists five levels: (1) the preconscious level noted above, at which, although there is no awareness of a subject over against an object, there is "a flux of sensations" that Dilthey called *Erleben;* (2) the awareness of certain kinds of sensations in certain patterns, which means the emergence of distinctions in our experience and therefore the beginning of consciousness; (3) the experience of these distinct sensations as the experience of a certain object or reality, an experience that depends on distinctions and arrangements provided by one's cultural context; (4) the more abstract forms of interpretation of our experience that give rise to science; and (5) the metaphysical level, which attempts to provide an overall picture of the world within which our experiences at the previous levels can be placed (40-41).

At each level of consciousness, at least beyond the preconscious level of *Erleben*, we do not simply experience the sensa that are there. On the contrary, even at the point of movement from the first to the second level, distinctions are possible because, using the power of attention, we focus on certain aspects of the total field and disregard other aspects. And this activity, in turn, is not possible without the work of imagination.

> Since our sensa are in time, they would always be carried away before we could really attend to them unless we could, through imagination, transform them into something no longer subject to the constant movement of time and hence, strictly speaking, no longer sensa. Through the dual activity of attention and imagination they become a complex product, a sensum conjoined and fused with the memory of previous data by the constructive power of imagination. (40)

This intimate cooperation of memory, attention, and imagination is present at each level. Indeed, "imaginative construction" becomes increasingly elaborate at the higher levels of consciousness, since each higher level must try to incorporate wider bodies of data than the prior level (42). Kaufman summarizes the nature of this operation in a few sentences.

> At each level in the movement of consciousness, selective attention, co-operating with constructive imagination, operates to draw certain elements out of the level immediately beneath, in order to construct a somewhat different but more inclusive set of relationships than are to be found there. In no case is the succeeding level "determined" by the preceding one, and yet it is always based on "clues" provided by the preceding level and on which we focus our attention, but which are interpretable in varying ways. Once attention has focused on certain clues as the significant ones to follow in moving from a lower to a higher level, and an appropriate imaginative interpretation of those clues has been made, the work need not be done over again in the same "original" fashion each time a similar situation arises. (44-45)

We see here, then, in regard to our epistemological limits, an inability to get to sensa, or experiences of anything, including our very selves, except through a tissue created by imagination, attention, and memory. As the last sentence quoted suggests, this tissue is not created anew in each moment of life but is given to us through our previous experience. Thus, our prior history has a profound influence on the way we see things. And not just our own personal histories, for our historicocultural context, which is mediated to us through language, fundamentally shapes our perception of our environment and ourselves (45-52).[15] Our limited viewpoint, which makes all our knowledge relative, is therefore not only the product of our individual, limited cognitive faculties—though this is the foundation for all other limitations. It is also the result of the limitations imposed by the perspective of our culture and its history. In light of the historical roots of our limited perspective, Kaufman refers to the limited nature of human life as the "historicity" of human life. We are, in a word, historical beings through and through because we are beings whose experience of the world is mediated through an imaginative construction that is in large measure given to us by our historicocultural situation.

As already suggested, this indirect relationship between our cognitive faculties and that which they cognize means that we lack any direct, apodictic knowledge of our environment or ourselves. For all experiences of the self or of objects in the world occur within an imaginatively constructed view of the meaning of these experiences. To be sure, we cannot make just anything of our world and ourselves. There are limits to the various possibilities for interpreting our experiences, since we do in fact encounter resistance from something beyond ourselves. Some interpretations, then, will be unable to account for the sensa that impinge on us. Nevertheless, a wide range of possible views remains. The many different outlooks of various cultures, which probably do not exhaust the range of plausible options, clearly demonstrate this fact.

Now if this variability is true of both our world and ourselves, of which we do have some (interpreted) sensory experience, how much more will it hold for our views of God, of whom we have no sensory experience at all? While some may wish to challenge Kaufman's insistence that God is wholly unavailable to our senses, he has been adamant on this point from the first. For Kaufman (clearly reflecting views of Paul Tillich), *God* refers not to an object among objects but to the ground of all existence. As such, God cannot be experienced as finite beings are experienced. Indeed, God cannot even be said to exist or not to exist, except in some symbolic use of this terminology, since such terminology generally refers to finite existents (114). Talk of God's existence—or any talk of God at all—is symbolic because all language comes from our experience of limited objects

---

[15]Language, which includes not only words but all meaningfully patterned actions, is the indispensable medium for the communication of culture and the formulation of our ideas and concepts. Hence it is an essential ingredient in our knowledge and perspective. Cf. p. 51.

in the world and hence, when taken literally, is an inadequate pointer to the unlimited ground of the world. A nonliteral, symbolic use of language, however, can help to convey something of this reality so that it can provide our lives with orientation and meaning. Now such an orientation is not simply given to us. Rather, it is an orientation that we have constructed with the use of memory, imagination, and attention. The justification of any particular orientation, therefore, cannot base itself on a simple appeal to what our senses perceive or our logic concludes—though neither experience nor logic is irrelevant (116). The ultimate court of appeal, Kaufman argues in his first book, is nothing other than our own subjective judgment, which is concerned to see whether any proposed metaphysical stance is sufficiently comprehensive, self-consistent, and coherent to be plausible (81-86).[16]

Under such circumstances, our contact with any reality beyond ourselves would seem to be tenuous at best. Some sort of reliable contact with an ultimate reality we call God would appear to be out of the question. Even in his early work Kaufman is clear on this point: we can have no contact with God through our experience or reason. If there is to be any contact between humanity and its divine ground, it can only be through a divine act of revelation. Prior to the publication of *An Essay on Theological Method,* Kaufman maintained that Christian faith and theology affirmed the reality of such a revelation and operated accordingly. Yet even in *God the Problem* one can see a significant attenuation of the relationship between the believer and ultimate reality, or God. In an essay entitled "God as Symbol," Kaufman had already begun to emphasize the imaginative nature of theological statements in such a way as to justify the work of theology without recourse to the idea of revelation.

Kaufman's stress on the imaginative nature of theological proposals here turns on a distinction between what he calls the "real God" and the "available God." The real God is the reality to which all talk of God ultimately refers, that is, the "real referent." This God is utterly transcendent, exceeding all human thought, so that it is an unknown and unknowable X. About the real God we can say nothing, not even that it exists. This inability on our part, it should be noted, is grounded as much in the nature of what we mean by God as it is in the limits of human knowledge. For God is by definition a reality that "transcends our knowledge in modes and ways of which we can never be aware and of which we have no inkling." Such a God cannot

---

[16]This is true in spite of the resistance subjects experience, since the meaning of such resistance is open to a number of interpretations.

provide a concrete orientation for life, since it is devoid of material content. At most, the real God serves as a "limiting idea," relativizing all our statements about God by constantly reminding us of their inadequacy in the face of an ineffable mystery.[17]

In spite of our ignorance, however, we do continue to speak about God, for only in this way can God function as a source of meaning and value for us. This God of whom we speak is the available God, who falls short of the real God, while at the same time mediating to us whatever knowledge we have of God. This trap of potential inconsistencies is escaped by Kaufman through an insistence that faith affirmations are life-policy affirmations rather than assertions about what exists in the realm of the transcendent. That is, a statement of belief in God (or the gods) is actually an affirmation that the world is ultimately congenial to human life, values, and purposes—that is, that our human purposing, valuing, and acting are not epiphenomenal but solidly grounded in the ultimate nature of things. The real meaning of theistic faith, then, is not its assertions about a God (or gods) but its expression of a life policy that is congruent with this understanding of our world and its metaphysical grounding. Moreover, this approach to the world is the result of an imaginatively constructed view of the way things are.[18]

Those who live by this faith indeed do not treat it as a mere hypothesis that may or may not be true. On the contrary, to live by this faith is to take it as the deepest and most important truth in life. Nothing is as real or as important for the believer as God. But when one takes this position, one is speaking of the material content mediated to us through the available God. When speaking in light of the real referent of God-language, the real God—in other words, when speaking formally about our concept of God—it is necessary to remember that "God" is our construct and that we cannot know God or even whether God exists. Kaufman sums up this tension-filled (if not contradictory) situation in these words:

> [The available] God will be the most objective or real element of the believer's phenomenological world, for, as the source and ground of all else, he provides the order or structure of all that has meaning and can be experienced, and he gives direction and purpose to the historical process. Thus, although formally (like any other cultural element) the available God is a human construct, created by men in the process of dealing with the exigencies of life,

---

[17]Kaufman, "God as Symbol," 85-86.

[18]Ibid., 86, 88-94, 101.

materially he is grasped as the most Real of all the Realities of experience and the world.[19]

This is not a mere shadow play put on by humans to amuse themselves
or to comfort themselves in the face of the abyss. It is, rather, an inevitable activity engaged in by beings who must act and who must therefore
project an ultimate environment in which to orient their actions.[20] Furthermore, this projection will not be understood as merely imaginary if
the "double-layeredness" of the idea of God is taken seriously. For the
tension between the real and available God means that God is not just a
"reality" of which we speak but is a symbol for the ultimate reality transcending even our talk of it and therefore relativizing that talk.

Thus, even though Kaufman insists that God is not merely imaginary,
the connection between the God in whom one trusts and the reality to
which it refers has become very difficult to maintain. In place of a confi-
dence in God's revelation has come a belief in the necessity of some metaphysical stance and in the appropriateness of a stance that views reality
as congenial to moral and personal existence. As before, Kaufman is convinced that human life runs its course within limits set by our historicocultural situation. We live on the basis of imaginative construals of the
world, the self, and ultimate reality. Unlike before, however, the imaginative construal of ultimate reality appears to be grounded only in human needs and possibilities and not at all in a revelation of the God who
transcends us. But this is to jump too far ahead. Before looking at the new
position that is foreshadowed in "God as Symbol" and emerges full-blown
in *An Essay on Theological Method*, we must say something more about the
nature of the human project as Kaufman describes it in his early work.

The Human Project

The limits under which we live should not be seen in a primarily negative way, for our historicity is in fact the basis for our creativity. Historicity is the essence of human life—so much so that it is the *imago Dei* that
sets human life apart from all other forms of life. God, too, has a history
in which the reality of the divine "person" comes to be through God's
own action. This is the meaning of God's "aseity." That is, God has aseity
not because of an impassivity that is unresponsive to what happens in
creation but because the divine reality has its basis in itself alone. God is
self-grounding. Moreover, this self-groundedness is the presupposition

[19]Ibid., 92.

[20]Ibid., 100-15.

for God's history with the world, since it allows for a dynamic under-standing of the divine reality, an understanding of God as coming to be through God's intratrinitarian activity, which is the basis for God's extra-trinitarian activity.

> Whereas God's aseity expresses the fact that God comes from noth-ing else than himself, God's history is the process through which this movement or development of the living God proceeds. This inter-pretation of God's aseity leads directly into the doctrine of the Trin-ity, which is simply the attempt to understand God's nature, in historico-ontological terms, through the notions of the relations of derivation and dependence among the three persons.[21]

Since humans are also beings whose nature comes to be through their histories, there is a sense in which human life, too, is self-grounded or self-created. To be sure, human life is grounded in other things as well, and ultimately in God's creative activity. Yet this self-creative dimension of human life, which is possible because of the historicity of human life, is a reflection of God's creativity and is therefore the image of God of which the creation account speaks. Thus, our historically limited position is an opportunity for creative activity as well as a restriction of our knowledge.

Not only are our limitations closely linked to our creative potential, they make talk about God a meaningful form of discourse. At one time people accepted the meaningfulness of theistic discourse because of a dualistic understanding of reality. That is, most people in the Western world believed that there were two worlds, the one in which we spent our allotted time on earth and another inhabited by God and the hosts of heaven. Such forms of thought have become increasingly unacceptable for people in modern society, so that another way of conceiving the meaningfulness of talk about God must now arise—unless we wish to abandon theistic language as a relic of the past. For Kaufman, a new basis for God-talk does exist in the fact that we know ourselves as essentially finite beings. To be finite or limited is to be bounded by something that sets limits to our activity. Now when we are so hemmed in by something that we cannot find a vantage point from which to view it, we have no way of knowing the real nature of such a barrier. We can conceive of it only in terms drawn from our experiences of finite barriers.

Kaufman classifies such barriers into four types: external physical lim-itations, internal organic limitations, personal restrictions coming from

---

[21]Kaufman, "The Imago Dei as Man's Historicity," *Journal of Religion* 36 (1956): 157-68, 163.

other selves, and normative constraints.[22] Theism emerges when the third type of barrier is taken to be the kind that sets the ultimate limit to human life. That is to say, when our finitude is taken to be the result of the activity of an agent who grounds our lives and gives them their limits, we are thinking in theistic categories. Furthermore, this way of conceiving ourselves and our world does not depend on the old form of dualism that believed in two worlds. Rather, it depends only on the idea that we are essentially limited beings who are restricted by a reality best characterized as an agent. To be sure, one is not forced to suppose that our finitude means that there is a God who grounds human life. But the recognition of human finitude does at least provide a foundation for the meaningfulness of discourse about God. To talk about God is to talk about the reality on the other side of the limit.

While we are not compelled to believe in God, Kaufman insists that some ultimate, metaphysical view of the nature of reality is necessary for human life. Early on, Kaufman made this claim on the basis of his definition of meaning as the perception of how something fits into a larger framework. This larger framework can and does expand to the point that it ultimately includes the whole of reality. On this basis, he argues, "the meaning of any assertion I can make presupposes a faith that my life has some sort of meaning, and the meaning of my life can be apprehended and understood only in relation to the whole of human history" (112). We need such a meaningful framework not only because of a cognitive need for meaning but also because of a moral need for the orientation that such a meaningful framework provides. Indeed, Kaufman maintains that any intentional human action requires at least an implicit view of the ultimate nature of things. In the earliest phase of his thought, his argument took the form of an insistence that our sense of the good is dependent on our understanding of the total framework for life. We do not have a given moral standard by which we can operate but require an understanding of the whole, an understanding that shapes our moral insight. In fact, from the Christian perspective, human moral insight has been distorted by sin, so that it is necessary to turn to God's act of revelation to discover the good and to God's act of redemption to enable us to accomplish it.[23]

To begin with our own conception of human possibility is therefore a serious mistake, since such a move fails to realize that God's revelation

---

[22]Kaufman, "Transcendence without Mythology," 56.

[23]Kaufman, *The Context of Decision: A Theological Analysis* (New York: Abingdon Press, 1961) 28-29.

reshapes all our ideas about human life and good.[24] Thus, the early Kaufman denied that one can begin from human ideals. "For Christian ethics, right and wrong cannot be decided merely in terms of the present situation in history, however impregnated with ideals our situation may appear to be. For the Christian ethic is historical-eschatological: it takes its bearings, not from what seems real and obvious in the present, but from the living past and the hoped for future." In fact, only in light of the Christian memory of the past and hope for the future does the Christian moral life seem reasonable; for without the hope that God is actually transforming the world "into his kingdom of love it would be meaningless and absurd for us to give our lives in absolute self-sacrifice and love."[25] In short, we live in conformity and response to what we take to be the nature of life's ultimate framework. For the Christian, this ultimate framework is an active, loving will.

In light of the need for such a meaningful context for life, Kaufman rejects contemporary philosophical arguments against metaphysical speculation, arguing instead that metaphysical construction is proper and necessary for philosophy (100-103, 114). He naturally does not mean that philosophy can in fact arrive at a definitive determination of the nature of reality. He merely means that philosophy must engage in the task of bringing "thinking going on in the cultural process to over-all unity from a definite point of view" (90).

Theology also has the task of developing such a unified point of view. However, whereas philosophy does so in terms of a rational philosophical tradition and strives toward universality in its terms, theology develops a unified viewpoint through the investigation and criticism of a particular religious tradition (though it intends to be no less universal than philosophy) (104, 133). Theology will therefore use theistic categories from the start in its effort to arrive at a comprehensive and unified view of life.

In this early period of his writing, Kaufman was sure that theology's statements about the ultimate environment of life were possible only on the basis of a revelation from "beyond" our spatiotemporal world. Since our knowledge cannot break out of its limited perspective on its own, it is dependent on what it receives from God's acts of self-manifestation for its affirmations. "Only if there were and is some sort of movement from beyond the Limit to us, making known to us through the medium of the Limit the reality of that which lies beyond, could we be in a position to

---

[24]Ibid., 51.

[25]Ibid., 62, 60.

speak of such a reality at all; only if God actually 'spoke' to man could we know there is a God."[26] The Christian claim is that such movement has in fact happened. In Jesus Christ and the history leading up to him, we have a revelational history in which God has made it possible for us to know and respond to the reality that grounds all life.

Now to state that revelation is the self-manifestation of God is to make a claim about a peculiar sort of knowledge, for, as we have seen, God is a reality of a different order than objects we perceive in our environment. God is not an item in our world but its very foundation and goal. When we consider knowledge of God, then, we are considering something other than information about objects or situations in the world. This is not to say that revelation is irrelevant to our world. On the contrary, it has great, even ultimately determinative, significance for everything that concerns us. However, it has such importance not because it conveys new information about ourselves and our world—if by "information" we mean new data that have to date been undetected by scientific research—but because it provides us with a definite point of view from which to understand whatever we discover about all finite realities. It is, therefore, the foundation for the self's fundamental orientation in life—that is, its basic structure of meanings and values.[27] In short, the concept of revelation has in view the foundational "reality" in a human life. "Revelation refers . . . to that locus in experience through which men discover themselves in relation to the ultimately real, the norm or standard in terms of which all other reality is defined for them, and beside which, therefore, all other realities are necessarily perceived as of lesser significance and meaning" (19).

For Kaufman, the Christian revelation, although possessing some characteristics unique to itself, is analogous to all foundations for human frameworks of value and meaning. For everyone must look to some ultimately unproven and unprovable basis for life's fundamental orientation—unproven and unprovable because such a basis is the presupposition for any type of demonstration and thus lies outside of all proof (21-22). In this context, revelation means "that process or event through which the Reality in terms of which we measure and judge all other realities encounters us" (22).

That the locus of revelation is always an event or process is a natural implication of the historicity of human life. For we are what our past—

---

[26]Kaufman "Transcendence without Mythology," 71.

[27]Cf. Kaufman, *Systematic Theology*, 18-27. Subsequent citations are noted in the text and refer to this edition.

both collective and individual—has made us. The history of our culture becomes ours through its linguistic and role systems, systems carrying categories, relationships, and interpretations that become our own as we are taught the language and roles of our society. Furthermore, each of us has an individual history through which we have come to view the world in a certain way. And, in both our collective and personal histories, certain events stand out as crucial keys to the meaning of the whole.

> This radically historical character of selfhood means that the ontological foundations of our deepest convictions are in history. Our beliefs and values, our criteria and norms, have come to us out of a social and personal past in which they first emerged in germ and gradually were formed. Thus, certain crucial events (of which we may be completely unaware) are the ontological ground of our values and norms. If these events had not occurred, our convictions and standards would be other than they are, and we would be different persons. (25)[28]

Using the term in a loose sense, such events "can be described as 'revelatory' in a special sense not only because their meaning and significance seems self-evident to the adherent of the perspective, needing no further explanation in terms of some other deeper or more intelligible ground, but also because they throw their light on all the rest of experience, 'revealing' its meaning" (27).

If everyone's structure of meanings and values is ultimately rooted in such events, it is also true that calling these events revelatory is not entirely proper in every case. The term fits in the senses already described. However, in one crucial respect only theistic frameworks can use the term *revelation* in its proper sense, for revelation refers to what happens between persons. That is to say, revelation has to do with the activity of self-manifestation, the unveiling of the inner being of a person. A unique quality of persons is their essential inaccessibility to mere external observation. Naturally, we can observe others and learn much about them in this way. Yet there is a part of a person, the most characteristic part, that can and will remain hidden from our view until that person chooses to reveal it through words and actions. Persons, after all, are not merely actors, but actors with a will. And it is the will, the intentions embodied in the actions, that constitutes a person's identity (33-40). The term *revelation*, then, most properly refers to the unveiling of those things that are

---

[28]The dependence on H. R. Niebuhr here is clear and explicitly acknowledged by Kaufman (see p. 23).

in principle unavailable to us until they are voluntarily made known by another person. It is this meaning that the term has for Christian faith, which speaks of the unveiling of the unique person, God.

In the case of Christian faith, the "person" who reveals something is not one among several subjects, a fact that presents some unique problems. Interpersonal communication takes place within a shared context of meaning, a common language and often a common cultural background. But what language do God and humans have in common? Clearly, God could not just come and speak to humans in order to make Godself known. Somehow, a conceptuality that makes it possible for people to come to know God had to emerge, something that, given the nature of human understanding, could come about only through a long, slow development. Kaufman argues that the history leading up to Israel and, finally, to Jesus includes precisely such a development. Prior to Israel's encounters with Yahweh, people gradually developed notions about a transcendent ground for life by formulating ideas about the gods. This process, according to Kaufman, was God's way of preparing people to recognize the hand of Yahweh in the events constituting Israel. Furthermore, this conceptuality was further refined throughout Israel's history, preparing the way for the recognition of God's revelation in the person of Jesus, who, for Christians, is God's definitive revelation.[29] Here something from beyond history, which we could not possibly know on our own, has entered into history to transform it by giving it new possibilities (41-56).

The transformation effected by revelation is of a sort that is consonant with free and spontaneous interpersonal relationships. God does not break into our world in a way that disrupts the chain of cause and effect or that coerces the one who receives the revelation into an unwilling response. Rather, just as two people respond freely to each other when they are engaged in open, spontaneous interaction, the recipient of a revelatory experience responds because the revelation has reached the center of the person and thereby brought a new, fundamental insight (38-39). Thus, in a revelatory experience an individual is confronted by a reality that comes from outside the self but that is so closely related to the self that a new person emerges from the experience.

Kaufman's belief in the centrality of revelation for Christian faith has far-reaching implications for the nature of the theological task. For, if Christian thought must root itself in God's revelatory acts, the church's

---

[29]Ibid., 41-56; "Revelation and Cultural History," in *God the Problem*, 148-70.

ideas and language must continually be examined and reformulated in light of those acts. In other words, "Christian theology is the critical analysis and creative development of the language utilized in apprehending, understanding, and interpreting God's acts, facilitating their communication in word and deed" (57). In light of the historically limited nature of all human thought, this task exceeds the grasp of any theologian or time. Furthermore, since God transcends all our experience, language, and ideas, theology is dealing with a reality that it cannot begin to contain in its systems of thought. Hence, theology, though necessary, can never suppose that it has completed its task. Rather, Kaufman insists that "theology remains forever a demand as well as an achievement" (80).

The goal of theology's work is the understanding of God's revelation in its relation to the theologian's own situation, and the understanding of the theologian's own situation in light of God's revelation. In the first place, then, theology must seek to uncover the historical acts that Christian faith takes as revelatory. That is to say, it is important to try to reconstruct, through an act of the historical imagination and with the help of all the critical tools at our disposal, the original revelatory events, since these events are the locus of God's self-manifestation. Moreover, theology must seek to understand these events in their revelatoriness, that is, in their function as the foundation of the Christian structure of values and meanings. To do so, one must turn to the primary source-document that tells of these events and of their significance for Christian faith—that is, to the Bible. The Bible thus rightly plays the central role in Christian theology.

Yet, while it has a pivotal role to play, the Bible's authority is not absolute, for it must remain subservient to the events to which it points. Furthermore, it is not the only authority in theology, for our understanding of the Bible depends in part on the community within which we live and interpret the biblical text. This community, then, also functions as an authority through the perspectives and categories it gives to the theologian. However, the theologian does not—must not—let the community think for him or her. On the contrary, it is important for the theologian to arrive at his or her own insight into the meaning of God's revelation, so that the theologian's own understanding also serves as an authority. Yet none of these authorities—the Bible, tradition, and the theologian— is anything more than a "proximate authority," since the only final authority is the event itself, that is, the historical event to which the Bible witnesses. Moreover, the role of each proximate authority is determined by its relation to this event (63-75). It is important to note that, at this period in his life, Kaufman was not afraid to speak of an authority to which theology is subject.

In this search for understanding, the ultimate authority of God's revelatory act over every phase of theological work must not be forgotten. Christian theology is not simply the work of autonomous man thinking whatever he pleases; on the contrary, it is produced when men seek deliberatively to subject their thinking to the authority of God's revelation. Since the revelation is apprehended as the right and proper source of the ultimate norms of meaning and truth, to work independently of it could only mean attempting invalid and finally meaningless intellectual activity. . . . everything . . . stands under some authority in the sense of more or less spontaneously turning in some particular direction to some particular locus when he seeks truth. . . . From a Christian point of view, however, if one's authority is less or other than the very revelation of God, it is idolatrous and enslaving. (65-66)

The authority of God's revelation does not mean that theology is interested in formulating systems that focus only on the revelatory events. Such an approach would deny an essential dimension of the revelatoriness of these events, namely, their power to illuminate all of life. If this power is taken seriously, the theologian will seek to bring every aspect of life into relation to God's revelation. In other words, the theologian will view revelation from the perspective of the situation in which he or she lives, and the situation in which he or she lives from the perspective of God's revelation (75).[30] All that comes to us from "the wide reaches of our world" is thus another source for theology. For, by bringing these materials into the work of theology, we show the meaningfulness of the Christian revelation; that is, we demonstrate that it makes sense. In light of this double-sidedness of the theological enterprise, it is apparent that theology operates with two "fundamental norms": (1) the historical norm, that is, the revelatory history; and (2) the experiential norm, that is, the experience to which our theology must be relevant (73-78).

Such a distinction does not mean that theology should, or even can, operate with criteria that come from outside of God's revelatory acts. On the contrary, since our basic orientation is grounded in what we take to be revelatory of the ultimately real, "our very criteria of adequacy are always rooted in the authority before which we have already bowed" (65). The experiential norm, then, is not a source of criteria that are independent of the Christian revelation. Rather, it refers to that realm within which God's revelation is to operate in an illuminating manner. It functions as a norm because a failure of the revelation to provide such illumination

---

[30]See also Kaufman, "Revelation and Cultural History," 168 n. 12.

would throw its revelatory power into serious question. That is to say, the way in which the Christian revelation impinges on the present situation displays its meaning (in a time-bound way). Thus, the significance of revelation cannot be viewed as a self-contained thing, which we merely explain in terms of itself. Instead, its significance lies in its meaningfulness for one's situation, so that every theological system must relate God's revelation to the present. Consequently, our present experience is normative in that through it we determine whether the revelation "makes sense." The Christian theologian operates with the conviction that the Christian revelation does indeed make sense, for he or she has experienced its power to illumine life. "To be a Christian theologian is to believe that a Christian interpretation does justice to the facts of experience and, indeed, illuminates them in ways other views do not. Such a one seeks, therefore, his defining categories in the Christian revelation and attempts to discipline his judgments and his criteria of judgment with reference to that (historical) norm" (76-77).

A significant implication of Kaufman's stress on revelatory events as the final authority for theology, as opposed to all proximate authorities, is the central role that thereby accrues to "the reconstructing 'historical imagination' (faith)" (71). Like the historian, the theologian has no direct access to the events with which he or she is primarily concerned. Instead, using whatever sources are available and the historian's critical tools, the theologian must try to reconstruct the event, to envision what it was like. This is an imaginative task. Yet the imagination is not in a position of preeminence on this account, for its role is to seek out the historical event as best it can. Still, since the event is not present to us, not even in the sources through which we learn of it, only the imagination can mediate it to us. Thus, although the event is primary, it can have this position only because we are able to bring it into our present through an act of "the reconstructing 'historical imagination' (faith)." Without this imaginative activity—or, in the case of the Christian, this act of faith that perceives both the event and its revelatory power—there could be no revelation from the past.

Whereas revelation is crucial to Kaufman's *Systematic Theology*, providing the epistemological basis for his theological work, his next book, *God the Problem*, gives indications of some important qualifications of this view. To be sure, he still notes that we cannot talk about God without a revelation that opens our eyes to God's existence and nature.[31] On the

---

[31]Kaufman, "Transcendence without Mythology," 71.

other hand, the ontological status of this revelation becomes quite problematic as a result of certain emphases that emerge here. In particular, the distinction that he draws, in the essay "God as Symbol," between the "real God" and the "available God" leaves open the question of the relationship between these two. For the available God is a human construct that is supposed to provide a framework for human life, whereas the real God so transcends human life that we can know nothing about such a God. The real God is a limiting concept that relativizes everything said about the available God. Even the existence of the real God is something we cannot affirm without falling into the contradiction of trying to say something about that which transcends our knowledge. In short, we seem to be left without any basis for believing that there is some sort of positive relationship between the real God and the available God.

Nevertheless, Kaufman does suggest that a positive relationship exists here. Specifically, our construction of God "is intended to be a symbolization of the ultimate reality with which we have to do; it is supposed to represent with some measure of adequacy 'how things really are.' " Since this statement comes in an essay devoted to an exposition of the idea of revelation, the positive connection between our construction and the real God is presumably made possible by the revelatory acts of God. But to say this is to highlight the problem we face, for claims about God's acts, even God's acts of revelation, put us in the realm of the available God, since we can say nothing like this about the real God. In other words, affirmations about God's revelation are also (nothing more than?) human constructs whose connection with the real God remains highly problematic. To assert, as Kaufman does, that those who live and think in terms of a faith in God "perceive him as the Real, the ultimate reality with which we have to do, the One in terms of whom all life and experience must be ordered" does not resolve the dilemma.[32] The same can be said of any construction of the ultimately real that one makes and in which one puts one's faith. Of course a believer will perceive the object of belief as real. This is a tautology. But if one is convinced that reality is beyond knowledge or speech, on what basis do we believe any construction?

Kaufman answers this question in *God the Problem* by speaking not of revelation but of the pragmatic power of a construction; a faith's ability to make sense of life, to provide a meaningful guide for one's actions, is

---

[32]Kaufman, "Revelation and Cultural History," 169 n. 13.

the real test of its trustworthiness.[33] Thus, the first question one asks about the Christian faith is not whether the God of whom it speaks exists but "whether this is an appropriate life-policy for men to adopt." In this sense, the real concern is not whether the Christian faith is true, but whether it is right. As Kaufman expresses it, "To say 'I believe in God,' I am suggesting, is more an expression of a life-policy one has adopted, an expression of how one does, or ought to, comport oneself, than it is an expression of what one believes factually to be the case." Thus, the imaginatively constructed symbol of God is intimately connected to moral action. Although Kaufman does not clearly spell out the nature of this connection, he does give a general description that suggests a different approach than the one he had articulated earlier. At one point the nature of this connection receives some attention in the context of considering the need to critique former ideas of God in order to construct a conception of God that will truly enhance human life.

> It is clear that not every conception of God—not even every "Christian" conception—helps to support, sustain, and develop man's moral sensitivity and activity by providing the indispensable metaphysical foundation for the vision of the world as a moral universe, an order within which personal existence finds ultimate metaphysical sustenance, and human and humanizing action is not only right but ultimately reasonable. For this reason (as well as others) a contemporary Christian doctrine of God dare not be constructed on the basis of an uncritical use of either traditional or biblical imagery: all such must be thoroughly criticized and reformulated in the light of criteria based on the image of that helpless, nonresistant suffering figure dying on a cross. Only such a radically loving, forgiving, suffering God can metaphysically sustain and further enhance our moral sensitivity in face of the terrifying evils in today's world.[34]

---

[33]Kaufman, "The Foundations of Belief," in *God the Problem*, 226-56. The difference at this point between *God the Problem* and *Systematic Theology* may in part be a difference in focus, the former being devoted to an exploration of the experiential roots of theology (see p. xii in the former). But Kaufman's statements in an essay such as "God as Symbol" betray a greater difference in principle between these two works than his explanation in the preface of *God the Problem* suggests.

[34]Kaufman, "God as Symbol," 107, 108 n. 26, 112 n. 31.

In its reference to the "suffering figure dying on a cross," this statement still reflects Kaufman's earlier insistence that our criteria of moral judgment are rooted in a revelatory event. Yet this "revelatory event" does not appear to be self-evident and capable of illuminating all other realms of life in the way such events are supposed to, for Kaufman provides a warrant for turning to the cross by appealing to what will "sustain and further enhance our moral sensitivity." That is to say, we already have some authentic and trustworthy "impulses toward the moral life," which "are supported and reinforced" by the idea that the world is a moral universe grounded in the reality of God.[35] In such statements as these, Kaufman implies that we already have a sense of what is humane and humanizing, a sense that provides criteria for judging that which would give us an "indispensible metaphysical foundation for a vision of the world as a moral universe." Thus, this "metaphysical foundation" does not function as the foundation of what we perceive as morally good but as a foundation for a moral vision of the world that can sustain and give important encouragement to our efforts to live in a way that we already know is good. Our metaphysical constructs, then, explicitly draw out the implications of our action for the ultimate nature of things. Kaufman does not yet provide a clear and unequivocal declaration of independence for our moral sense. Nonetheless, he does indicate an important move away from his earlier understanding of the relationship between metaphysics and morals and, in so doing, foreshadows the self-conscious shift in theological method that clearly emerges for the first time in his next book, *An Essay on Theological Method.*

Kaufman's argument in "God as Symbol" has a distinctively Kantian character. Like Kant, he assumes a moral sense that can then become the basis for making nontheoretical statements about God.[36] Unlike Kant, however, Kaufman does not explain what this moral sense is or how it arises. Another problem in Kaufman's discussion (in this case, a problem shared by both Kaufman and Kant) is the inconsistency involved in positing God as the ground of the moral life, when the moral life grounds itself. Why should we introduce the concept of God when the moral life itself expresses its demands and demonstrates its possibility through concrete action in accordance with those demands? Whatever the problems in this essay, however, "God as Symbol" foreshadowed what was to come.

---

[35]Ibid., 109.

[36]Kaufman explicitly appeals to Kant at several points. See ibid., pp. 101, n. 21, 109 n. 28, 114 n. 33.

• Kaufman's Recent Work •

In his *Essay on Theological Method*, Kaufman notes at one point that he now regards "the methodological foundations of theology" that were set forth in his *Systematic Theology* "as seriously misleading," especially in the "somewhat simplistic view of 'revelation' " that he had presented there.[37] He thereby explicitly alerts his readers to the fact that this work signals a new stage in his thought.[38] The degree to which this is true is indicated by his statements about revelation quoted above. Whereas he had earlier claimed that Christian faith and theology must look to revelation as the foundation for talk about God, a foundation beyond which there is no appeal, he firmly rejects such ideas in this later work. All efforts to begin with God's revelation, he argues, presuppose something that needs explanation and justification, namely, the very concepts of God and revelation (2).

Calling theological approaches that begin with revelation "theological positivism," Kaufman insists that theology, as a critical discipline that is concerned to speak intelligibly to its own time, must penetrate more deeply into the foundation of theistic language.

> Like any others, these concepts [of God and revelation] have been created and developed in and through human processes of reflection on life and interpretation of experience. It is only because some persons at certain times and places found it useful and meaningful and perhaps even necessary to speak of "God's revelation," in order to make sense of the life and history which they were undergoing, that these terms and concepts were developed and employed within the human sphere at all. (2)

Kaufman goes on to note that, because of such developments, these concepts are available to us now. Yet we cannot merely presuppose them

---

[37]*Essay on Theological Method*, 19 n. 10. Subsequent citations are noted in the text and refer to this edition.

[38]Cf. also his statement that, at the time of *Systematic Theology*, he "did not fully realize how radically Christian theology must be reconceived if it is understood as essentially imaginative construction" (p. 19 n. 10), and his statement in the preface that the dissolution of "the neo-orthodox consensus in protestant theology, which had made so much of the authority of 'God's revelation' as the ultimate court of appeal, forced me, like others of my generation, to think through afresh the task of theology and to search for new and more adequate foundations. My teaching and writing in recent years reflects this search, but it has not been until recently that I have felt sufficiently confident about my emerging understanding of theological method to publish it" (p. x).

and use them as they have been used in the past. On the contrary, it is necessary to decide how we can reconstruct them by examining how and why they initially emerged and by determining what that means for their continued significance in the present. There is, then, a direct correlation between our understanding of the origin and function of religious concepts and our understanding of how we should go about constructing and reconstructing them for our own situation. And, since ideas such as God and revelation have a human origin, being grounded in our imagination, and are useful to humans for human ends, theology must therefore understand itself as a human enterprise operating according to human criteria and objectives. In other words, theology's dependence on human terms and concepts to interpret human events and experiences according to human modes of thought radically undercuts all claims to a transcendent foundation (3). Rather than presupposing religious concepts and terms, as theology has been wont to do, we must examine their origin and function in order to arrive at a better understanding of their potential significance for us.

My contention that Kaufman here exhibits an important change in his thinking should not be taken to mean that he had earlier argued for a form of "theological positivism" that simply asserted the idea of a revelation without any attempt to analyze and justify the use of this concept. As is abundantly clear from my analysis of Kaufman's thought prior to *Essay on Theological Method*, he certainly did try to show the meaning, intelligibility, and necessity of some sort of revelatory basis for human life and thought. However, in *Essay on Theological Method* he characterizes his earlier development of the concept of revelation as naive and labels all attempts to begin with revelation as "theological positivism." It is noteworthy that he apparently places Paul Tillich—who certainly had much to say in a preliminary way about the idea of revelation and who therefore did not simply posit the concept of revelation as something beyond challenge and analysis—among those who presuppose what needs explanation and who are thus theological positivists (2).

Kaufman's treatment of Tillich and his criticism of his earlier stand on revelation suggest that the label "theological positivism" is meant to apply to more than those who begin with revelation without any effort to explain or justify such a move. Indeed, the general development of his thought in this essay indicates that the label applies to any position that takes revelation as a necessary part of "the methodological foundations of theology," that is, as something that theology requires in order to say something about God. Theology requires an understanding of the logic of the culture's use of the terms *God* and *world*, the materials for constructing/reconstructing these concepts (materials provided by tradition and contemporary understanding), and the criteria of humanization and relativization as guides for this constructive activity. These factors, rather than revelation, form the methodological foundations of theology. Revelation, then, can never be a part of the methodological basis for theological work, even though it can be a concept that theology concludes is important and that theology speaks of as a foundation in some sense (3).

The idea of revelation, then, still has a possible place within Kaufman's system. But it is important to keep in mind that the notion of revelation will be a conclusion of theology and not its beginning premise, a conclusion that "rests upon prior foundations in experience, reflection and reasoning" (3-4). How, in light of Kaufman's earlier discussions of the meaning of revelation as the ultimate foundation of life and thought, it is possible to reach a conclusion, on the basis of our own experience, reflection, and reasoning, that something is in fact a revelation from God (who, we should remember, transcends our thought and experience), Kaufman does not say. Perhaps some concluding statements in the essay help to shed a little light on Kaufman's meaning, even if they fail to resolve the logical difficulties. At the end of the third chapter, he notes that there is some merit in the claim that divine revelation is the ultimate ground of theological knowledge. He does not mean, though, that theologians who take revelation as their point of departure are right. Rather, he reiterates his view that certain ways of speaking about God—specifically those that speak about God as an agent—depend on the concept of revelation, since we can come to know personal agents only if they choose to reveal themselves (67-68).

Therefore, within the framework that wishes to build an image of God according to the model of agent, one can and must speak of God's revelatory activity as the foundation for theological knowledge. At the same time, theology remains a creation of our imagination, a human construction that operates according to rules that we devise through our analysis of the way the word *God* functions in our language. How do we reconcile these two claims? According to Kaufman we do so by realizing that "it is precisely through the constructive work of the human imagination that God—ultimate reality understood as active and beneficent, as gracious— makes himself known." He continues: "From this point of view the concept of God itself . . . is to be understood as rooted in and the vehicle of divine revelation. And theological work . . . should be understood as seeking to take God's revelation of himself with maximal seriousness" (68). Again, this assertion does not explain how we can *conclude* that God is actually involved in our work. But, on careful examination, one can see that Kaufman is not really speaking of a conclusion based on evidence and reasoning here. Instead, he is speaking of how a particular point of view understands the concept of God. That is, he appears to have moved from a discussion of theology's foundational concerns about the origin of its concepts to a consideration of the way things appear from within the framework defined by those concepts.[39]

The only conclusion that could be involved here is that the whole framework of which the concept of God as agent is the center is viable because it is pragmatically useful. At any rate, this reference to revelation is not methodologically significant, since one should continue, according to Kaufman, to construct and reconstruct the concept of God rather than engage in an interpretation of a tradition that mediates God's revelation. Does this indicate that theology has a critical mode, in which the idea of revelation is merely one of the concepts that undergoes criticism and re-construction, and another mode, in which one takes it upon oneself to view the world from the framework that one has imaginatively con-structed (without ultimately losing sight of the fact that it is essentially a human construction)? Or perhaps the difference here is the difference be-tween theology and faith: the former operates critically, whereas the lat-ter, though chastened by theology's realization of its human nature, existentially lives within the framework constructed/reconstructed by theology. Although Kaufman never explicitly defines the distinction be-tween theology and faith in this way, his discussion sometimes implies it (see, for example, p. xi). However this difference may be explained, the crucial point is that revelation has, for all practical purposes, been elim-inated as an important methodological principle. It is a concept that a rel-atively autonomous subject finds useful in building a certain view of God and the world, but it provides no basis for assuming some sort of referent for *God* and no justification for starting with revelatory events in our statements about God.

With the rejection of revelation as a basis for theology's work comes a rejection of any appeal to the language of the church as the primary con-text for theology. Rather, in view of the fact that *God* is a concept in the ordinary language of Western culture, the primary linguistic context for

---

[39]In interpreting Kaufman, one often discovers that it is difficult to tell when he is writing as a theologian who is asking critical questions about the Christian faith and when he is writing as one who is viewing things from the perspective of faith, i.e., when he is displaying the existential meaningfulness of the Chris-tian point of view. The passage under discussion here apparently belongs to the latter group, as the phrase "from this point of view" suggests.

theological reflection must be the ordinary language of a society. That is, the function of the word *God* within the ordinary use of language is determinative for our own understanding of its formal properties, if not its material content. The language of the church depends on this more general use of the word, being a variation, refinement, or transformation of society's language. Although the church's use of God-language is important, therefore, it is not the final arbiter but a contributor to theological reflection, which can be properly appreciated only within the larger context of a culture's common language. Thus, the real key to the way in which God should function for us—and therefore the clue to how we should construct/reconstruct the concept of God—lies in the ordinary use of language (8-15).

While the common language of our culture provides certain constraints and guidelines for theology, it is essentially a constructive work of the human imagination. From the beginning Kaufman stressed the role of the imagination in human knowledge in general, and in theology in particular. Now, however, imagination becomes the central concept for theology. Indeed, it takes the place of revelation as the foundation for theological reflection.[40] Whereas in his earlier work Kaufman wrote of a given for theology—namely, the revelation that is theology's self-evident point of departure for making claims about God—he now argues that the material for theological reflection arises from the constructive work of the imagination. In other words, the human imagination, in order to provide a framework of meaning for life and resist tendencies toward idolatry, makes use of images and concepts drawn from experience to project a picture of that which grounds and limits human life (10-15, 27-37).[41] This picture, then, is grounded in what people have found useful for the construction of an ultimate environment for life. Although a certain framework of understanding may wish to view this picture as grounded in revelation, theology should concern itself with the degree to which various images and concepts serve their intended function and should reconstruct them to enable them to achieve this function more effectively, rather than try, through the hermeneutical retrieval of a tradition, to understand the meaning of some revelatory events for our time.

---

[40]Cf. Garrett Green, "Reconstructing Christian Theology," *Religious Studies Review* 9 (1983): 220.

[41]See also Kaufman, "Metaphysics and Theology," in *The Theological Imagination: Constructing the Concept of God* (Philadelphia: Westminster Press, 1981): 250-51.

For Kaufman the function of the concept of God is clear: it serves to relativize and humanize life. As already indicated, he reaches this conclusion through his understanding of the manner in which the word functions in ordinary language. In its ordinary use, we see that the word *God* serves to indicate the ultimate point of reference for life. As a result, it has a peculiar logical standing, for the ultimate point of reference cannot be a part of the empirical world but must transcend all that we can experience. Unlike objects and situations in the world, therefore, we cannot check our ideas of God against that which we experience of God— there is no experience of God as such. This idea is not a new one for Kaufman, for it was a central theme in his earlier work as well. What is new is the conclusion he now draws from this premise, namely, that we should not think of God as a distinct entity at all. Instead, God is a concept that focuses a set of images and concepts that defines a certain orientation toward life.[42] It is, in other words, the central element in an overarching vision of the whole within which humans live. As such, the concept of God "is created by the mind for certain intra-mental functions" rather than a concept that refers to an object (25). When theologians fail to realize this limitation and speak of God as an existing being or distinct entity of some sort, they are illegitimately reifying, or treating in an objectivist manner, this mental construct.[43]

In spite of his strong rejection of objectivist treatments of God, Kaufman makes a curious move when dealing with the question of the ontological status of that which God symbolizes. Even though God is not a being or object to which God-language directly refers, this concept does symbolize that which provides a metaphysical grounding for moral existence. We must remember that the use of God-language is supposed to provide an ultimate environment for life. And, if we assume that God is no more than a fanciful notion that we have created out of thin air, we will never really commit ourselves to the framework grounded by the concept of God.

In other words, our talk about God must have an aura of reality if it is to serve its purpose. But how can it achieve this status when we realize that God is not something that we can experience or to which we can point with our language? Kaufman suggests that the answer lies in contem-

---

[42]Kaufman, "Constructing the Concept of God," in *Theological Imagination*, 28-29. It should be noted that Kaufman tends to use *concepts* and *images* interchangeably, sometimes using the expression "image/concept."

[43]Ibid., 28-29.

porary ideas about the movement of history toward greater and greater humanization. Such views make plausible the idea that there are cosmic forces working toward human fulfillment—and this can therefore serve as the ontological grounding for the "reality" of talk about God. Kaufman argues that this view is harmonious with Christian affirmations about God, since the real purpose of such affirmations is to express the faith that God will bring about the Kingdom, in which humans will find their complete fulfillment. Hence the achievement of humanization through the movement of history is the underlying meaning of Christian language about God, so that the question of the ontological status of such language, at least in our time, is best answered by referring to the movement of cosmic forces tending toward humanization.[44] Nevertheless, at this time, Kaufman also maintained that the more personal mode of speaking about God is an important way of expressing this metaphysical grounding of human moral life, for it "represents with great vividness and power the fact that we are created, sustained, and fulfilled as human and humane, not by our efforts alone, but from beyond ourselves, from resources in the ultimate nature of things."[45]

Kaufman's argument here presents some difficulties in view of statements he has made about both the logical standing of metaphysical language and the transcendence of God. Starting with the latter, it is not clear how the transcendent God can, in effect, be identified with forces at work within the world. And, in this light, it must be asked whether Christian affirmations about God really are reducible to ideas about cosmic forces. The second issue, the logical status of metaphysical language, renders problematic the very effort to explain the reality of God in terms of cosmic realities. For Kaufman has argued repeatedly that metaphysical language is no more directly descriptive of how things really are than is theological language.[46] Why, then, should we appeal to the equally imaginative metaphysical claims about cosmic forces to ground claims about God? Apart from its supposedly "nonobjectivist" nature, the only reason ap-

[44]Ibid., 37, 46-51; cf. idem, *Theology for a Nuclear Age* (Philadelphia: Westminster Press, 1985) 40-46. See especially p. 44, where God is described as "this whole grand cosmic evolutionary movement" that has led to the emergence of human and humane forms of life.

[45]Kaufman, "Constructing the Concept of God," 51. As we will see, Kaufman has changed his mind on this point.

[46]Kaufman, *Relativism, Knowledge, and Faith*, 95-103; idem, "God as Symbol," 102-106; idem, "Metaphysics and Theology," 241-49.

pears to be that people today are supposed to find talk about cosmic forces more plausible than talk about God.[47] The major concern in Kaufman's discussion at this point, then, *may be* what will give God-language an aura of reality rather than what actually does give it an ontological grounding. Such a concern would arise out of Kaufman's belief that moral life will have a better foundation if people believe that it is in harmony with the ultimate nature of things. But the belief is apparently more important than the reality.[48]

If this interpretation is correct, Kaufman's argument is not that we actually can provide a permanent metaphysical grounding for the idea of God but that the idea of God can be given plausibility in our time by appealing to these metaphysical concepts. On the other hand, he also claims that there must be some congruence between an orientation that works for humans and how things really are. This comment, however, does not mean that the particular metaphysical concepts that he employs are valid for all time. To be consistent, it seems that Kaufman would need to argue that they, too, are imaginative construals that another time might wish to reject in favor of some other type of construal. For the present, however, this sort of metaphysical conceptuality provides a reasonable way to speak of the ontological ground of talk about God. In short, although the practical usefulness of Christian faith suggests that it has some sort of contact with metaphysical reality, no set of concepts, whether theological or metaphysical, can claim to be a direct and eternally valid representation of the true nature of things. In spite of Kaufman's claims about an ontological foundation for theism, therefore, the real issue here seems to be "the viability and appropriateness of this whole frame of orientation"— that is, whether it is pragmatically useful for the humanization of life.[49] For the real test of an orientation is not whether we can prove, through science or philosophy, that its metaphysical claims are true (an impossible task) but whether it works for us. In the end, its pragmatic power grounds its metaphysical claims rather than vice versa.

On the other hand, Kaufman's recent book *Theology for a Nuclear Age* makes this interpretation of his thought a little more difficult to maintain.

---

[47]This, of course, is a view that is by no means beyond dispute, since it is not clear that many really would find the idea of cosmic forces all that plausible and there seem to be a number of people who still find talk about God meaningful and believable.

[48]See, e.g., Kaufman, "Constructing the Concept of God," 38-39, 47.

[49]Ibid., 47-48.

There he speaks without reservation of God as the "grand cosmic evolutionary movement" that has given birth to human freedom and self-consciousness and that seeks to progress even further through the advance of human history. This movement encompasses physical, biological, and historicocultural dimensions of life, through which unanticipated results of human action have come into being. Because human action does in fact lead to unforeseen, creative consequences, Kaufman argues that "there is a hidden creativity in the historico-cultural process" that has resulted in human life as we know it. However, he does not identify this creative process alone with God. Rather, this process depends on physical and biological preconditions, which leads Kaufman to state, "God should today be conceived in terms of the complex of physical, biological and historico-cultural conditions which have made human existence possible, which continue to sustain it, and which may draw it out to a fuller humanity and humaneness."[50] Only devotion to this sort of God will avoid idolatry, Kaufman continues, since any other type of "God" would not be the reality that created and sustains us.

Such an argument raises a number of questions. By linking the idea of divine creation and sustenance to our connection with and dependence on physical, biological, and historicocultural forces, Kaufman has managed to transform the classical meaning of God's creative and sustaining activity. However, this transformation is not without some serious difficulties. For the classical view, which distinguishes God's creating and sustaining act from such cosmic forces by making it the ground of these forces, would provide reasons for regarding Kaufman's description of God as resting on a serious confusion of God and creation. Although Kaufman's description of God in terms of historicocultural processes may not exactly be treating God as an object, it certainly tends to view God as a reality that can be circumscribed and explicitly defined. This is a strange argument, in light of Kaufman's own position, as articulated in earlier writings, that God is a transcendent reality that we cannot adequately conceive or define. There is no hint here of the double-layeredness of the concept of God. There is also no suggestion that these metaphysical claims are imaginative constructs that are bound to their time.

Nevertheless, it may be that Kaufman is here offering a construction of God for the faithful to affirm (that is, expounding the existential significance of the concept of God) and therefore not operating at the level of discourse in which it is necessary to point out the imaginative, con-

---

[50]Kaufman, *Theology for a Nuclear Age*, 41, 42, 44.

structive nature of all such metaphysical proposals. In that case, my suggested interpretation of Kaufman's talk about cosmic forces would hold. Still, Kaufman's manner of expressing himself has left this ambiguous at best.

At any rate, Kaufman has not abandoned his emphasis on the importance of imaginative construction. He also continues to argue that the principles according to which the imagination should function are humanization and relativization, since the pragmatic function of theistic concepts is to guide the way we construct them. Again, since these concepts are humanly constructed for human ends, they should be judged by criteria that are grounded in those ends.

When Kaufman wishes to summarize in a word what those ends are, he invariably uses the term *humanization*. To be sure, he clearly rejects the notion that we should fashion God to fit whatever wishes and needs we may have, for they may be distortive of what is truly humanizing (56). Indeed, human idolatrous tendencies often lead to inadequate views of God; hence these tendencies can and must be combatted with the help of the formal dimension of the idea of God—that is, God as the ultimate point of reference that relativizes all else. This formal principle means that we can never take our wishes and needs, our knowledge, our accomplishments, or even our understanding of God as final and without inadequacies. To do so would be idolatry, something Kaufman strongly condemns throughout his writings. It is essential, then, for any concept of God that we construct, to relativize everything in human life.

Such relativization, however, should be joined with the principle of humanization, since the concept of God is supposed to provide an ultimate point of orientation and devotion for human life. To do so, of course, our idea of God must be more than abstract and formal. It must be given a content that is relevant to human life and leads life to a fuller realization of its possibilities. Now the concept of God can achieve this end best through anthropomorphic images and ideas (55).[51] It is possible to use such a conceptuality without falling into idolatry if we keep in mind that there must always be a balance between humanization and relativization, so that each can "qualify and correct the other in constructing the concept of God" (56). If one maintains this balance, the anthropomorphic aspects of the concept of God will not be a mere extension of "the empirically human." Rather, they will be "an idealization or perfection of the human which opens up new possibilities of understanding the human itself" (55).

---

[51]See also Kaufman, "Attachment to God," in *Theological Imagination*, 58-79. Again, this is a view that Kaufman has now significantly modified. See below.

Both of these motifs function as criteria that the imagination uses in its construction and reconstruction of the concept of God. But there is also a third criterion, which emerges from the need to make the concept of God relevant to our lives: *presence.* The concept of God must impinge on us in such a way as to provide orientation in our concrete situations. By adding this third criterion, Kaufman is able to relate the criteria for theological construction to traditional trinitarian views of God. First, God is the transcendent ground of everything, the One who relativizes all our ideas, projects, hopes, and achievements; second, God is the One who comes to redeem, who humanizes life; and third, God is the One who dwells in the believer, who is present to us in such a way as to bring this relativization and humanization into our lives. In light of statements he has made about imagination as the medium of revelation and about the metaphysical reality with which our pragmatically useful concepts are in contact, one might think that Kaufman would use the motif of presence to develop the thought that God, in some ontologically real sense, is in fact present to us through our theistic language and ideas. However, his rather brief discussion of this criterion never moves in that direction. Instead, he uses the motif of presence as a formal principle that can be subsumed under humanization, that is, as a way to stress that one's concept of God must relate itself to the full range of life. Thus, he argues that any adequate construction of God must show

> the way in which God is related to every segment and every dimension of our experience and world. The theologian, thus, must develop an understanding of the world, of human culture and human life, which takes into full account what is known and believed about each of these matters in modern wisdom and science; no domain of culture or of learning may be overlooked if God is to be not only "the God of the fathers" but also the proper and true ultimate point of reference for our time and our world.[52]

Now the fact that the concept of God that one constructs must truly be able to function as the ultimate point of reference for life has important implications for the way one should relate to the history of thought about God. For any theological proposal that departs too dramatically from received notions will not be able to elicit assent from people generally. Unless one's proposals are perceived to be in fundamental harmony with the theological tradition, then, one is merely engaging in speculative exer-

---

[52]Kaufman, "Christian Theology as Imaginative Construction," in *Theological Imagination*, 275.

cises rather than in a meaningful construction/reconstruction of the concept of God. Consequently, it is essential to make use of tradition when formulating new theological proposals. We of course should not simply repeat the tradition, but we must show some sort of continuity between our own proposals about God and the manner in which the tradition has spoken about God. If this connecting is done successfully, genuinely new formulations can be accepted by believers and can help to transform their insights and loyalties (33).[53]

In many ways, Kaufman's most recent work shows a great suspicion of the ability of tradition to help us in our contemporary situation. On the other hand, he sees tradition as more than something of which we must take account because we deal with people who are consciously committed to a tradition. Even when he argues that our situation in the nuclear age is so radically new that tradition provides no great help without a radical deconstruction and reconstruction of it, he adds that past insights and knowledge remain important and useful.[54] Furthermore, he is well aware that even the continuing use of the word *God* makes one indebted to tradition, which has bequeathed the word to us. He also notes that we all depend on an inherited framework of interpretation for the categories we use in dealing with our experience, thought, and action.[55] Moreover, the continuing importance of tradition can be seen in the way Kaufman proceeds in his theological reflection. For example, the use of the Christian categorial scheme—God, the world, the human, and Christ—reflects the influence of Christian tradition in his theology.[56] Also, Kaufman still argues that the history of Jesus Christ can be of significant help in constructing an adequate picture of the human and of God.[57]

In his use and qualified appreciation of tradition, Kaufman seems to make possible at least a limited acknowledgment of the disclosive power of tradition and hence of our dependence on tradition as an ongoing stream within which human life is lived. Indeed, at one point he speaks of the power of the image of Jesus to *reveal* something about the nature

---

[53]See also Kaufman, "Constructing the Concept of God," 23, 31; and idem, "Attachment to God," 74.

[54]See especially Kaufman, *Theology for a Nuclear Age*, 10-14.

[55]Kaufman, "Constructing the Concept of God," 31.

[56]Kaufman, "The Christian Categorial Scheme," in *Theological Imagination*, 99-122.

[57]Kaufman, "Toward a Contemporary Interpretation of Jesus," in *Theological Imagination*, 123-56; and idem, *Theology for a Nuclear Age*, 47-63.

of human life. "The theological significance of Jesus is to be found in what his life and death reveal, or can reveal, about the nature of the human and the possibilities of the human." Furthermore, in response to the question of why theology should concern itself with Jesus, he states that modern Western understandings of God and humanity have been deeply influenced by the image of this person. As a result, whether we accept or reject the picture of human life shaped by the image of Jesus, we must deal with that image.[58]

These intimations of the disclosive power of tradition are never developed. In fact, Kaufman's stress on imaginative construction, without any exploration of the possibility and implications of a receptive dimension to the imagination, keeps the idea of disclosure from becoming a significant part of his system. And this is apparently a deeper problem than merely overlooking a dimension of our relationship to tradition. For his view of how we come to accept and make use of the image of Jesus (and of other parts of tradition) presupposes some understanding of humanization that we can use to judge the adequacy of that image as a resource for building a picture of the human and of God. Thus, he notes that we will decide whether commitment to Jesus is appropriate on the basis of whether Jesus exemplifies what is truly human and whether devotion to him further enhances our humanity. Our response to these issues, he further notes, will "depend on our conception of Jesus, our conception of what is 'truly humane,' and our conception of what is required to create or bring about the truly humane."[59]

This statement is not problematic in itself. A problem does arise, however, when one asks how we arrive at this determination of what is humane and humanizing. In light of our dependence on inherited frameworks of understanding, it seems evident that our ideas of humanization inevitably presuppose something that is supposed to be the result of our reconstructing activity—that is, a concept of the human, but also the larger framework within which this concept has its place and significance—in which case the picture of a constructing subject must undergo far-reaching qualification. That is, the power of tradition to disclose possible understandings of humanity and the world apparently has a fundamental role here. Construction would thereby be conjoined with disclosure, and a significantly different picture than that of a subject's building images or concepts of God, the world, and the human would emerge.

---

[58]Kaufman, "Contemporary Interpretation of Jesus," 143 (quotation), 127.

[59]Ibid., 150.

However, Kaufman clearly does not approach this issue in this way. In fact, he never directly addresses this particular problem at all. Yet he does make statements that are not compatible with the view that the understanding of humanization by which we make our judgments is itself dependent on the disclosive power of tradition. He insists that we must depend on our own decisions, which he contrasts with what tradition "predetermines."[60] This contrast between tradition and our own responsible decisions (which are based on our understanding of humanization) moves in the direction of treating tradition as a source of building blocks that we, as controlling subjects, use to construct pictures of God, the world, and humanity, rather than viewing tradition as an ongoing stream encompassing human life, within which human life becomes what it is as it is borne by that stream into the present and toward the future. In short, Kaufman's approach to tradition, within the context provided by his essentially constructivist understanding, is largely instrumentalist. That is, he basically treats tradition as one of the instruments that controlling subjects use to reach the goals they decide are important. In such circumstances, the disclosive power of tradition can play no more than a very subordinate role.

In a very brief way, Kaufman also suggests at one point that the aesthetic dimension of imaginative construction has certain implications for the way we construct the concept of God. That is, the theologian's work must to some degree be shaped by "aesthetic considerations of harmony and balance, consistency and contrast" (32). However, Kaufman never expands on this idea, so that its significance for the concept of God remains undeveloped.

In addition to developing criteria for judging theological proposals, Kaufman has argued that the development of theological proposals takes place according to a threefold structure, which he calls three "moments." The use of this terminology should not be taken to mean that theology always occurs in the same temporal sequence. Rather, these moments are dialectically related (69 n. 7, 65). Yet they can and should be distinguished for the sake of clarifying the process through which a theologian goes in the formulation of his or her proposals. The first moment is the development of an idea of the world, a conception of "the overall context within which experience falls" (47). This concept has such a fundamental place in the order of theological construction because, according to Kauf-

---

[60]Ibid., 125. It is significant, perhaps, that Kaufman does not distinguish here between being shaped by a living tradition and being caught in traditionalism.

man, "all conceptions of God presuppose notions of the world" (48). That is, the idea of God is a counterpart to the idea of a "whole" (the world) within which one lives, since the concept of God emerged in order to provide a ground and point of orientation for that whole.[61]

The second moment of theological construction is the formulation of a concept of God. This is important because the idea of a world can easily become absolutized, which then makes it an idolatrous and humanly destructive concept (45). The concept of God, however, serves to relativize all conceptions of the world and therefore keeps any view of the whole from overdetermining our thought. The word *God* is well suited to this purpose because it is a symbol of that which transcends the whole, that than which nothing greater can be conceived, the mystery that always eludes our grasp. On the other hand, as we have noted above, *God* is also the ultimate point of orientation for human life, and for this purpose our concept of God requires material content. Such content is provided through the use of models drawn from experience and applied to the relation between God and the world.

> The concept of God—like the concept of world—is always constructed with the aid of models drawn from ordinary experience. In accordance with the formal requirement that our idea of God be developed in relation to our notion of the world, the initial move will be, with the help of finite (experienced) relationships as models, to attempt to conceive the (unexperienced but imaginatively constructed) relationship between the world and God. With a bridge from the world to God thus provided, the terms or relata of the finite relationship(s) can then in turn become models for constructing more fully the concepts of God and world. (52-53)

The sorts of relationships that have provided models for this purpose are cause/effect, wholly other/familiar, ground/superstructure, and agent/act. At the time he wrote *Essay on Theological Method*, Kaufman believed that the last relationship was of central importance for Christian conceptions of God, for it provides a model for conceptualizing God in a way that is particularly appropriate to God's function as a focus of orientation for human life.[62]

If we are to conceive of God in such a way as to make God an appropriate focus of devotion and commitment, it is important to develop a view

---

[61]In fact, Kaufman argues that the idea of "world" is more essential for human life than the idea of "God" (30).

[62]He has now modified this view significantly. See below.

of the human as a part of one's construction of the concept of God. It is so important, in fact, that in one essay Kaufman gives it independent status alongside the concepts of world, God, and Christ.[63] In his discussion of the three moments of theological construction, however, the idea of self or humanity is subsumed under that of God.[64]

The third moment of theological construction arises from the need to reformulate the original concept of world in light of the concept of God that one has constructed (59-65). Here there is a dialectical interplay between the two concepts that is weighted on the side of the concept of God. "Simply adjusting each of these concepts to the other, compromising a bit on both sides, is not all that is required here. The concept of God, as the idea of that which limits and relativizes the world, must be given a certain priority, with the concept of world adjusted to and rebuilt on the basis of fundamental requirements which the notion of God imposes" (59). One cannot, however, merely deduce the concept of world from that of God (a practice that Kaufman attributes to Karl Barth). Such a step ignores the fact that the concept of God presupposes an original concept of the world. Furthermore, it overlooks the fact that our theological vocabulary is related to our experience in the world. Any efforts to construct a vocabulary that is initially unrelated to ordinary experience can only leave us with abstract and empty formulas (60). What is required, then, is a recognition of the need to relate both concepts in a way that gives priority to "God" yet still recognizes the integrity of the "world," especially to the degree that the latter is built on our ordinary experience.

As a constructive work of the imagination, theological construction is ultimately based on the decision of the theologian. No other person or thing can serve as the final arbiter of one's work.

> Once we recognize that our theology is fundamentally our own construction of a notion of God believed appropriate for our time, we will see that we cannot divest ourselves from taking full responsibility for our theological work. *We* are the ones who must

---

[63]Kaufman, "Christian Categorial Scheme," 99-122. Here Kaufman lists self, world, God, and Christ as the four central components, or fundamental categories, of a Christian worldview. The idea of Christ, however, has a different status than the other three, since it serves to give shape to each of them.

[64]The difference between *Essay on Theological Method* and *Theological Imagination* here may be attributable to the fact that the former has a cosmological starting point for its theological proposals and the latter has an existential point of departure. In the latter case, one would expect the concept of self to be more prominent.

persuade ourselves what the principles of absoluteness and humaneness can and must mean for our time and our world and our experience, and we are the ones who must decide how their conjunction in a reality appropriate to focus the worship and devotion of modern men and women can be understood. We are the ones, in short, who must construct the conception of God which will be meaningful and significant for our day. There is simply no one else to do it. To be called to the vocation of Christian theologian is to be called to just this task of construction.[65]

Kaufman argues that this constructive task requires a radical reconceptualization of the concept of God, since the traditional theological concepts have become "intuitively implausible" for many today.[66] To what extent traditional concepts must be rejected or overhauled, he does not say. However, in recent works he has provided some indications of what he now thinks may need to be done to personal images for God. In his presidential address to the American Academy of Religion, "Nuclear Eschatology and the Study of Religion," he argued that notions of God as personal agent encourage us to think that God will bail us out of the nuclear peril we face, thereby encouraging us to think that we do not have to shoulder full responsibility for solving this world-threatening problem. Such attitudes are extremely dangerous, indicating that a fundamental reconceptualization of God is needed in this situation. We live in a time when humanity has a destructive power at its command that is far beyond anything dreamed of before. As a result, old concepts and symbols are no longer sufficiently illuminating, and new ones are desperately needed.[67]

In his recent book *Theology for a Nuclear Age*, Kaufman carries some of these thoughts even further. Arguing that God is the reality that "gives us our humanity and such fulfillment as may come our way" and that "limits and restricts and judges us when we overreach ourselves or seek that which can only harm or destroy us," Kaufman states that this reality is constituted by the physical, biological, and historicocultural factors enabling human life. Hence God is to be identified with the "whole grand cosmic evolutionary movement" that has given birth to human life.[68] Fur-

---

[65]Kaufman, "Christian Theology as Imaginative Construction," 274 (emphasis his).

[66]Kaufman, "Metaphysics and Theology," 261.

[67]Kaufman, "Nuclear Eschatology and the Study of Religion," *Journal of the American Academy of Religion* 51 (1983): 8-9, 12-13.

[68]Kaufman, *Theology for a Nuclear Age*, 37, 41, 44.

thermore, God should be imaged in this way rather than in personalistic terms, since our contemporary situation can no longer be illumined by the "dualistic and asymmetrical" point of view that is a part of personal images such as Father, Lord, King, and Creator.[69] That is, Kaufman contends that these personal images for God present a picture in which God is dominant and we are subordinate and obedient. Moreover, in this view God is fully in control and will ultimately carry out the divine purposes, which are characterized by caring and love. However, our contemporary understanding is that we are not "at the disposal of mysterious cosmic powers that impinge on us unilaterally from beyond." On the contrary, we can modify and adjust the forces that impinge on our lives. In fact, with the creation of the nuclear threat, "the cosmic order which is the source and context of our lives and our well-being suddenly seems to have no way to protect itself from the onslaught with which we humans now threaten it."[70] Thus, we belong to a unified ecological order, and our conception of God must be framed in these terms, which means that personal and political images of God must be eliminated or at least relegated to secondary status.[71]

Here Kaufman deals with the question of the truth of language about God in terms of its connection with cosmic forces. However, he has not consistently dealt with the truth question in this manner. In *God the Problem* he made a distinction between "true" and "right," treating the former as the question of correspondence between idea and reality and the latter as the question of whether certain ideas express appropriate life policies. He then argued that theology should ask not whether its formulations are true but whether they are right. If they are right, and if one's life is shaped by them, then one believes in God in the most basic and meaningful sense.[72]

In an epilogue to *Essay on Theological Method,* however, he drops the distinction between true and right and argues that, in view of the kind of concepts involved in theological language, a theological construct may be regarded as true "if it in fact leads to fruitful life, in the broadest and full-

---

[69]Ibid., 32-33, 38-39.

[70]Ibid., 38-39.

[71]Ibid., 53-57. Kaufman never treats the question of whether other personal images besides images of Father, Lord, King, and Creator may alter the impact of personal images. He also never addresses the issue of how his current argument affects earlier claims he has made about the transcendence of God.

[72]Kaufman, "God as Symbol," 107-109, 113.

est and most comprehensive sense possible" (76). Such a statement seems to be an effort to place the issue of truth in a pragmatic context and thus to leave aside all questions about the correspondence between concepts and external reality. Yet, in his discussion of these matters in *The Theological Imagination*, he suggests that the truth of God-language may lie in its ability to symbolize, in a humanly meaningful way, certain cosmic forces. In spite of his criticism of objectivist language, even in this context, such an argument appears to be an attempt to find an object or process to which to refer the concept of God, as well as to respond to questions of truth in terms of correspondence between ideas and external realities rather than in pragmatic terms. In short, though his thinking seems to have been influenced by pragmatism, his treatment of this issue remains fraught with ambiguity.

• Kaufman on the Imagination •

Although Kaufman uses the concept of imagination repeatedly in his writings, even in his earliest work, he never provides an extended discussion of its meaning and role in human thought in general or in theology in particular. In fact, he never provides a definition of the concept. Nevertheless, his scattered references to imagination do describe what he believes it does and also provide an implicit definition of it. In order to focus the issues arising from the imaginative nature of theology, as Kaufman sees it, an analysis of his various statements about imagination is called for.

In his first book, Kaufman linked imagination with attention and memory. All three human capacities are essential for conscious perception because without them we would have only fleeting sensa, which would be lost as soon as they occurred. But with these capacities, it is possible to lift sensa out of the flux of time and thus to make them the object of our attention. The central faculty in this process is imagination, for through its constructive power sensa become "a complex product, a sensum conjoined and fused with the memory of previous sensa." Thus, imagination's power of synthesis, coupled with memory's power to hold past sensa for later recall, makes it possible for us to focus our attention on certain aspects of experience and thereby to build an increasingly comprehensive and complex picture of our world. The link between imagination and attention allows the former to isolate certain aspects of experience and to unite them with other aspects in an imaginative construction. And the link between memory and imagination enables imagination to link things that are separated by time yet joined through our ability to bring the past into the present.[73]

Kaufman's point seems clear enough in a general way. But it is difficult to see exactly how these three capacities are to be distinguished from each other. Does attention operate without the imagination at any point? Or is the act of attending to some dimension of experience already an imaginative act? Again, does the memory function alone? Or is the act of remembering an act of imagination? The closest that Kaufman comes to providing a distinction between memory and imagination is a statement that our personal histories are "preserved in memory" and "activated" when our present *Erlebnis* (or preconscious experience that functions as the basic foundation for all conscious experience) "is imaginatively interpreted."[74] This comment suggests that memory is some shadowy repository of past experiences, which can be activated at any moment by imagination. This treatment of the workings of the human mind is vague, if not naive. And because Kaufman leaves such questions unanswered, his concept of imagination, as well as of memory and attention, is not well defined.

This vagueness continues in his later discussions of theology as imaginative construction—while the kinds of activity in which the imagination engages are the same. For example, he compares the constructive activity of imagination to the act of building a house: imagination takes raw materials provided by experience and builds something according to its own design rather than according to something inherent in the materials themselves (28, 39). Creative imagination, then, is essentially a synthesizing and constructing power that uses images, concepts, metaphors, and models drawn from our experience of finite realities to construct a picture of the world and God,[75] a construction that may or may not take place consciously.[76] Furthermore, it is able to envision possibilities that do not actually exist "and hence to serve as the foundation of the humanly created world of culture and history."[77]

---

[73]Kaufman, *Revelation, Knowledge, and Faith*, 40-52.

[74]Ibid., 46.

[75]Cf. Kaufman, preface to *Theological Imagination*, 11; idem, "Constructing the Concept of God," 22, 28, 281 n.1; idem, "Metaphysics and Theology," 247-48; and idem, "Christian Theology as Imaginative Construction," 267.

[76]Kaufman, "Christian Categorial Scheme," 109.

[77]Kaufman, "Attachment to God," 60.

These activities of synthesis and construction can be free of all rules or pragmatic considerations.[78] However, the theologian cannot indulge in the mere play of fantasy. Rather, the work of theology requires a disciplined construction that follows certain rules inherent in the logic, or grammar, of the concepts and images with which it works. That is to say, theology works with a public language that carries meanings that can be violated only at the expense of theology's own interests (10, 33, 36).[79] Consequently, the theologian must carefully consider what language about the world and God is trying to do and say "so as to enable us to say and do them better—more accurately, more precisely, more effectively" (9). In other words, theology derives rules for its operation by coming to a clear understanding of the function, in the life of a society, of the language to which it attends.[80] As we have seen, these functions can be reduced to two: humanization and relativization. Now because the purpose of theological concepts is to bring fulfillment to human life, pragmatic considerations can and must help to guide our imaginative construction. Among these pragmatic considerations are not only questions about whether a certain perspective enhances human life but questions about whether a given constructive proposal is in sufficient continuity with the tradition of a society to be accepted as believable (32-33).[81] Tradition, then, cannot be rejected but must be reconstructed with a view to what people can accept as expressive of reality.

Imagination, therefore, can be free or rule governed; in the case of theology, it should be the latter. And what, precisely, is imagination? Although Kaufman never answers this question, his discussion implies that he views it as "that which creates mental images," which Mary Warnock describes as "the most ordinary sense of the word 'imagination' that there is."[82] For example, imagination focuses on certain aspects of *Erlebnis* to formulate images of the objects impinging on us. Moreover, at the highest level of consciousness, it uses materials drawn from its imaginatively interpreted experience at lower levels of consciousness to formulate a picture of the world and of God. Thus, everything revolves around picture images that are the result of the constructive activity of the imagination.

---

[78]Kaufman, "Contemporary Interpretation of Jesus," 142.

[79]See also Kaufman, "Constructing the Concept of God," 23, 30-31.

[80]Ibid., 30-31.

[81]Ibid., 23; and idem, "Metaphysics and Theology," 257-60.

[82]Mary Warnock, *Imagination* (Berkeley and Los Angeles: University of California Press, 1976) 10.

• Some Central Issues •

Kaufman's recent proposals raise numerous issues. Those that are central to his own work, and that will be central to the rest of this book, revolve around the question of the nature and role of imagination in theological reflection and construction. Whether or not one agrees with his proposals, it is evident that he has touched upon a crucial question for theology today, and has done so in a way that sharply raises certain matters that demand our attention. In particular, his emphasis on the imaginative nature of theological work confronts us, in a way that we cannot ignore, with the question of what it means to say that theology is a human enterprise that involves the imagination. That is, he has made it clear that theology must accept the imagination as a central component of its work and must come to terms with the implications of this increasingly inescapable fact.[83]

The issues that Kaufman raises emerge not only from his insistence that theology is an imaginative undertaking but also from his emphasis on the linguisticality and historicity of human life. Because we must operate within certain definite limits on our knowledge, limits grounded in the twin facts that our language shapes all our experience and our historical situatedness circumscribes our horizons, our imaginations must build an environment in which to live. This is true at every level of existence, in Kaufman's view. And, at the level at which theology operates, that level in which we are concerned to construct an ultimate environment for life, the imaginative dimension of human thought becomes especially important, since the subject matter, God, has a unique logical standing—that is, it refers to the ground of all there is. To sharpen these issues a little, I will now take a closer look at Kaufman's treatment of them, with a concern to see what he has established and what he has left unclear or failed to demonstrate.

In the first place, there can be little doubt that Kaufman has rightly argued that theology is an imaginative enterprise. The construction of finite models, concepts, metaphors, and symbols that we can use to refer to an infinite reality, which transcends all that we can experience, does indeed appear to be a highly imaginative undertaking. As we have seen, however, it is not entirely clear what Kaufman means by *imagination* and exactly how it functions in this context. He merely assumes that, if he can

---

[83]Cf. Ronald F. Thiemann, "Revelation and Imaginative Construction," *Journal of Religion* 61 (1981): 242-43; and Green, "Reconstructing Christian Theology," 221.

show that theological proposals are essentially imaginative, this will prove that they are essentially our own construction. But can we assume that imagination is an essentially constructive power? Could it also be receptive in some way?[84]

When dealing with our imaginative understanding of what we experience, Kaufman does not assume that our concepts are imaginative constructions through and through. For in that case we have an experiential check on our concepts, so that they must "correspond" in some sense to our percepts (75). This contrast between theological concepts, which have to do with things of which we have no perception, and empirical concepts, which are meant to relate to and represent things that we experience in our world, is grounded in Kant's distinction between concepts that are filled by intuitions (that is, experience) and empty concepts that can only pretend to represent what is metaphysically true.

Ronald Thiemann has noted this theme in Kaufman's thought and has criticized Kaufman for failing to realize the degree to which all our ideas about the world are imaginative. Noting that Kaufman has posited a sharp dichotomy between activities of description and construction, Thiemann attributes Kaufman's view that God is only a construct to a naive view of empirical concepts.

> Kaufman's appeal to Kant in order to establish his symbolic theory of theological discourse, with its separation between construction and description, revolves around an argument about the logical uniqueness of the concept "God." Kaufman asserts that the concept "God" is "of a different logical order" because it does not correspond to any "percept." The clear implication is that other disciplines are descriptive because they employ concepts which correspond to percepts, while theology, because of the uniqueness of its noncorresponding concepts, must forgo description and be purely constructive.

Against this naive view of the correspondence between ordinary concepts and objects in the world, Thiemann argues that "all concept formation is the result of imaginative construction." As a result, it is wrong to suppose that the truth of any of our concepts lies in their correspondence with items "out there" in the "real world." Instead, since all experience is dependent on our imaginatively created concepts, we have no way of arriving at a concept-independent view of things in order to check these concepts against "reality." Thus even disciplines such as the sci-

---

[84]Cf. Green, "Reconstructing Christian Theology," 221.

ences do not "depend on any simple correspondence of . . . concepts with percepts"; we actually check our concepts by relying on the framework they provide rather than by checking to see if they correspond to items in the world.[85]

Thiemann further argues that, once the sharp distinction between description of things we experience and construction of concepts dealing with what we do not experience is removed, or at least softened, it is possible to reconsider "the methodological fruitfulness of the revelation model," for the separation between construction and description collapses. I do not say that Thiemann wishes to defend what Kaufman calls the "objectivist" approach to theology, in which theological concepts are supposed to be some sort of direct description of God. On the contrary, Thiemann's whole argument has criticized such an objectivist approach in all disciplines, including the sciences. Nevertheless, he does wish to argue that theological proposals can be both constructive and descriptive without falling into this objectivist trap. This duality can occur if theology takes itself to be about the business of bringing God to speech, not through the description of a given percept, but through a conceptual redescription of a narrative text in which we come to see the presence of God for us. God's presence in the biblical text is not direct, since it comes through a double mediation: the humanity of Jesus, and the witness of the biblical narrative to Jesus. In other words, God is hidden in the text that witnesses to Jesus Christ and must be brought to speech through our efforts to follow the logic of this text. This is an imaginative task.

> Precisely because the knowledge of God is indirect, a space is opened which can only be filled by the imaginative act of the theologian. The theologian does not simply repeat the biblical narrative but rather interprets it or conceptually redescribes it. That redescription requires an imaginative act which begins with what David Kelsey has called an "imaginative construal of the presence of God pro nobis," but the imagination continues to function as the theologian depicts the world as seen through that construal.[86]

Thus, through a denial of Kaufman's separation of description and construction, and through an understanding of revelation that tries to avoid the objectivist trap, Thiemann tries to bring imagination and revelation together.

---

[85]Thiemann, "Revelation," 248, 249, 252, 254-57.

[86]Ibid., 252, 258-60. 262-63.

Thiemann's criticism of Kaufman has some merit, especially in his insistence that Kaufman has no warrant for positing a sharp dichotomy between description and construction and in his argument that a dependence on revelation need not fall into objectivism. On the other hand, Thiemann's critique fails to hit the mark squarely because it overlooks two important factors in Kaufman's thought. First, by jumping too quickly to the conclusion that Kaufman has a naive view of truth as correspondence between ideas and realities, he fails to realize that Kaufman is well aware of the imaginative nature of all our perception. Second, Thiemann misconstrues Kaufman's argument when he states that Kaufman believes that the concept of God is of a different logical order "because it does not correspond to any percept."[87] This is only partly true. The other dimension of Kaufman's argument at this point, which Thiemann never acknowledges, is that the concept of God has to do with that which is the *ground* of the world and therefore of all percepts. This, rather than the fact that we have no direct experience of God, is the fundamental reason that the concept of God has a unique logical status.

The relationship between our ideas and things "out there" is of course a matter of considerable dispute. Some have criticized Kaufman for being too pessimistic about the possibility of knowing the nature of reality and of speaking about this reality.[88] Thiemann, on the other hand, finds Kaufman too willing to speak as if our language corresponds to items in the world. Is this merely a matter of different perspectives? To some degree it is. Yet it is also a matter of failing to appreciate Kaufman's position on its own terms. Although Thiemann's article is well argued, he caricatures Kaufman's epistemology. Thiemann too quickly passes over certain indications in Kaufman's *Essay on Theological Method* that Kaufman does in fact realize that all our concepts are imaginatively constructed. At one point, Thiemann acknowledges that such indications are to be found, but he concludes, on the basis of the contrast that Kaufman draws between God and ordinary percepts, as well as on the basis of Kaufman's use of "correspondence" language, that Kaufman does not take the imaginative character of concepts seriously.[89]

---

[87]Ibid., 248.

[88]See, e.g., D. R. Griffin, "Gordon Kaufman's Theology: Some Questions," *Journal of the American Academy of Religion* 41 (1973): 554-72; and Kevin J. Sharpe, "Theological Method and Gordon Kaufman,"*Religious Studies* 15 (1979): 173-90.

[89]Thiemann, "Revelation," 250.

Against Thiemann's conclusion, we have already seen that Kaufman's distinction between God and other concepts rests on more than the fact that God is not a percept. Furthermore, although Kaufman's use of the language of correspondence is vulnerable to criticism, the way in which he uses it suggests that Thiemann has based too much on the presence of this terminology. For example, one critical passage uses the language of correspondence, yet does so in a way that indicates that Kaufman is using this language loosely.

> The question of whether theological claims are true, and if so in what respects, has not been straightforwardly addressed in this essay. This is because this question, as usually understood, presupposes what I have called the "perceptual model" of reality, where the correspondence of our ideas with the reals "out there" is a proper issue. It is appropriate to raise the question of truth in this form with regard to every object or quality in the world, for here we are concerned with the way in which one item in our conceptual scheme relates to and represents one item *in what we call (also in our conceptual scheme) experience or the world.* (75; italics mine)

While Thiemann rightly criticizes the idea expressed here that there is some kind of one-to-one relationship between concepts and items in the world, the last sentence shows that we should be careful about putting too much weight on what Kaufman says about correspondence. That is, Kaufman's statement suggests that even our experience is understood in terms of our conceptual scheme. Thus, it is not some sort of raw sensation to which we can appeal for confirmation of our concepts. This idea is fully consistent with Kaufman's argument against theologies that try to ground themselves in religious experience. They will not work, he insists, because there is no such thing as raw experience. Rather, all our experience is understood in terms of concepts that we have created, so that, in effect, such theologies are appealing not to our experience but to the concepts we have constructed (4-8). Moreover, this argument is what one would expect in light of Kaufman's discussion in *Relativism, Knowledge, and Faith* of the imaginative character of all our knowledge.[90]

Should we conclude, then, that Thiemann's critique rests wholly on a misunderstanding, that Thiemann and Kaufman actually agree at this point? Not at all, for there is a basic point of disagreement between them, one that is rooted in a Kantian distinction. Kaufman does indeed want to argue that there is some sort of difference between concepts that deal with

---

[90]Kaufman, *Relativism, Knowledge, and Faith*, 27-38.

our empirical world and those that lack empirical content. Thiemann, however, rejects this view, or at least tries to soften the distinction. In his argument against it, Thiemann refers to Kant's distinction between sensibility (*Sinnlichkeit*) and understanding (*Verstand*) and maintains that this distinction will not hold, since "it is necessary to establish the priority and independence of percepts" if one is "to claim a correspondence between concepts and percepts."[91] This ordering is no doubt true for any claims about correspondence between concepts and percepts. However, the issue of the distinction between sensibility and understanding is not thereby settled. Rather, Thiemann's criticism has merely shown the shortcomings of one way of dealing with the distinction. It does not necessarily lead to a rejection of the distinction itself.

Perhaps this point will be clearer if we consider the distinction in light of a basic dictum of Kant: "Thoughts without content are empty, intuitions without concepts are blind."[92] That is to say, the percepts received through our sensibility require language to be meaningful, yet our language needs the content provided by sensibility to be anything other than empty ideas. The point seems too obvious to belabor. Yet one brief example may be in order. If one is given directions to a spot in a strange city, the meaning of the language is clear. On the other hand, what could one make of directions to a spot in the heavenly New Jerusalem? This does not mean that there is, in the first case, a *correspondence* between the (linguistic) directions and some sort of percept. It merely means that the directions are given meaningful content through an empirical relationship of some sort between the language and the city in which we wish to find a spot. If one denies this, an extreme solipsism would seem to be the result.

It is interesting that, in spite of his criticism of Kaufman and Kant, Thiemann does in fact operate with some kind of distinction between sensibility and concepts. This can be seen in at least two places in his argument. First, Thiemann speaks of our concepts as coming from a conceptual framework bequeathed to us by a "linguistic community."[93] Now to speak of a community giving us a conceptual framework, that is, to note that in some way our concepts come to us through experiences of something or someone outside ourselves, is to raise anew the question of the relationship between those concepts and sensibility. For if experience is

---

[91]Thiemann, "Revelation," 251.

[92]Immanuel Kant, *Critique of Pure Reason*, trans. Norman Kemp Smith (New York: St. Martin's Press, 1929) A51 = B75 (p. 93).

[93]Thiemann, "Revelation," 253.

created or completely shaped by one's concepts, it is difficult to see how one can be given concepts by a linguistic community. Rather, the linguistic community itself would have to be the creation of one's own conceptual construction (thus, the solipsism mentioned above).

Second, in his treatment of the imaginative character of theology, Thiemann notes that for Barth the knowledge of God is indirect. He continues, "Precisely because the knowledge of God is indirect, a space is opened which can only be filled by the imaginative act of the theologian."[94] This is a curious statement in light of Thiemann's earlier criticism of Kaufman. One would have expected him to argue that, since the imagination is involved in all concept formation, it is involved in the same way here. Instead, in a manner similar to Kaufman, he states that God's hiddenness opens a space in which imagination can be active. The imagination, then, is more active (or active in a different way) in this case than in those cases having to do with things that are not hidden. Again, do we not find here a tacit dependence on the distinction between sensibility and understanding? If so, even Thiemann's own arguments lend some support to the distinction Kaufman has made.

On the other hand, Thiemann's criticism of Kaufman's discussion of this distinction still has some merit. For, as already noted above, Kaufman does at times speak as if there were a one-to-one relation between concepts having to do with our experience of things in the world and percepts. As Thiemann has correctly argued, however, conceptual frameworks are actually validated by relying on them as a whole rather than by checking to see whether each concept has a corresponding percept. And this qualification does in fact suggest that the distinction portrayed by Kaufman should be softened. It should only be softened, however, rather than removed, since the difference between ideas with an empirical content and those that lack such a content remains valid. Thus, some of the problems associated with the fact that we have no experience of God remain. Still, the function of our conceptual frameworks in everyday situations has some similarity with the function of theological frameworks, so that the former may provide clues for dealing with problems associated with the latter. In this sense, Thiemann's argument is well taken.

Thiemann also makes an effective criticism of Kaufman's argument that the proper context in which to understand language about God is the context provided by "ordinary language." Thiemann rightly points out that Wittgenstein, who is the inspiration for this argument, was critical

---

[94]Ibid., 262.

of generalizations such as "ordinary language." Instead, he argued that the meaning of language is to be found in its relation to a "form of life," which in this case suggests that the meaning of language about God is to be found in religious forms of life.[95] Along the same lines, Kevin J. Sharpe has shown that Kaufman makes unwarranted assumptions about our ability to know exactly what the "ordinary" meaning of "God" is.[96] In short, Barth's claim that theology is grounded in the church's talk about God is not as easily dismissed as Kaufman supposes.

• Conclusion •

Kaufman himself once held to Barth's view on the basis of one of the primary implications of the linguisticality of human life, namely, its historicity. By *historicity* Kaufman means that our historical location gives our lives a particular perspective that we cannot simply leave behind as we wish. This perspective is mediated to us through language, the instrument for the transmission of culture. In his early writings Kaufman used this fact as a basis for arguing that revelation was a foundation for theology's affirmations about God, insisting that everyone had to turn to some revelation as a ground for orientation in life. For the Christian, of course, this revelation is centered in Jesus Christ, who is transmitted to us through the tradition of the church. By the time of the publication of his *Essay on Theological Method*, however, Kaufman had undergone a dramatic change of mind. Although he continues to argue for the historicity of human life, he now denies that this feature means that Christian theology must begin from a revelation. On the contrary, our historicity is a basis for arguing that our ideas of God are our own construction. Furthermore, since we live and operate in contexts shaped by tradition, we must use our tradition as we try to construct/reconstruct our ideas about what is ultimately real. We are not simply bound to our tradition, however, for we must address our current needs, and this action may require a radical break from the past. Yet even in such a case, the tradition provides material that we can use as we try to further the humanization of life.

Two questions must be raised about Kaufman's discussion of historicity. First, can he consistently argue, on one side, that we are historically determined beings who must operate with the categories given to us from the past and, on the other, that our tradition is basically material for us

---

[95]Ibid., 247-48.

[96]Sharpe, "Theological Method," 175-79.

to use in constructing something that is intended to lead us to a goal that is apparently understood at some point and to some degree apart from tradition (humanization)? Whence comes this goal? How do we know how to define it? Second, has Kaufman therefore found a nonhistorical (and therefore nonlinguistic) foundation for his thought? Or has he, instead, found a new "revelation?" In terms of his discussion of revelation in *Systematic Theology*, the latter seems to be the case. For, if in fact what is revelatory for us is whatever we take to be a self-evident starting point given to us from the past, then the apparently self-evident idea of humanization has become Kaufman's revelation (though he himself does not acknowledge this fact). The historical ground of this idea seems to lie somewhere in the Enlightenment and its aftermath. We must ask about the adequacy of his revelation. This is an extremely difficult question to answer, since there is no neutral vantage point from which to make a judgment. On the other hand, the question cannot be avoided. Also, one can legitimately ask and answer the question from an avowedly Christian point of view, especially since Kaufman intends to be writing about what Christian theology should be doing.

In sum, the linguisticality and historicity of human life mean the imagination is involved in all knowledge. In the case of theology, however, Kaufman argues that the imagination is especially prominent because we have to do with a reality of which we have no experience and, even more, because we have to do with the reality that is supposed to ground all experience and is therefore not an object among objects. Thus, we cannot check our concepts of God against our experience of God. Furthermore, we should not think of God in objectivist terms, for to do so would be to violate the unique logical status of the ground of all existents. Instead, we should realize that, as the concept that focuses our understanding of the ultimate foundation of all existence and that therefore provides the ultimate framework of orientation for our lives, God is an intramental concept, a regulative idea that provides a structure for our experience. Alternatively, Kaufman argues that God can be understood in terms of cosmic forces tending toward humanization. How the understanding of God as intramental and the understanding of God as "cosmic forces" are to be related to each other, Kaufman never explains. At any rate, the concept of God is the result of a highly complex and abstract imaginative act. That is, it draws on our already imaginatively constructed concepts of finite realities in order to apply some of them to this infinite reality that transcends our experience and understanding.

Kaufman rightly stresses that God has a unique logical status and is not an object among objects, or even a being among beings. In this light, he rightly calls into question claims of a direct experience of God. His claim, then, that the imagination has an especially prominent role to play in our talk about God is well supported. However, it does not necessarily follow that God is only an "intramental" concept and that all attempts to think of God as having independent existence are illegitimate forms of objectivist thought. Surely those who profess faith in God, even when they have insight into the fact that God can be never properly be thought of as one of the beings or objects of our universe, mean to profess their trust in and commitment to a reality, a mystery, that transcends not only their experience and understanding but also their existence— a reality that is truly self-grounded and that is the ground of all existence. It is one thing to argue that we have no direct experience of God, quite another to maintain that the word *God* lacks a referent.[97] Thus, even though theology is not dealing with a given object that it is to describe, this admission does not force us to the conclusion that God is essentially an imaginative construction that we have built for our own purposes. In this context, despite his caricature of Kaufman's view and his questionable rejection of the distinction between sensibility and understanding, Thiemann may well be right when he suggests that the "foundation" metaphor has beguiled Kaufman into assuming that theology must be engaged in either imaginative construction or description of an object.[98] Could the imagination be both constructive and descriptive (in the sense not of describing an object but of making God present through, for example, the "conceptual redescription" of a narrative)?

This question highlights a problem pervading Kaufman's recent work, namely, a failure to give careful attention to the notion of imagination. The resulting vagueness in his use of the term leaves several questions hanging. For example, what is the relationship between imagination in "ordinary" perception and in theology? Between faith's apprehensions and theology's constructions? Between imagination and the linguistic/historical nature of human life? Between imagination and tradition? Also, his concentration on the role of imagination in theology fails to consider what it would mean to highlight the imaginative nature of the concept of humanization. As a result, one is sometimes left with the impression that theological concepts are imaginative, whereas the concept of humanization is basically empirical and can therefore serve as a guide for the imag-

---

[97]Perhaps this fact has now been acknowledged by Kaufman in his definition of God in terms of cosmic forces.

[98]Thiemann, "Revelation," 254.

inative construction of the former. This, of course, is not Kaufman's stated view. Yet his actual discussion of these issues gives one cause to wonder. At any rate, the point I wish to stress is that Kaufman needs a more rigorous understanding of imagination.

The rest of my efforts in this book are directed toward a careful consideration of the imagination and some of its implications for theology. My purpose is not to shore up Kaufman's proposals. Rather, I consider the imagination with a view to reconsidering some of the issues Kaufman's work raises. At the heart of these issues is the question of the relationship between theology's imaginative constructions and the realities affirmed by faith. That is to say, the central issue raised by Kaufman and addressed here is the problem of the relationship between imagination and faith. Is the imagination in theology an essentially constructive activity, or does it have a significant receptive dimension as well? In answering this question, I give some (mostly indirect) consideration to the nature and role of revelation. I focus, however, on the imagination and how it relates to faith and theology. Such consideration will provide a framework within which revelation could (in another book) be further examined.

KANT ON THE
IMAGINATION

When one approaches the issue of the imagination, it quickly becomes apparent that an overwhelming number of different aspects could be considered. Fortunately, the focus of this work does not require a thorough investigation of all aspects of the imagination. In particular, the psychological and physiological aspects of the imagination, while undoubtedly of some interest, are not directly relevant to my purposes. Rather, I explore, in practical terms, how the imagination *functions* as we orient ourselves and find our way in the world.

The particular angle from which I approach the imagination is largely shaped by the questions raised by Kaufman's recent work. To provide a basic framework for my development of a theory of the imagination, I begin with an analysis of Kant's treatment of this theme. I have chosen this starting point for a number of reasons. First, Kaufman frequently appeals to Kant. It is interesting to note that, even though Kaufman appeals to Kant's work as a basis for his understanding of the limits and possibilities of human life, he does not directly make use of Kant when treating the imagination. This neglect is curious, since Kant made much of the imagination in his *Critique of Pure Reason* and *Critique of Judgment.* If Kaufman had made use of Kant at this point, it may have led to a significant modification of his understanding of the imagination, for Kant tried to balance its constructive and receptive dimensions. This fact makes Kant especially interesting and significant as a starting point in my own analysis of the imagination. A second reason for beginning with Kant is that he recognized the pivotal role that imagination plays in human life and perception. His recognition was distorted by his attempts to reach an ahistorical, a priori level of human cognition in his analysis. Nevertheless, he managed to uncover some fundamentally important insights into the nature of the imagination's operation in human life. Finally, because Kant develops some of the basic features of the imagination and connects them with its essential role in human life and perception, he provides a point of departure for some more recent analyses of the imagination, which I consider in the next chapter.

I first examine Kant's treatment of the imagination in *Critique of Pure Reason* and then turn to *Critique of Judgment* to see the development there of his understanding of the imagination. Finally, I compare briefly Kant's and Kaufman's views of the imagination. Throughout these analyses, it will be apparent that Kant's presentation suffers from some important weaknesses, although he also provides some valuable insights into the nature and role of the imagination in human life.

• The Imagination
in *Critique of Pure Reason* •

Immanuel Kant used several words for imagination, but the most frequent and most important was *Einbildungskraft*. Mary Warnock states that this term "suggests a power of making images, pictures or representations of things."[1] And, in fact, Kant's use of the word throughout his first and third critiques supports her definition. Furthermore, at several crucial places in *Critique of Pure Reason*, Kant clearly connects this power of making images with a power of synthesis, of bringing together a number of ideas, sensations, and so forth to create a whole. Indeed, this is the imagination's primary function at the most fundamental level of perception, as Kant depicts it.

The Transcendental Imagination

The imagination is able to operate at this fundamental level of perception because it is both a "transcendental" (or "productive") faculty and an "empirical" (or "reproductive") faculty.[2] At the transcendental level, the imagination is said to mediate between the categories of the pure understanding (*Verstand*) and the manifold intuitions of the faculty of sensibility (*Sinnlichkeit*).[3] Here Kant follows the lead of philosophers such as Hume, who assumed that we receive a multitude of discrete sensations

---

[1]Mary Warnock, *Imagination* (Berkeley and Los Angeles: University of California Press, 1976) 26.

[2]Immanuel Kant, *Critique of Pure Reason*, trans. Norman Kemp Smith (New York: St. Martin's Press, 1965, c. 1929) A118-30 (pp. 142-50).

[3]Ibid., A124 (p. 146).

from the external world. The connection between these sensations, moreover, depends not on what comes from the external world but from the activity of our own minds. Now for Hume this connection is arbitrary, for it depends on the choice of our imaginations, which synthesize a variety of sensations that we originally experienced as a chaotic multiplicity. This choice is influenced by factors such as what kinds of sensations usually occur together and similarities between sensations, yet at base the combination of sensations rests on no more than the subject's decision. Kant did not question the idea of a multiplicity (a "manifold") of originally unconnected sensations. But he did deny that we are ever consciously aware of such a multiplicity, since a series of unconnected sensations could provide no real experience. For experience requires a subject who endures through time, and such an enduring subject requires a world of enduring, self-subsisting objects to provide a basis for the development of self-consciousness. Consequently, Kant argued that the multiplicity of sensations ("manifold of intuitions") described by Hume impinges on us at a preconscious level and that we become aware of these sensations only after our transcendental imaginations have synthesized them into a meaningful unity.

The imagination is eminently qualified to perform this task because it has contact with both sensibility and understanding. On the side of sensibility, it has a sensible dimension in that it synthesizes appearances into a representation or image. On the side of understanding, its synthesis is rule governed, taking its lead from the categories supplied by the understanding.[4] Thus, the imagination is able to take the chaos of sense impressions and bring it into a unity by following the lead of principles supplied by the understanding. And all this it does at a transcendental level, that is, at a level preceding our conscious activity and making such activity possible.

Kant here seems to offer us a way to introduce the imagination into a primordial level of human consciousness. Such a view would give strong

---

[4]This exposition, though true to the scheme delineated by Kant here, is in some ways clearer than Kant himself was in *Critique of Pure Reason*, for his discussion is filled with ambiguity about the exact place of the imagination. Thus, at times he treats the imagination as an independent faculty at work between understanding and sensibility, and at other times he treats it as a part of the understanding. Or in some contexts he suggests that sensibility and understanding spring from a common root—the imagination. See *Critique of Pure Reason*, A15 = B29, A835 = B863, A124, B151-52, A78, and A141; Norman Kemp Smith, *A Commentary to Kant's "Critique of Pure Reason"* (London: Macmillan, 1966) 77, 225, 264-66.

support to treating the imagination as a fundamental factor in all human activities. Unfortunately, Kant's discussion becomes suspect once some of his basic presuppositions are brought under scrutiny. For example, in terms of the limitations that he himself has placed on human knowledge, he has claimed much more about the transcendental operations of the human mind than he is allowed to say. How are we to know what happens, empirically speaking, at the preconscious level at which the external world impinges on us? Is he not attempting to say something empirical about that which is a foundation for our empirical knowledge? For example, how can we claim that our original intuitions are manifold rather than, say, a unity? As P. F. Strawson has seen, Kant's view is vulnerable to "the ad hominem objection that we can claim no empirical knowledge of its truth; for this would be to claim empirical knowledge of the occurrence of that which is held to be the antecedent condition of empirical knowledge."[5] Strawson's criticism is of a piece with his general objection to Kant's effort to ground the nature of knowledge entirely in our cognitive faculties.[6] Thus, Kant erroneously supposed that the legitimate distinction between our experience and our ideas about our experience serves to justify claims about "faculties" of sensibility and understanding and about the contribution that each faculty makes to our consciously unified experience of the world.[7] The alternative, of course, is to start with our experience in an analytical exploration of limitations to, and necessary general features of, human experience, without supposing that this approach opens a way to make empirical statements about its transcendental ground in our cognitive constitutions. That is, the alternative is to examine features of experience without becoming involved in questions about its necessary conditions in some a priori realm.

---

[5]P. F. Strawson, *The Bounds of Sense: An Essay on Kant's Critique of Pure Reason* (London: Methuen, 1966) 32.

[6]See ibid., 15-16: "Wherever he [Kant] found limiting or necessary general features of experience, he declared their source to be in our own cognitive constitution; and this doctrine he considered indispensable as an explanation of the possibility of knowledge of the necessary structure of experience. Yet there is no doubt that this doctrine is incoherent in itself and masks, rather than explains, the real character of his inquiry; so that a central problem in understanding the Critique is precisely that of disentangling all that hangs on this doctrine from the analytical argument which is in fact independent of it."

[7]Ibid., 20-21.

Kant did not proceed in this direction, because he had accepted the "idea idea" that had been formulated by Descartes.[8] He could have made his point against Humean atomism by rejecting this "Cartesian-Humean notion that you could get away from common sense to a 'philosophical view' according to which 'only perceptions are present to the mind.' '"[9] That is, this dualistic approach rests on some questionable assumptions about human perception and experience, and Kant could have approached the problems he wanted to resolve by examining those assumptions in a critical light.[10]

Such an alternative was closed to Kant, however, at least partly because he wanted to make room for a "noumenal" realm within which he could place God, the immortal soul, and free will. Having made the distinction between phenomenal and noumenal realms in *Critique of Pure Reason*, Kant then postulated God, immortality, and freedom in his discussion of the categorical imperative in *Critique of Practical Reason*. The effort to postulate God, a soul, and free will as necessary implicates of moral existence fails in light of Kant's own claim that the categorical imperative confronts us as something we must simply obey. That is to say, it demands obedience regardless of whether we can understand the world as ultimately rational. Moreover, it is hard to see how Kant could get around the point that any effort to posit God as the ultimate foundation of the moral life is an illegitimate application of the phenomenal category of causality to the noumenal realm. The noumenal realm, then, needs more than the categorical imperative as its justification. Unfortunately for Kant's system, that justification is also lacking in *Critique of Pure Reason,* as Strawson rightly argues. At any rate, since his system tried to make room for the noumenal realm by treating human perception as a product of both the understanding, which processes only ideas, and the sensibility, which processes only sensations, he needed something to mediate between them—namely, the imagination. The question facing us now is whether the failure of Kant's dualistic approach to experience makes his discussion of the imagination useless for us.

---

[8]Richard Rorty defines the "idea idea" as "the notion that people came in two halves, a mind and a body, and that one could focus the eye of the mind on 'inner space' and find 'ideas' there." Unpublished notes handed out by Richard Rorty in class, Princeton, New Jersey, 7 February 1980.

[9]Unpublished class notes distributed by Rorty, Princeton, New Jersey, 12 February 1980.

[10]For a thorough, critical analysis of this type of dualism, see Gilbert Ryle, *The Concept of Mind* (New York: Barnes & Noble, 1949).

Imagination and Synthesis

The failure of Kant's "psychological" approach to the nature of human experience and understanding certainly does undercut his treatment of this particular activity of the imagination. Nevertheless, his discussion may still be of some value. For his view of the imagination as a power of synthesis that can operate in a rule-governed manner is a sound intuition—especially if we speak in terms of powers or capacities rather than of faculties and if we avoid transcendental pretensions. Hence we may still discover that the imagination has a crucial role to play in human cognition, even if we arrive at that conclusion in a different way than did Kant. In other words, though any analysis of imagination today must eschew Kant's transcendental approach, his treatment of other aspects of our imaginative powers remains instructive for contemporary analysis.

Even Kant's transcendental analysis offers some suggestive insights, since he, fortunately, did not remain consistently transcendental in his explanation of the a priori synthetic activity of the imagination.[11] Thus, he states that the idea of "dog" "signifies a rule according to which my imagination can delineate the figure of a four-footed animal in a general manner, without limitation to any single determinate figure such as experience, or any possible image that I can represent in concreto, actually presents."[12] The manner in which this happens, Kant asserts, "is an art concealed in the depths of the human soul." But we do know enough about it to say that the image we receive of any particular object, such as a dog, is never completely congruent with the concept under which it is subsumed—for example, any particular dog will in some ways have its own distinctive characteristics that do not belong to the general concept of dog.[13] And yet, through the activity of the imagination, particular objects are subsumed under general concepts—a four-footed animal with certain features is seen as a dog. Here Kant is on firmer ground, for he is dealing with empirical, rather than transcendental, dimensions of perception.

---

[11]Norman Kemp Smith notes that at A141-42 "Kant speaks of the empirical faculty of productive imagination, and so is led, to the great confusion of his exposition, though also to the enrichment of his teaching, to allow of empirical as well as of transcendental schemata [for Kant the schemata are rules for the production of images and are therefore of central importance in the imagination's mediating work], and thus contrary to his own real position to recognise schemata of such empirical objects as dog or horse" (*Commentary*, 337).

[12]Kant, *Critique of Pure Reason*, A141 = B180 (pp. 182-83).

[13]Ibid., A142 = B181 (p. 183).

Kant's point is compelling. Particular objects in our experience, when viewed in their individuality, are indeed unique in some ways. Yet they often share many things in common with other individual objects of our experience. Our general concepts come from the abstraction of these common features into a class of objects to which we assign the individuals. Hence, both the formation of the rules for the production of an image (that is, the creation of an abstract notion of a class of objects, which provides us with principles for the representation of a general image of those objects) and the subsumption of any individual existent under that class are activities of the imagination, according to Kant.[14]

Now if we think of the imagination as a faculty of the mind, there is still reason to question Kant here. For how do we know that we have some single "faculty" in our minds that has this particular function? Are we even sure that this is the right way to view the mind? On the other hand, if we think here not of a faculty but of a functional power, whose possible source in our cognitive constitution is not important for the issue at hand, then this is a helpful and promising approach. That is, it suggests that our activities of concept formation and of subsumption of individuals under general categories stem from our imaginative power to see things in our world as possessing some sort of significance that goes beyond the individual. This understanding brings us into contact with Mary Warnock's definition of imagination. Partly in dependence on Kant, she defines imagination as the power of "seeing as" and connects it with the ability to construct images of things.[15] Such creative ability entails the power of synthesis, of bringing together the similar in the midst of the dissimilar.

This power of synthesis and image construction is certainly not transcendental in the sense that Kant assigned to the "transcendental imagination." Yet this imaginative capacity remains an essential and basic aspect of human cognition, albeit at the empirical level. Now to suggest that this constitutive activity of the imagination is an empirical rather than transcendental activity is to suggest that it is a historically shaped activity. That is to say, once one abandons the transcendental, a priori claims made by Kant, one had left behind the realm of that which is supposedly above the flux of history and brought the imagination, as well as the rest of our human cognitive powers, into the sphere of historical continuity and change. Thus, if one defines imagination as the power of "seeing as," one must add that how we see our world and all it contains is profoundly

---

[14]Cf. Warnock, *Imagination*, 27-28.

[15]Ibid., 138, 140.

shaped by our sociohistorical location. And, by pressing the historicity of the imagination a bit further, it becomes apparent that the metaphor of "seeing as" may be somewhat misleading, for it implies that the imagination does its work primarily, if not wholly, on the level of individual, conscious perception. However, as I argue later, we are most deeply shaped by the part of our tradition that we are not conscious of. Can we not then find here a warrant for understanding the imagination as more than an individual, conscious power and activity? And do we not have reason to suggest that the ocular metaphor of "seeing as" is helpful but not finally sufficient?

• The Imagination
in *Critique of Judgment* •

These questions will emerge again as important guides in my attempt to develop an understanding of the imagination as it relates to faith and theology. Before following their lead, however, there is still more to learn from Kant's treatment of the imagination, for his third critique also provides an insightful discussion of the imagination. There the free play of the imagination is his primary focus of concern.

Beauty and the Free Play of the Imagination

The free play of the imagination, operating apart from the constraints of any rules, is perhaps the most common way that people tend to understand its role in human life. It is the power by which we engage in daydreams and by which we enter into the most far-flung flights of fancy. Kant, of course, also recognized that this was a part of the imagination's powers. However, his concern in *Critique of Judgment* is not with flights of fancy but with a free and spontaneous activity of the imagination that is nevertheless in harmony with the rules of the understanding. In this spontaneous yet ordered play of the imagination, Kant locates the experience of beauty and the sense of nature as a purposive whole.

According to Kant, whenever we encounter a beautiful object, we receive the impression that it is purposefully ordered, yet, to the degree that we view it as an aesthetic object, we are unable to assign a definite conception of purpose to it. That is, the way in which the various parts of a beautiful object fit together gives it the appearance of a purposive structure; and in this way the representation of the object in our imaginations is in accord with the ordering rules of our understanding. Nevertheless, this appearance of purposiveness is purely immanent to the object; that is, the viewer does not see the aesthetic object as having been made for an external purpose that determined its design. In this sense, the imagination, as it uses its representational power to play with the object, is free from what Kant calls "concepts," so that it is not subject to the understanding in this case. Thus, the imagination operates freely yet remains in harmony with the understanding. In Kant's view, this harmony gives rise to the feeling that we know as the experience of beauty. This feeling is free from all "interest," that is, from all concern about other possible uses and benefits of the object, and rests entirely on the harmony between imagination and understanding. The ability to judge whether an object will give rise to a harmony between the free play of the imagination and the understanding Kant called "taste." He further argued that at base we all have the same cognitive structure, so that the imagination and understanding in everyone will operate in the same way. Hence the experience of beauty should be the same for all (even though it often is not), and true judgments of taste are universally true (that is, demand assent from all).

Kant's treatment of beauty concerns itself primarily with the beauty of nature. Indeed, for him the beauty of art is derivative from this more fundamental form of our experience of beauty. Of course, whereas natural beauty is produced apart from our intentional activity, leaving only the experience of beauty a matter for philosophical concern, artistic beauty is the product of human creativity. Thus, a critique of aesthetic judgment must in this case deal with both the experience and the production of the beautiful object. Structurally, the experience of a beautiful work of art is the same as that of a beautiful "work" of nature—that is, a spontaneous harmony between the imagination's free play and the understanding's rules.

But how do we explain the production of the work of art that gives rise to this delightful harmony? Kant was sure that the work of producing a beautiful object must in some way parallel the experience of its beauty. That is to say, there must also be a free play of the imagination in the production of a work of art. Yet this play must be in harmony with the understanding. Only in this way can a work of art yield the impression of an order that arises freely, that is, without being subject to the constraint of rules. Those who are able to produce beautiful objects through a free play of imagination Kant called "geniuses." Through considering their works, which serve as exemplars for the further production of aesthetic objects, we refine our judgments of taste. That is, through the sensitive and intelligent experience of great works of art, we hone our ability to judge whether other works of art are beautiful. However, Kant does not mean that the artist who is a genius can dictate standards of beauty for the rest of us. On the contrary, according to Kant the genius is not in a position to engage in arbitrary construction, or even to explain to others what makes his or her work great. For the genius, in a spontaneous and unconscious way, receives rules for the production of art from nature. "*Genius* is the talent (or natural gift) which gives the rule to art. Since talent, as the innate productive faculty of the artist, belongs itself to nature, we may express the matter thus: Genius is the innate mental disposition [*ingenium*] *through which* nature gives the rule to art."[16]

Furthermore, even the genius is ultimately dependent on the faculty of taste (which, we must remember is developed in our experience of nature as well as of the previous history of art), for through taste's judgments the talent of genius is refined, and the works produced by genius are judged to be beautiful or not. In short, Kant grounds the experience of beauty in nature, so that the production of beautiful art must be viewed in its dependence on nature to be properly understood (sec. 46 [pp. 150-51]).

If one searches for a reason for Kant's relegation of art to the status of a handmaiden of nature, one does not have far to look. In the introduction to *Critique of Judgment*, he indicates the need to find some way to mediate between the phenomenal world of nature, subject to the categories of the understanding, and the world of ethics, discovered by us through the dictates of practical reason. If one were to leave things as they stood at the end of his first two critiques, these two worlds would remain wholly unrelated, and one would therefore have no reason to suppose that the free world of the categorical imperative could actually impinge on the phenomenal world of mechanistic causes and effects. Consequently, motivation for ethical action would be vitiated, if not destroyed. However, this problem can be overcome through a consideration of the faculty that mediates between (theoretical) understanding and (practical) reason, namely, the faculty of judgment. Now, once our faculty of judgment discovers that the representations provided by the imagination's free play are in accord with understanding's rules, we are encouraged to think the possibility that the phenomenal world of appearances is in fact in harmony with the realm of ethical demands. This correspondence, to be sure, is not something that we can know but only something we are encouraged to think by the experience of beauty. Yet for beauty to have this effect, it must come from nature. Otherwise, we would simply have to attribute the harmony between representations and the understanding to the artifice of human production and not

---

[16]Kant, *Critique of Judgment*, trans. J. H. Bernard (New York: Hafner Publishing Co., 1951) sec. 46 (p. 150); cf. sec. 50 (pp. 163-64). Subsequent citations are noted in the text and refer to section and page numbers in this edition.

to a hidden unity of reason and nature. When natural beauty is given priority, however, such a hidden unity can be thought, though not known. Furthermore, the production of art then finds its place as that which helps us to see the beauty in nature and therefore to think its unity with both understanding and reason.

The Sublime

The same concern to mediate between the phenomenal and noumenal realms is operative in Kant's treatment of the sublime. The sublime has to do with a capacity in our minds that becomes evident through an encounter with those things in nature that overwhelm us with their awesome size or power. Kant's view here is complex. First, he defines the sublime as "that in comparison with which everything else is small." However, nature itself cannot provide us with such a reality, since the size of natural objects is a relative thing. That is, everything can be seen as either small or large, depending on the perspective one adopts. Thus, no object of the senses can properly be called sublime. Yet the reason strives toward the idea of an absolute totality, "in comparison with which everything else is small," and the imagination makes an (always unsuccessful) effort to represent it. Now the imagination's inability to represent this idea of reason leads us to view the reason as a "supersensible" faculty that is greater than and has dominion over the (sensible) faculty of imagination. The sublime is therefore actually located in the capacity of our reason to formulate the idea of an absolute totality. Things in nature are sublime only in a derivative sense, when they excite our minds into striving after this idea of reason. Thus, Kant states, "it is not the object of sense but the use which the judgment naturally makes of certain objects on behalf of this latter feeling [of a supersensible faculty] that is absolutely great, and in comparison every other use is small. Consequently it is the state of mind produced by a certain representation with which the reflective judgment is occupied, and not the object, that is to be called sublime." Kant thus amends his earlier definition and states that "the sublime is that, the mere ability to think which, shows a faculty of the mind surpassing every standard of sense" (sec. 25 [pp. 88-89]).

The possession of a faculty that surpasses "every standard of sense," and that therefore surpasses the imagination, makes the sublime an important mediating link between the phenomenal and noumenal realms. Kant explains this mediation in two different and complementary ways, depending on whether we are dealing with the "mathematically sublime" (having to do with magnitude) or the "dynamically sublime" (having to do with force). When we imaginatively represent the greatest possible size to ourselves, we discover that reason can always add to the size of this representation, even though we are unable imaginatively to comprehend this greater size (cf. secs. 26-27 [pp. 89-90, 96-99]). We can think it but not visualize it. As a result, we become aware of the fact that the (supersensible) reason is greater than the imagination and has dominion over it.

As for the dynamically sublime, in this case we encounter awesome forces in nature (such as a storm or the ocean) that vividly bring home to us our own small and insignificant physical stature. Yet, in the face of nature's overwhelming might, we also discover in ourselves a power of resistance—on a different level than the physical. That is, we discover a nonsensuous standard of judgment, residing in our rational faculty, by which we can judge everything in nature—including our own physical well-being—as small and insignificant. These standards are those that are concerned with "our highest fundamental propositions," that is, the demands for ethical action that our reason places on us (sec. 28 [p. 101]). Here again, we discover the superiority of reason over sensibility and the need for the latter to conform to the former, a discovery enabled by the very inability of the sensible to be adequate to the rational. Thus, whereas the experience of beauty arises from a harmony based on the spontaneous agreement of the imagination and the understanding, the experience of the sublime arises from a conflict between the imagination and the reason. However, in this conflict there is also a harmony of sorts, for it is in accordance with the viewpoint of reason that sensibility should be inadequate to it (sec. 27 [p. 97]).

Now the imagination remains essential in the experience of the sublime, even if it is finally inadequate. For it is the imagination's finally unsuccessful efforts to represent ideas of reason that excite these ideas in us and show the superiority of the supersensible realm of reason. In other words, the imagination presents to the mind, through its power of representation, those representations that suggest these ideas of reason but cannot contain them (cf. sec. 29 [pp. 109-10]).

Aesthetic Judgment and the Moral Life

Through the experience of the beautiful and sublime, then, we are encouraged to think the harmony between the phenomenal world and the ethical life, so that it appears possible to realize the demands of the latter in the context of the former. Another way of expressing the point is to say that the beautiful and sublime provide analogies to the operation of practical reason. In fact, Kant at one point suggests that the beautiful acts as a symbol for the moral life, since the experience of beauty has some sim-

ilarities with the experience of moral demands. Just as we, in the judgment of the beautiful, give the law to ourselves in relation to the objects
that we view, the practical reason legislates to itself through the categorical imperative. Also, the harmony between the imagination and the understanding reminds us of the harmony of the will with itself in the
legislative activity of the practical reason. Furthermore, the beautiful provides one with an immediate experience of pleasure that is devoid of any
personal advantage (any "interest"), which parallels the sort of pleasure
one derives from obeying the categorical imperative. And the experience
of beauty is an experience of something both subjective and universal,
which is also true of the categorical imperative. Thus, the experience of
beauty is well suited to point us to the moral life (cf. sec. 59 [pp. 199-200]).

Each of these characteristics, with the exception of the harmony between imagination and understanding, is also true of the sublime. And
the one difference that does exist gives the sublime an even closer connection with the good.

> A feeling for the sublime in nature cannot well be thought without
> combining therewith a mental disposition which is akin to the
> moral. And although the immediate pleasure in the beautiful of
> nature likewise presupposes and cultivates a certain liberality in our
> mental attitude, i.e. a satisfaction independent of mere sensible
> enjoyment, yet freedom is thus represented as in play rather than
> in that law-directed occupation which is the genuine characteristic
> of human morality, in which reason must exercise dominion over
> sensibility. But in aesthetical judgments upon the sublime this do-
> minion is represented as exercised by the imagination, regarded as
> an instrument of reason. (sec. 29 [p. 109])

As an instrument of reason, the imagination is able to represent things in
a way that maintains our independence of nature (as explained above) and
thereby "to place the absolutely great only in the proper destination of
the subject."

Kant speaks of symbols in this context. For him a symbol is something
we use to guide ourselves in reflecting on the operation of something else.
That is, a symbol operates analogically, shaping the way we think of the
operation of that to which the symbol is applied. Formally speaking, then,
it operates in the same way as the schematism of a concept. However,
unlike a concept, it does not provide theoretical knowledge. Instead, a
symbol provides rules for "the practical determination of what the idea

of it [the object in view] should be for us and for its purposive use" (sec. 59 [p. 198]).[17]

In short, the imagination's power to produce representations, which are freely created yet ordered in a way that is harmonious with the understanding and reason, is an important element in human moral life. The experience of the beautiful cultivates a sense of satisfaction in something other than the gratification of the senses. And the sublime illustrates the power of reason over sensibility. Furthermore, without it we would seem to be living in two entirely separate worlds, one mechanical and subject to the inexorable laws of cause and effect and the other free and subject only to the laws legislated by the free will. With it, we can think the harmony of these two worlds, so that the former gives the appearance of being congenial to the ends of the latter. Here the representational powers of the imagination are in the forefront of Kant's thought, rather than the synthetic.[18] Furthermore, in this sphere the imagination is capable of producing ordered, rather than chaotic, representations, without being subjected to constraints from the understanding and reason.

Teleological Judgment

The harmony between the phenomenal and noumenal worlds receives further support from Kant's critique of teleological judgment. Here he is concerned to analyze a form of reflective judgment that regards nature as purposive—not in the wholly nonconceptual sense of the purposiveness of a beautiful object (that is, "purposiveness without purpose"), but in the sense of viewing nature as the result of an intelligent, purposive cause working according to a design. Kant is quick to point out that there is absolutely no way, either a priori or a posteriori, to demonstrate that nature is in fact the product of such a cause (sec. 61 [pp. 205-207]). Yet this way of looking at nature can help us to organize our investigation of it and thereby further our scientific inquiries. When so used, the concept of teleology is a "regulative idea" formulated by the reflective judgment (secs. 61, 67 [pp. 205-207, 224-28]).

Kant does not suggest that one has a warrant for adopting from the outset a teleological view of the whole of nature. On the contrary, nature

---

[17]Kant makes a point of saying that the knowledge of God is symbolic in this sense of the term.

[18]Of course, these two should not be separated. They can be distinguished, however, and in this case the representational work of the imagination receives Kant's major attention. Thus *Vorstellung* and *Vorstellungskräfte* are frequently used terms in his discussion of aesthetic judgment.

as a whole can be seen in a mechanistic rather than a teleological way (secs. 63-65 [pp. 212-22]). However, when we encounter organisms whose internal organization is such that, through the interdependent relationship of their various parts, we find ourselves compelled to think of them as the products of a cause operating according to a purposive design, then we have a warrant for investigating them in a way that is guided by the notion of purpose. For in such cases we seem to be dealing with more than a mere succession of efficient causes, as is the case in mechanistic structures. We seem, instead, to be dealing with a reciprocity by which the organism maintains each of its parts and forms itself into the individual that it is. According to Kant, we find this sort of reciprocity comprehensible only in terms of human purposive action. In such cases we cannot attribute purposive causality to nature itself, for the idea of purpose comes from the structure of our own thinking rather than from nature itself. We cannot make such organisms intelligible to ourselves, however, without treating them as if their existence were dependent on purposive causes (secs. 64-65 [pp. 216-22]).

Having made this point, Kant returns to the idea of viewing the whole of nature teleologically and argues that, when we begin with the teleological appearance of organisms, we do indeed have a basis for taking the rest of nature in this way. In his view, the introduction of the idea of purpose into any part of nature brings into play a principle that is at variance with the principle of mechanistic causality. Moreover, any attempt to judge nature by both principles at once would deprive us of any "certain rule of judging," so that "the purpose of nature must be extended to everything included in its product" (sec. 66 [pp. 223-24]). At another point Kant makes his point succinctly. "By the example that nature gives us in its organic products we are justified, nay called upon, to expect of it and of its laws nothing that is not purposive on the whole" (sec. 67 [p. 226]).

Curiously, Kant says nothing about the role of the imagination in the operation of the teleological judgment. He writes, instead, about the conjunction of understanding (the source of a priori, universal laws of nature) and reason (the source of ideas of purpose). Nevertheless, there does seem to be some warrant, in light of Kant's discussion of the imagination elsewhere, for suggesting that the imagination is intimately involved here. For surely the synthesis involved in formulating the idea of purposive organisms and a purposive nature is the work of the imagination, since the imagination is the power of synthesis. This view receives some support from the fact that Kant does at times speak of representing (*vorstellen*) nature as a purposive system (secs. 61, 81 [pp. 206, 271]). In the critique of aesthetic judgment, the activity of representation is connected with the work of the imagination. In other words, even though Kant himself never put it this way, it does not seem to be straining his discussion here to suggest that this activity of the reflective judgment, in which we form the general idea of purposive nature, is also a work of the imagination.

Kant's real concern in all of this, of course, is not to articulate the imagination's functions. Rather, as he suggested in the introduction to the third critique, and as his concluding paragraphs make clear, he is concerned about the relationship between nature and freedom. To this end, he argues that nature as a teleological system appears ordered toward human culture, and in particular human ethical action, as its final goal (secs. 83-84 [pp. 279-86]). Consequently, the teleological judgment leads us to think about the complete harmony between nature and freedom—which is in accord with faith in God, the immortality of the soul, and a free will. Such faith is warranted by practical reason, even if it cannot be proved by theoretical reason or reflective judgment.

• Kant and Kaufman on the Imagination •

There are some interesting similarities and differences between Kant's and Kaufman's treatments of the imagination. The most striking similarity is that both argue for the importance of seeing the world as congenial to humans and human ends. Moreover, both regard the imagination as an important element in our ability to construe the world in this fashion. However, the specific way in which the imagination is said to operate is not the same for each. Whereas Kaufman regards the imagination as primarily a constructive activity by which we construct or reconstruct our world, Kant views the imagination as both constructive and receptive. Kant certainly did not believe that the imagination puts us in touch with "things in themselves." Furthermore, he regarded the imagination as operating freely in the aesthetic judgment. Nevertheless, for Kant the judgment of beauty is the result of a free yet orderly play of the imagination as it is stimulated by forms provided by nature. Even in the case of beautiful art, its connection with nature, through both the genius who produces it and those who appreciate it, means that the creative originality of the imagination is not merely constructive. That is, imagination in aesthetic production and experience is ultimately a matter of attuning ourselves to beautiful and sublime forms in nature—even though these forms do not put us in touch with "things in themselves."[19] And in his critique

---

[19]Actually, Kant's insistence that we have no contact with "things in themselves" becomes somewhat attenuated at some points in *Critique of Judgment*. For

of teleological judgment, Kant carefully tried to base teleological judgment on something in our experience of nature that compels us to think teleologically. The teleological judgment, then, is not just our construction but a response to the way that nature impinges on us.

Does Kaufman or Kant have the better argument here? In light of the historicity of human thought (which is far more pervasive than Kant recognized), it is evident that Kant's understanding at this point cannot simply be adopted as it stands. That is to say, the historicity of human life makes questionable the claim that scientific inquiry requires the idea of intelligent purpose and that judgments of beauty are ahistorical and universally true. In both cases, we have to do with historically contingent orientations to the world. Kaufman, in other words, is more on the mark than is Kant on this point. Yet it does not follow that Kaufman is right to view imagination as primarily constructive. For, even though we may not be able to follow Kant in his essentially ahistorical understanding of aesthetic and teleological judgments, we may still find reasonable an understanding of the imagination that views it as both constructive and receptive. Unlike Kant, however, we will have to view the receptive dimension of imagination in the context of the historicity of human life. If the imagination is receptive, its receptivity belongs within the stream of history. In this view, the receptivity of imagination is connected with the power of tradition to disclose truths about life in the world, rather than with the ability to have some direct contact with things in the world.[20]

In fact, Kant's discussions in the third critique of symbols and regulative ideas are instructive in regard to the question of the disclosive power of tradition. For the suggestion that symbols provide ways of organizing our understanding of things, if solidly placed in the context of history and praxis, shows how the imagination's representations can open up a way of being in the world. Not every way of being in the world is justifiable, of course, and not every representation is a symbolic disclosure of truth. But a possibility for genuine disclosure is located in the power of symbolic representation, a representation based on the imagination's power of understanding something as something. As for the notion of regula-

---

example, his assertion that the experience of the sublime suggests ideas of reason seems to imply that here we do get some intimation of what lies on the other side of the divide. So, too, does his discussion of the presentation of ideas of reason through aesthetic ideas. Cf. Warnock, *Imagination*, 64-65.

[20]One upshot of this view is the historicization of our view of what is humane and humanizing, so that Kaufman's seemingly independent criterion is discovered to be "paradigm dependent" after all.

tive ideas, it is too rigidly presented by Kant, since he has a firmly established view of which regulative ideas should be valid for all time. Yet the
idea that we need to assume some coherent view of things as a whole,
some system, to progress in our understanding of the world is well taken.[21]
Moreover, such historically contingent views of the whole can also have
consequences for our understanding of what constitutes appropriate ethical action.[22] Again, to note the contingent and imaginative character of
these systems and views of the whole is not to decide in advance whether
they are essentially our creative constructions. That question must be answered through a careful analysis of imagination and tradition and their
relation to life in the world. In other words, it remains an open question
at this point whether imagination is essentially constructive or depends
on disclosures of truth not subject to our own constructions.

• Conclusion •

Before we can move to a consideration of the disclosive power of tradition and of the role of the imagination in relation to it, it will be necessary to
analyze more closely the function of the imagination. Even though his ahistorical, a priori claims cannot be accepted, Kant's treatment of the imagination has done much to provide a foundation for this closer examination.
His analysis of the imagination's power of synthesis and of its indispensable
role in our perception of things remains valid and valuable, even when we
eliminate its objectionable features. That is, even if we make no assumptions about a priori and unchanging structures grounding our conscious
dealings with the world, and even if we do not presume to make pronouncements about epistemological foundations for human experience and
activity, it is clear that the synthesizing power of the imagination is essential
to human understanding and activity as we know it; for through this synthesis we derive and use forms by which we identify and deal with parts of
our world and the world itself. Furthermore, Kant's third critique makes it
clear that the imagination plays a crucial role in our understanding of the
world as congenial to human goals and values. In particular, his arguments
that we need coherent systems to guide our scientific reflection and that there

---

[21]Cf. Warnock, *Imagination*, 43-66. Her interpretation of Kant is more generous
than mine. But her view of the continuing truth to be found in his position is a
helpful appropriation of his work at this point.

[22]Cf. Gibson Winter's discussion of the nature and importance of root metaphors, in *Liberating Creation: Foundations of Religious Social Ethics* (New York:
Crossroad, 1981) 1-28.

are reasons to view the world as a purposive whole within which we can realize our fullest potential are stimulating and instructive, in spite of their questionable details.

Although Kant provides an important starting point for an understanding of the imagination, his treatment is not fully adequate, as has been noted throughout this chapter. Is there any way to bring his authentic insights into a more adequate framework that takes seriously the historicity of human life and thought and that speaks in terms of powers and functions rather than of faculties? I believe that there is. The next chapter considers such a framework.

THE PLAY
OF IMAGINATION

The continuing significance of Kant's treatment of the imagination is indicated by the important role it plays in Mary Warnock's development of a theory of the imagination. Even though she also makes use of other thinkers, such as Coleridge, Wordsworth, and Wittgenstein, her discussion makes extensive use of Kant and concludes that the sound intuitions in his theory of the imagination can be brought into a more adequate framework by defining imagination as the power of "seeing as." This provides an excellent provisional definition of the imagination. It can serve only as a transition, however, since it needs further development and modification before we have come to an adequate understanding of the imagination, one that can provide the basis for an exploration of how the imagination is related to faith and theology. Such development and modification will take place through an examination of the thought of Paul Ricoeur and Hans-Georg Gadamer as it relates to this issue. Gadamer's development of a theory of understanding through the models of play and the fusion of horizons actually provides the most comprehensive framework for my own articulation of a theory of the imagination. Nevertheless, I deal with Ricoeur first, for a couple of reasons. In the first place, since he links imagination with metaphor and metaphoric process, his discussion provides a natural first step in the further development of the notion of "seeing as." Second, Ricoeur's discussion of metaphor provides a perspective from which we can locate the imagination in Gadamer's models of play and the fusion of horizons. This contribution is important because Gadamer has very little explicit to say about the imagination. In short, Ricoeur provides a bridge from Warnock's discussion of imagination to Gadamer's articulation of the act of understanding.

Before we can completely cross that bridge, however, it will be necessary to pass through a brief critique of the ocular metaphor used by both

Warnock and Ricoeur. After examining these thinkers and noting the shortcomings of the ocular metaphor, we will be prepared to see how Gadamer helps us to locate the imagination within the historicity of human life. His models of play and the fusion of horizons, along with the related ideas of effective-history and disclosure, will be pivotal at this point. Finally, the examination of Warnock, Ricoeur, and Gadamer will set the stage for a brief exploration of imagination and disclosure, which is central to an understanding of the receptive dimension of the imagination. By the end of this chapter we should have an understanding of the imagination that allows us to modify Kaufman's constructive view of its operation by joining its constructive activity with its receptivity to disclosures mediated through tradition.

• A Provisional Definition •

Even though the way in which Kant tried to establish the pivotal role of imagination in all human perception and thought is seriously flawed, it does not follow that he was wholly mistaken. For a healthy understanding of the historicity of human life can lead to a similar conclusion, without making the same questionable foundational claims. At this point, there is much agreement between Kaufman's argument and my own. I believe that Kaufman has a sound intuition when he argues that human life is not lived in a realm of "raw experiences" that serve as the foundation for knowledge and action. Rather, human life is lived in a world of inherited meanings that profoundly shape cognition and praxis. We are not rigidly bound by these meanings; our own thoughts and actions are not mere repetitions of what has gone before. Yet we are placed in a situation by these meanings, so that the things that we know and do, as well as how we know and do them, receive an indelible stamp from what has come to us from the past. The categories by which we think, what we tend to deem important, the aspects of things that stand out for us, how we relate to others and to things in the world—all these and much more besides are given to us from the past.[1] To

---

[1]This is a crucial point that receives confirmation from many quarters in many different ways. For example, Thomas Kuhn, *The Structure of Scientific Revolutions*, 2d ed., enl. (Chicago: University of Chicago Press, 1970), argues that the scientific tradition shapes the work of scientists (without denying the possibility of change in that tradition). Hans-Georg Gadamer, *Truth and Method*, trans. Garrett Borden and John Cumming (New York: Continuum, 1975), argues for the formative influence of tradition and language in human thought and action. And Gibson Winter, *Liberating Creation* (New York: Crossroad, 1981) 44-51, stresses the shaping power of the past by focusing on symbols, which come to us from the past, as organizing forces in human life and perception. Much of the rest of the next two chapters is a variation on this theme.

be sure, Kant also insisted that we do not relate to the world through direct and uninterpreted experiences that could serve as the building blocks for all our knowledge. His mistake was to try to transcend the limits that he himself articulated and to make claims about the ahistorical, transcendental foundations of experience.

Given the inescapable historicity of human life, Kaufman has good grounds for arguing that the imagination is involved in all human perception, knowledge, and praxis. For one does not merely experience what is there to be experienced but experiences things in terms of meaningful patterns brought into every aspect of life. And, as Kant noted, the activities of synthesis and subsumption underlying these meaningful patterns, most of which activities occur apart from our conscious awareness, are the work of the imagination.

The centrality and scope of this work of imagination emerges with even more clarity when we consider the dimension of the future. That is, our life in the present is shaped by the past, in light of expectations for the future. The past, in other words, does not force us to repeat what has been. Instead, in combination with what we experience in the present, the past engenders hopes for what is to come—hopes that, while not confined to what has been, are given shape and direction by it. For example, when the Hebrew prophets envisaged the coming rule of God, they spoke of it in terms of a new and better Davidic ruler, a transformed Mosaic covenant, a New Jerusalem, an exodus far surpassing the first exodus. Thus, the imagination, by refining and resynthesizing images from the past, creates visions of what can be.[2] In this way, the imagination helps to make human freedom possible, for the illumination of the horizon of the future gives us a certain distance from the state of things in the present and thereby enables us to act with a limited measure of freedom.[3]

---

[2]Winter, *Liberating Creation,* 56-64, argues that the symbol mediates both the past and the future and is therefore that through which human life becomes intrinsically temporal—not in the sense that we are in time but that time is in us. Furthermore, he maintains that symbols open up a space for human life in the present by placing us in a world of others, of nature, of technology, and of sociopolitical structures. Through symbols, then, human life becomes spatiotemporal.

[3]Cf. Mary Warnock, *Imagination* (Berkeley and Los Angeles: University of California Press, 1976) 181: "In thinking, 'I can change this situation,' I necessarily envisage the situation as containing some feature which it does not at the moment contain. Freedom of action and freedom to envisage the non-existent are the same." Subsequent citations are noted in the text and refer to this edition.

The importance of the imagination for human perception, knowledge, and action becomes clear when we join the realization of the historicity of human life with the understanding of imagination as that by which we see something as something. That is, even when we see a familiar, everyday sort of thing as something with a certain meaning for us, we are engaged in the imaginative activity of "seeing as." For example, even a seemingly straightforward sort of perception, such as seeing a house as a house, is an imaginative act, since it focuses on certain familiar features of the object and construes it accordingly. Mary Warnock makes this point through a comparison between the perception of familiar objects and the recognition of someone's portrait. That is, we recognize a portrait as familiar by viewing it in terms of the image of the person it represents, by seeing it as that person. This is also the way we deal with the world as a whole. "We cannot draw a hard line between perceiving the world as familiar, as where we live, as full of remembered objects, and perceiving a portrait of a familiar face, of recognizing the Duke of Wellington in the canvas. Into both these kinds of perception it seems that imagination enters" (194).

As already noted, such acts of "seeing as" are shaped by the horizons of the past and future. Hence, the imaginative act of "seeing as" depends in large measure on our past and on the expectations for the future that the past has engendered. However, it is also possible to turn this assertion around. That is, it is the capacity to "see as" that enables the past and future to impinge on the present. For the ability to have meaningful experiences, that is, to see things as meaningful, gives us both a tradition and a relationship to the present in which the tradition can be effective. It is therefore no exaggeration to say that the imagination is a sine qua non of human life.

Warnock connects imagination's work of "seeing as" with its image-forming ability.

> Imagination is our means of interpreting the world, and it is also our means of forming images in the mind. The images themselves are not separate from our interpretations of the world, they are our way of thinking of the objects in the world. We could not do one of these things if we could not do the other. The two abilities are joined in our ability to understand that the forms have a certain meaning, that they are always significant of other things beyond themselves. (194; cf. 152-60, 173, 198-99)

Thus, the ability to create an image of something, a form that possesses a certain significance, and apply that image or form to things we experience is what makes it possible to see something as something meaningful. Has Warnock fallen into a trap of using something now widely discredited (by, for example, Ryle and Wittgenstein), namely, the idea of a mental image? If she were using this term to mean something that has its own independent existence, just as, for example, a house is perceived as something with an independent existence quite apart from our own subjective experiences of it, then she would be falling prey to what Ryle called a "category mistake": that is, treating mental events as if they were the same sorts of things as physical entities, such as bodies. However, Warnock is well aware of this potential pitfall and has carefully avoided it through a definition of the image that ties it inextricably to the act of perception. When she speaks of image, she has in mind something that has its existence only "when we think imaginatively about something," rather than something that is an independent object (152-60). This fact has implications for the way in which we come to understand the nature of the image. "It thus becomes clear that the question how we are to describe an image as it presents itself to us, inevitably turns into the other question of what we are doing when we imagine something. We cannot isolate the question of images and try to answer it by itself. . . . In order to understand the image, we need to understand the diverse but related functions of imagination" (172-73; cf. 158).

In accordance with this approach, Warnock describes images as whatever our minds reproduce in order to identify and focus on objects of our experience. That is, the importance of images lies not in what they are themselves but in how they enable us to relate to our world. In some cases, that which our minds reproduce, "through which we aim toward the object of our thought," are "visual thoughts"; but not in all cases. For example, in the case of sounds, such as a musical note, the image is not visual at all; yet such sounds are still mentally reproducible and hence are identifiable through the image that we reproduce in our thoughts. One may wish to question whether the term *image* is the best one, in light of such considerations, but Warnock nevertheless uses it in this context. At any rate, her point is clear and persuasive: the imagination reproduces the images (or forms) of things, thereby enabling us to connect present experiences with those meaningful forms and to see that which we experience as having a certain significance.

Two caveats are necessary here. First, Warnock is not arguing that every recognition of something involves the explicit awareness of an image with which we connect it. Rather, her point is that it is the ability to reproduce images of things, if necessary, that makes possible the perception of things in our world as significant in some way. Thus, one may see a house as a house without explicitly having a "visual thought" of a house.

Yet, it is the ability to reproduce the image of a house, when called on to do so, that gives one the ability to make this identification. For this identification depends on knowing what constitutes a house and therefore being able to reproduce a house in one's mind. The second caveat: Warnock does not intend to say that we see the image instead of whatever we are experiencing at any given moment. When, for example, we see a line drawing that we identify as a duck, we are not merely seeing a mental image of a duck. Instead, we are seeing lines on paper that we, by means of the image of a duck, see as a duck. Images, then, do not take the place of objects of perception, of a world transcending our subjectivity, but mediate between the world and the self in a way that opens the self to the world.

As seen earlier, Warnock argues that a full understanding of imagination calls for an understanding of the functions of the imagination. At least four functions are pivotal for an adequate appreciation of the nature and role of imagination in human thought and perception. The first has already been indicated but bears repeating: through the imagination we see everyday objects as everyday. The familiarity of people, places, things, events, and so forth depends on associating them with familiar images. Through its capacity to form these images and subsume objects under them, the imagination enables this sort of familiarity with our world. This familiarizing function of imagination goes hand in hand with another function: the imagination enables us to focus on a particular aspect of what we experience. That is, images are not full pictures of things as they are in themselves but reproduce certain aspects of our world that are important for us.

> The images we form are necessarily incomplete, but they are ways of representing for ourselves some of the features of the object of our thought, those features which will identify what we are thinking of (though of course we may not successfully identify the object of our thought—that is, we may not be able to attach a name to it or connect it with other things). The image, that is to say, relates to the aspect of the object which we are for the time being concentrating on. (173)

Thus, a lumberjack would generally have a different image of a tree than a bird watcher or a city dweller, just as the image of a tree in the mind of a city dweller would differ to some degree from that of the bird watcher. To be sure, their respective images of trees would have much in common, yet in each case different aspects of trees would be of primary concern. Because each focuses on different aspects, each has a slightly different image.

On the other hand, if a lumberjack comes to see a tree through the image familiar to the bird watcher, the experience could be defamiliarizing, an experience that brings us to the third function of imagination. In view of its ability to focus on certain aspects of things, the imagination can engender new views of even everyday sorts of realities by focusing on their hitherto hidden or largely ignored features. Through its ability to synthesize it can also combine things in unfamiliar ways and thereby generate new insights and points of view. This function of the imagination is an important ingredient in creative imagination.

To this point the discussion has centered on what appear to be cognitive functions of the imagination. It also has an important affective dimension, which has an influence on its cognitive activities. Wordsworth and Coleridge both stressed this function of the imagination. In their view, the ability to bring an image of something to mind carries along with it the ability to feel the significance of it, to be affected by it. Conversely, the ability to feel the significance of something we experience depends on the ability to reproduce an image of it, to see it as something with a certain significance for us and therefore as something that carries a certain affective impact. Furthermore, in Wordworth's view this activity of the imagination works below the conscious level, so that it becomes difficult in this connection to distinguish between feeling in the mind and in nature (124-26). Hence the cognitive and affective significance of things in the world for us, in this view, is more than our subjective reaction, since it has its root in a largely preconscious relationship between self and world through which possible ways-of-being-in-the-world are exemplified. This relationship naturally has a direct bearing on what aspects of our world stand out for us and become imaged through the imagination, and hence on what we know about the world. Such considerations also suggest that images are not necessarily just our subjective creations but can exemplify qualities possessed by things in their relation to us. And these qualities that are significant for us are important to both the intellect and the heart. (169, 173, 196).

One further qualification must be kept in mind with respect to Warnock's understanding of the imagination. She does not suppose that she is dealing with a "faculty of the soul." Whether the imagination is rooted in such a faculty, or what psychologists and biologists might discover about the workings of the mind and the brain that has relevance for the questions related to imagination and faculties of the mind, are unimportant for Warnock's purposes. She notes: "I am claiming the intelligibility of finding similarities between certain aspects of intelligent perception, and thinking of things in their absence, and so on. My thread of connexion can be conceived just as a series of similarities; and the name of the whole series is 'imagination' " (196; cf. 195). Her discussion of imagination, therefore, has to do with a series of acts of perception that can be held together through their similarities, whatever diverse biological and psychological dynamics lie behind them. When she speaks of imagination, then, she is speaking in terms of a function of human life rather than of a faculty of the mind.[4]

• Imagination and Metaphoric Process •

Paul Ricoeur also defines imagination as the power of "seeing as" and in so doing joins it inextricably to metaphoric process. For metaphor also consists of the activity of "seeing as," or seeing one thing in terms of certain relevant aspects of another.[5] Thus, a consideration of metaphor, especially as Ricoeur analyzes it, should help to clarify what is involved in imaginative activity.

The Meaning of Metaphor

Ricoeur carefully distinguishes between his view of metaphor and a prevalent view that treats it as a case of "deviant denomination." In the latter view, metaphor is simply the substitution of a figurative word for a literal word that would express the meaning more directly. In this case, metaphor functions as a sort of window dressing, a way to make one's speaking or writing more colorful. But it provides no new information and can be fully translated into other words that are literal and direct. Against this common view, Ricoeur insists that metaphor is a phenomenon of discourse, that is, something that transpires at the level of the sentence or higher, rather than at the level of isolated words. It is a case of "impertinent predication."[6] That is, metaphor is the result of an intentional contradiction at one level of discourse for the sake of the emergence of a new meaning at another level. This abstract statement needs some concrete explanation to become clear.

---

[4]I also intend to speak of the imagination in just this way.

[5]Paul Ricoeur, *The Rule of Metaphor: Multidisciplinary Studies of the Creation of Meaning in Language,* trans. Robert Czerny et al. (Toronto: University of Toronto Press, 1981) 6, 199, 212-13, 231; cf. Philip Wheelwright, *Metaphor and Reality* (Bloomington: Indiana University Press, 1962) 72-91.

[6]Ricoeur, *Rule of Metaphor,* 4, 99, 180; see also Ricoeur, *Interpretation Theory: Discourse and the Surplus of Meaning* (Fort Worth TX: Texas Christian University Press, 1976) 46-53.

In the first place, metaphor is a statement, a combination of noun and verb with their modifiers, that speaks of one thing in terms of another.[7] Views of metaphor as deviant denomination overlook this aspect of metaphor, since they see it not as a statement but as a substitution within a statement. Consequently, whereas substitution theories of metaphor see its duality in terms of a figurative word taking the place of a literal word, Ricoeur sees metaphor's duality in terms of a figurative meaning that arises from the ruins of a literally contradictory meaning. That is to say, when metaphor is located at the level of discourse rather than words, one's concern is primarily with the meanings connected with the statement as a whole instead of with the meanings of individual words. In the case of metaphor, the meaning of the statement, when literally interpreted, is logically absurd. For example, Shakespeare wrote:

> *Time hath, my lord, a wallet at his back*
> *Wherein he puts alms for oblivion,*
> *A great-sized monster of ingratitude.*[8]

An interpretation of this statement at the literal level leaves one without a logically coherent meaning.[9] Literally speaking, time has no wallet and no back to put it on, collects no alms, and shows neither gratitude nor ingratitude. The meaning of the metaphor, therefore, can emerge only when one allows its literal meaning to self-destruct.[10] The destruction of its literal meaning paves the way for an interpretation on another, figurative level. This conflict between literal and figurative interpretations of a metaphor "sustains the metaphor," for the "process of self-destruction or transformation . . . imposes a sort of twist on the words, an extension of meaning thanks to which we can make sense" of a literally nonsensical statement.[11]

---

[7] See Ricoeur, *Interpretation Theory*, 45-69.

[8] Cf. ibid., 51, and 98.

[9] When Ricoeur speaks of literal interpretation, he does not mean that words have inherent meanings. Rather, a literal interpretation is one that operates according to the meanings commonly ascribed to the words in a statement. Cf. *Rule of Metaphor*, 96. Subsequent citations are noted in the text and refer to this edition.

[10] Cf. Ricoeur, *Interpretation Theory*, 50.

[11] Ibid. Because a metaphor that still shocks us with its absurdity operates in this way, it is called a "tensive metaphor." Those that no longer strike us as absurd, because we have grown so familiar with them that we merely assume their meaning, are "dead metaphors" and are a part of the common coin of a language.

It should be clear by now that the essence of metaphor has nothing to do with the typical grammarian's definition. That is, it does not matter whether a statement uses *like* or *as* in its comparison. Although in some (but not all) cases the explicit use of comparative terms can diminish the vividness of a metaphor, the metaphoric twist does not depend on the absence of such terms. Whether the grammarian would call something a metaphor or a simile, then, has nothing to do with whether a statement is metaphoric in the sense described by Ricoeur (cf. 26).[12] Furthermore, the metaphoric process, as described above, can also be said to characterize larger units than the individual statement, for example, paragraphs or even entire works (229-46). Ricoeur likens the essence of the metaphoric process to Gilbert Ryle's notion of a "category mistake," that is, the treatment of something belonging to one category as if it belonged to another. For Ryle's concern, namely, the concept of mind, the category mistake of treating minds as if they were material things (like bodies) is an egregious error, resulting in numerous logical confusions. The category mistake of a metaphor, on the other hand, is deliberate and carries fruitful consequences. "It is, in effect, a calculated error, which brings together things that do not go together and by means of this apparent misunderstanding it causes a new, hitherto unnoticed, relation of meaning to spring up between the terms that previous systems of classification had ignored or not allowed."[13] By working against familiar points of view, therefore, a metaphor has the power to bring to light overlooked resemblances between things and thereby "to establish new logical frontiers on the ruins of their forerunners" (197, 21-22).[14]

This type of category mistake works because metaphor has the power to uncover resemblances in the midst of and in spite of differences. Metaphor, in other words, makes no claim that two things usually viewed as far apart from one another are in reality close together. Differences are acknowledged and preserved. Yet such recognition does not prevent the perception of a resemblance between certain aspects of two things that are otherwise different. Such aspects include quality, structure, locality, situation, and feeling (cf. 189, 194-200). These aspects emerge through the

---

[12]See also Wheelwright, *Metaphor and Reality*, 71.

[13]Ricoeur, *Interpretation Theory*, 51.

[14]Ricoeur also suggests that this operation provides a hint that our existing classifications are the result of the work of metaphor. Cf. Hans-Georg Gadamer, "Semantics and Hermeneutics," in *Philosophical Hermeneutics*, trans. and ed. David E. Linge (Berkeley and Los Angeles: University of California Press, 1976) 85-86.

clash of "semantic fields" and the "new pertinence" answering the challenge of this contradiction (cf. 58-59, 194, 199). That is, the intersection of usually divergent meanings, or "semantic fields," opens up the possibility of seeing some features of that which is under consideration in a new way. For example, when Shakespeare compares time to a beggar, there is certainly no claim that time and beggars are, after all, ultimately the same. Yet there is a resemblance between the way each relates to us, a resemblance whose unique qualities can come to light only through the metaphor itself. In other words, the insight conveyed by a metaphor belongs inextricably to it. To express the thought in another way is to lose something in it. For living metaphors provide a unique angle of vision whose complete meaning—that is, whose fecundity—cannot be defined in advance (cf. 98-99).[15] For this reason, a true, living metaphor (that is, one that has not lost its tensive quality through becoming too familiar) cannot be exhaustively paraphrased. Paraphrases can, of course, express some of the meaning in a metaphor. But they cannot capture the fullness of the metaphor.[16]

Another important implication of metaphor's unique combination of identity and difference is that it cannot be turned into a foundation for apodictic pronouncements. Hence a metaphor cannot be an occasion for logical coercion but only an invitation to look for oneself. Another way of putting this point is to insist that a metaphor retains both the "is" and "is not" that characterizes its identity in difference (cf. 247-56). And, since we cannot draw logically precise lines between the "is" and "is not"—to do so would amount to an exhaustive paraphrase—metaphors provide no foundation for logically coercive arguments. They can, however, open our eyes to ways of construing the world and guide us in articulating such construals. In this way, they invite us to participate in their redescriptions but give us no clubs to use against others.[17]

Metaphor and Reality

We come now to a work of metaphor that is the heart of imagination's creative power, namely, the redescription of "reality" (cf. 7). Like lan-

---

[15]See also Ricoeur, *Interpretation Theory*, 52.

[16]Cf. ibid., 52.

[17]Cf. Sallie McFague, *Metaphorical Theology: Models of God in Religious Language* (Philadelphia: Fortress Press, 1982) 19; and Winter, *Liberating Creation*, 24: "Metaphors do not settle everything, but they are guides to the rich possibilities of life and nature."

guage in general, metaphors stand open to the world in which we live, and they do so in a way that reorganizes our understanding of the world. As Wheelwright expresses it, "What really matters in a metaphor is the psychic depth at which the things of the world, whether actual or fancied, are transmuted by the cool heat of the imagination."[18] Now, such transmutation concerns much more than the redescription of objects in our world. For metaphor is also a dynamic event disclosing the dynamic character of human life in the world. That is to say, metaphors disclose possible ways-of-being-in-the-world through situating the human in relation to the world and the world in relation to the human. Ricoeur states, "To present men 'as acting' and all things 'as in act'—such could well be the ontological function of metaphorical discourse, in which every dormant potentiality of existence appears as blossoming forth, every latent capacity for action as actualized." (43). This dimension of metaphor is given some further articulation by John Dixon, who notes that the metaphoric process is one of linking things to functions and purposes.[19] For example, seeing a stick as a club that can be used as a weapon is a metaphoric act that relates the stick (thing) to a potential use as a club (function), and this act carries with it certain possibilities of social organization and domination (purpose). Dixon thus concludes, "Every purposeful form is not simply a tool but a metaphor, a transformation of thing into meaning and purpose, the condensation of meaning and purpose into a thing."[20]

This power of metaphor includes an affective dimension. For the situation of the human in the world entails more than "objective facts" about selves and things. Indeed, such objectivity is an abstraction from our more primordial rootedness, which is characterized by a prereflective relation to the world—that is, a way-of-being-in-the-world. Now, if they are not reduced to psychological states of mind, feelings are a central element in this way of being. As Ricoeur notes, they are "a way of finding or sensing oneself in the midst of reality" (229; cf. 245-46). Thus, metaphor can and often does locate feelings in things, such as, for example, when one speaks of a sad picture. Ricoeur argues that such cases, which are the result of a metaphoric transfer of feelings from persons to things, involve the rec-

---

[18]Wheelwright, *Metaphor and Reality*, 71; cf. Ricoeur, *Rule of Metaphor*, 6, 74, 304.

[19]John W. Dixon, Jr., *The Physiology of Faith: A Theory of Theological Relativity* (San Francisco: Harper & Row, 1979) 22-23; he also speaks of this process as an imaginative act (p. 20).

[20]Ibid., 162; cf. 167.

ognition that things in our world exemplify or express certain emotions. For example, when one speaks of the "joyous undulation of the waves," there is no implication that the waves feel joy. Nevertheless, the waves do in fact "possess" the feeling of joy in that they exemplify or express that feeling (even for someone who may not be feeling joyful when viewing the play of the waves) (229-39). On the other hand, metaphors can also represent feelings within a person in terms drawn from the external world: for example, when speaking of a "lake of ice" within. In both cases, metaphors depict feelings as neither objective nor subjective. "Poetic feeling in its metaphorical expressions," notes Ricoeur, "bespeaks the lack of distinction between interior and exterior" and presents "the reciprocity of the inner and the outer." Consequently, metaphoric redescriptions have the power of touching the full scope of human life in the world, including its intimate "participation in things" (246).

Clearly, such metaphoric redescriptions carry us away from scientific approaches to reality (without denying that scientific conceptions have an important place in human life), which depend on an objectification of things that leaves such poetic points of view without apparent justification. However, it does not follow that metaphoric redescriptions and their affective points of view are wholly without warrant. As long as one remains within the framework of a positivist conception of reality and its concomitant "verificationist" notions of truth, one will never see metaphor as more than either an escape to naive forms of life or an "as if" treatment of things that are more directly known in other ways (cf. 247-56, 303-13). But metaphors refer to the world in a manner that such positivist approaches cannot adequately comprehend, for metaphors, through their indirect reference to actual and potential self-world relationships, make contact with a level of being that the positivists overlook or ignore. "Poetic discourse brings to language a pre-objective world in which we find ourselves already rooted, but in which we also project our innermost possibilities. We must thus dismantle the reign of objects in order to let be, and to allow to be uttered, our primordial belonging to a world which we inhabit, that is to say, which at once precedes us and receives the imprint of our works" (306).

This statement by Ricoeur does not amount to a claim that, unlike the positivists, we have some sort of direct access to our primordial way of being and that we have therefore found a new basis for knowledge of things as they are in themselves. Even to think in such terms is to reintroduce correspondence notions of truth that the metaphoric view eschews. For metaphor is an indirect approach to the world through the verbal iconicity of the metaphor and presents realities that are uncovered only through the metaphor.[21] Furthermore, even though they are extensions of meaning, metaphors grow out of and depend on inherited networks of meaning. If we can speak of a primordial belonging to the world, then, it is in the sense that we are rooted in a past that has already situated us in the world and has shaped us before we try, in our finite freedom, to shape ourselves. The primordial rootedness of human life is a rootedness in a tradition that places its stamp on everything human, including our free and creative activity (cf. 303-304).

However, we cannot say that we are trapped within a windowless room constructed of language and its meanings, for tensive metaphor—like language in general—refers to an extralinguistic reality. Moreover, it does so in a way that is intended to redescribe that reality (cf. 7, 304).[22] There is certainly no extralinguistic standpoint that we can adopt in order to judge whether language adequately relates to a reality outside of itself. Nevertheless, as Ricoeur notes, language is a self-transcending phenomenon; that is, it has a "reflective capacity to place itself at a distance and to consider itself, as such and in its entirety, as related to the totality of what is." As a result, language brings with it a consciousness of openness to a world of being; not in a way that allows one to stand outside of language but in a way that allows us to come into contact with being through the openness of language. In Ricoeur's words, "Something must be for something to be said" (304). If so, it is permissible to think of an extralinguistic reality mediated to us through language. This claim is another way of insisting that, although language may shape experience to some degree and even make some experience possible, language does not create the reality of experience itself. Thus, even though we have no "raw experience," language mediates and does not merely create.

The other side of the language-world relation must also be emphasized: language creates a "world." That is, language is a shaper of our world; and metaphor in particular is a creative redescription of reality. Yet it need not, on that account, be pure creation rooted in human inventiveness. Some fanciful presentations of the world can be pure creations. But we mark such free creations as fanciful and thereby remove them from the world in which we live. On the other hand, significant metaphoric redescriptions of our world have a quality of fittingness about them. They have the power to open our eyes to possible relationships to, or ways of

---

[21]Cf. McFague, *Metaphorical Theology*, 133-34.

[22]Ibid., 132.

being in, the world.[23] They thus have the dynamic quality of showing how life can "blossom forth" in the world (308-309). In this sense, metaphor is a *creation* that *discovers* a possible way of being through its power of redescription. Its creativity, then, resides not so much in its power of constructing, which is rooted in the human subject, but in its ability to mediate between self and world—to be, in other words, disclosive. Here it may be that "creation and revelation coincide" (246).

The lack of a direct perception of things and of an extralinguistic place from which to stand in judgment complicates the question of whether one has any warrant for making such claims. The fact that our experience of the world is not infinitely malleable, while pertinent, does not provide any easy resolutions to the dilemma. For the intractability of experience is not such as to make apparent the true nature of things. One is still faced with a welter of possibilities.[24] But the claim of metaphoric disclosure in no way tries to avoid this fact. Multivalency is one of the important implications of metaphoric redescriptions of reality. On the other hand, metaphor also makes a claim to fittingness, which is not compatible with the notion that all points of view are equally justifiable. There are distinctions to be made, but distinctions that are inevitably tied to the stance one adopts. The question of warrant for claiming a truth in metaphoric disclosure, therefore, must accept this limitation, one that precludes the possibility of proof or verification. Yet it does not preclude the possibility of justification or the elaboration of criteria of justification within one's context. Such criteria are clearly not neutral, since they are tied to a stance and the context to which it belongs; but they are not therefore merely subjective or have no logical impact on those who do not share the stance. The contextual nature of justification suggests that whether a stance is justifiable can be determined only in the situation calling for justification and through conversation with others who do and do not share one's stance (since a context necessarily includes one's relationship with others and may be optimally understood only through dialogue). There are, in other words, no a priori criteria of justification. Thus, only after metaphoric disclosure makes its indirect yet significant claim on us are we in a position to raise the question of its fittingness or justification.

Metaphor and Imagination

How do these considerations illumine imagination? The implications for imagination—where we define imagination as the power of meta-

---

[23]Ibid., 134-37; Dixon, *Physiology of Faith*, xxix.

[24]Cf. Richard Rorty, *Philosophy and the Mirror of Nature* (Princeton NJ: Princeton University Press, 1979) 324-56.

phoric process, on the basis of the connection of both to the activity of "seeing as"—are undoubtedly more numerous and far-reaching than this discussion can indicate. For my purposes, several important implications stand out.

One such implication is the definition of imagination's power of synthesis in terms of the metaphoric activity of bringing near what is far apart; that is, pointing to the similar in the dissimilar. This process is at the heart of imagination's creative activity and suggests that the uncovering of hitherto unrecognized relationships is what generates new insights. Moreover, this function is also central to imagination's more pedestrian work of recognizing the everyday as the everyday, for this activity of subsuming the individual under a general category is also, to a lesser degree, recognizing a similarity in spite of dissimilarity. That is, the individual is not in every respect like other individuals that are assigned to the same class, yet their likeness is recognized in spite of individual differences. Even the recognition of something as something we have dealt with before is a recognition of its similarity in spite of different circumstances. This observation provides support for Ricoeur's suggestion that our everyday classifications may be the result of the codification of past metaphors (197-98).[25] At any rate, the operation of metaphors provides illumination of imagination's synthetic activity.

The conjunction of imagination and metaphoric process also implies that imagination is not just a matter of imagery, in the sense of faded sense impressions, but has a linguistic aspect as well. That is, through metaphoric activity we can see that the creation and discovery of similarity in dissimilarity is the consequence of an intersection of "semantic fields." For metaphor is first of all a clash of meanings embedded in language, through which a new meaning emerges. Thus, the metaphor is a "verbal icon" that serves as "the matrix of the new semantic pertinence" arising out of the self-destruction of the literal meaning (199). As a verbal icon, a metaphor is a description rather than a presentation of an icon, through which our attention is directed to the important aspects of whatever it indirectly represents. In this way, it guides the new production of meaning. The image is not thereby eliminated, since the verbal icon points to the image through its description. Indeed, the description of an icon is, in effect, the presentation of "a formula for the construction of icons" (189). But these icons remain connected to the verbal description—not in the

---

[25]I am not arguing that the recognition of the everyday takes place through living metaphors. My point is, rather, that the metaphoric process of "seeing as" is relevant even in these cases.

sense that every image visualized in the mind requires an explicit verbal component but in the sense that such images are susceptible to description in this way, so that they can be communicated to others or reproduced. That is, they are meaningful images in that they are open to explanation or description in language. In short, the image-producing ability of imagination goes hand in hand with metaphor and its semantic qualities. Thus, the ability to call to mind an image, which Warnock connects with the ability to recognize something as meaningful, entails as well the ability to present a formula for the construction of the image.[26] "Seeing as" is inextricably connected with language, without being limited to it.

The metaphoric power of "seeing as" has far-reaching consequences because it carries with it "the power to elaborate, to extend the parallel structure" (189). That is, through its deliberate categorical error, metaphor makes possible the articulation of certain aspects of a new situation by following the relevant structure of a more familiar situation. Ricoeur further illuminates this elaborative power of metaphor through a comparison between metaphors and scientific models (239-46). Following the lead of Max Black, he notes that there are three basic types of scientific models: (1) scale models, which help either to reduce or enlarge things to human size and show how they look or work; (2) analogue models, in which the model and original resemble each other in their structures, rather than in their sensible features, and rules of interpretation govern the manner in which the pertinent structures in the model will be applied to the original; and (3) theoretical models, which also operate according to similarity of structure but which consist of verbal description rather than constructed models. Clearly, the operation of metaphors most closely resembles that of theoretical models. A significant dimension of this comparison is the fact that it highlights the ability of metaphors, like models, to operate according to a logic of discovery rather than of deduction. They guide the imaginative articulation of a less familiar domain by providing a structure from a more familiar domain. In this way, metaphors and models act as heuristic fictions that harbor the power of redescription. Ricoeur succinctly states these points as follows: "The central argument is that, with respect to the relation to reality, metaphor is to poetic language what the model is to scientific language. Now in scientific language, the model is essentially a heuristic instrument that seeks, by means of fiction, to break down an inadequate interpretation and to lay the way for a new,

---

[26]All is not therefore reducible to straightforward description, for the formula, let it be remembered, is the verbal icon of metaphor, with its indirection and its meaning that resists exhaustive paraphrase.

more adequate interpretation . . . the model is an instrument of redescription" (240).

In addition to underscoring the link between description and heuristic function, Ricoeur sees in this comparison between models and metaphors an indication that the most significant metaphors are located not in statements or sentences but in extended metaphors (such as a tale) and in metaphoric networks organized around "root metaphors."[27] For a model is not a single statement or image but "a complex network of statements" that guides investigation. Hence, the most profound redescriptions are effected by the application of a network of metaphors to the new situation. Furthermore, the use of radical metaphors that have the power to bring about a profound reorganization of thought is also important for significant redescriptions. In this light, we can see that creative imagination is an activity of synthesis that is far more complex than connecting simple ideas. On the contrary, it operates in a realm of multiple networks and interconnections and of radical visions that enable profound and far-reaching breakthroughs in insight (244). This fact suggests a complexity that we must constantly strive to understand yet that continually eludes our grasp. We may be able to trace the operation of the imagination; we are not likely ever to capture it.

Another important implication of this convergence of imagination and metaphoric process is that the creative dimension of imagination has the same disclosive power as that of metaphor. That is, if it is proper to view metaphor as both creation and discovery, imagination must also be so viewed. To think of it as the constructive activity of the human subject, then, catches only part of its meaning and potential. As with metaphor, imagination's embeddedness in a tradition that mediates a world to us implies that, for historically rooted human beings, construction is profoundly shaped by the past. Our past, our tradition, is mediated to us through language. And language, both in the content of the past that it brings to us and in its implicit view of the world, guides our thought. To be historically rooted, then, is to be linguistically rooted (cf. 303-304).[28] And to be linguistically rooted is to have the world mediated to us through language, even in the work of creative imagination. This understanding is in line with the semantic dimension of imagination that was examined above. It also underscores the fact that there is no way for us to arrive at an extralinguistic point of view. Yet, like language, imagination is open

----

[27]Cf. Ricoeur, *Interpretation Theory*, 64.

[28]See also Winter, *Liberating Creation*, 54-91.

to the world, and through its power of metaphoric process imagination is able to mediate something of the world. Again, this raises the issue of the justification of any supposed disclosures. Although this is a difficult issue, it is a different way of seeing imagination than understanding it as essentially a constructive power. It at least leaves open the possibility that the imagination could also be receptive, that is, open to the world through its metaphoric power.

• We Are More Than We See •

Even though joining imagination with the activity of "seeing as" helpfully advances our insight into imagination's function in human life, it also suffers from some serious limitations. In his analysis of the history of Western philosophy since Plato, Richard Rorty traces the baleful influence of the use of ocular metaphors to characterize knowledge. Because Western thought regarded knowledge as a form of sight, albeit an inner sight, it tended to conceive of correct knowledge as a correspondence between idea and object and to think of the foundation of all true knowledge as the subject's ability to reflect the external world accurately. Indeed, the epistemological concern at the heart of much philosophy can be interpreted as an effort to find something in the subject that enables such accurate reflection and that therefore provides a foundation for human knowledge. However, once the ocular metaphors for knowledge are abandoned, many of the problems that have traditionally occupied epistemology become moot. In particular, there is no longer any need to understand knowledge as the correspondence between idea and object; as a result, the search for a foundation that will make such a correspondence possible loses its raison d'être. Knowledge, in short, is not a direct reflection of the world but a collection of propositions by which we organize ourselves and accomplish our goals.[29]

While Rorty's analysis is helpful, it still does not resolve what is perhaps the most serious problem associated with connecting imagination to sight: namely, the tendency of such a metaphor to encourage a subjectivist understanding of imagination. By *subjectivist* I mean the location of imagination wholly within the individual's subjective consciousness, with the result that imaginative activity is taken to be entirely at the subject's discretion. Such an understanding of imagination is at odds with what we have already said about the role of imagination in everyday types of perception. For understanding the everyday as everyday is something that

---

[29]Rorty, *Philosophy and Mirror of Nature*, especially pp. 3-13.

occurs, for the most part, apart from our conscious choice and aware-ness. It is the result of the framework of understanding inherited from our past and our own personal histories through which certain things, events, situations, persons, and so forth become routine for us. Whereas our personal histories, and what becomes familiar through them, may seem to be based on our own personal, subjective outlooks, this can only be partially the case, since the way we interpret and respond to our en-vironment is largely shaped by the framework that comes from the past. This framework, in turn, is mediated to us through the community (or communities) to which we belong.

Thiemann, then, is right when he insists that knowledge "involves the adoption and skillful use of a conceptual framework which is the posses-sion of a linguistic community."[30] However, he fails to draw the conse-quences of this insight for imagination, since he continues to regard imagination as entirely the work of the individual subject, who must put this conceptual framework to use in personal existence. Although this is surely a part of imagination, the fact that the subject's orientation to the world is largely given to it through a community suggests that the imag-inative construal of the world is more than the work of the individual subject. It is already at work in the subject's preconscious life in the world, in the way in which the subject is "thrown" into the world. Thus, before we begin in a conscious way to conceive the world imaginatively, we are already rooted in an imaginative world of meaning through which the world is mediated to us. And what is thereby opened to us is pivotal for all our more conscious imaginative efforts. Hence, even our creative ef-forts are not altogether our own personal construction but arise out of the creative power of the tradition to which we belong. In short, although imagination is personal, it is also more than personal. It is transpersonal. Furthermore, to the degree that conceptual frameworks uncover a world, and are not just the subjective creations of communities or individuals, the imagination is not merely a human power of construction or projec-tion.[31] It could, perhaps, be defined in this case as a power of attunement that is finally located in neither subject nor subject matter but in the play between them.[32]

---

[30]Ronald F. Thiemann, "Revelation and Imaginative Construction," *Journal of Religion* 61 (1981): 253.

[31]Of course, whether it is proper to speak of a conceptual framework as un-covering a world is open to debate and not yet justified here. But it is a possible point of view that I discuss later.

[32]See Winter, *Liberating Creation*, 110-11.

We cannot say, however, that the metaphor of "seeing as" has simply led the discussion astray. On the contrary, it conveys some sound intuitions into the power of imagination. The point of the above arguments is that "seeing as" is not fully adequate. What this ocular metaphor conveys is in fact a part of the imagination's powers, but only a part. The use of the term *construal* points in this direction, since it encompasses "seeing as" but is not confined to it. Yet the idea of construal, too, tends to center on the subject's own powers of insight, so that it is not finally adequate as a metaphor for imagination. A more adequate metaphor is provided by Hans-Georg Gadamer's discussion of play.

• Imagination and Play •

In his discussion of play in *Truth and Method*, Gadamer is concerned to propose an alternative to the understanding of art that has become predominant in aesthetic theory since Kant. This predominant understanding is, according to Gadamer, guilty of subjectivizing art; it takes works of art to be objects that are entirely divorced from the world, placed in a realm all their own, and experienced as aesthetic forms without cognitive content.[33] Their value, therefore, lies in their ability to give rise to an aesthetic experience, that is, to a purely subjective enjoyment of them as forms. They teach us nothing about our world or ourselves; rather, they are the occasion for pleasurable experiences lacking cognitive value. In this view, "the connection of the work of art with its world is no longer of any importance to it but, on the contrary, the aesthetic consciousness is the experiencing centre from which everything considered to be art is measured" (76).

Against such views, Gadamer insists that no true experience can be only an experience of form. On the contrary, any experience or perception "remains related to knowledge" if it is to be experience or perception in the full sense, for there is no such thing as "pure hearing and seeing" (81). Such notions are "dogmatic abstractions which artificially reduce phenomena," since they overlook the fact that "perception always includes meaning" (82). A proper appreciation of art must not ignore the unity of form and content and hence the unity of experience and knowledge in the encounter with a work of art.

> The pantheon of art is not a timeless presence which offers itself
> to pure aesthetic consciousness but the assembled achievements

---

[33]Gadamer, *Truth and Method*, 73-90. Subsequent citations are noted in the text and refer to this edition.

of the human mind as it has realised itself historically. Aesthetic experience also is a mode of self-understanding. But all self-understanding takes place in relation to something else that is understood and includes the unity and sameness of this other. Inasmuch as we encounter the work of art in the world and a world in the individual work of art, this does not remain a strange universe into which we are magically transported for a time. Rather, we learn to understand ourselves in it, and that means that we preserve the discontinuity of the experience in the continuity of our existence. Therefore it is necessary to adopt an attitude to the beautiful and to art that does not lay claim to immediacy, but corresponds to the historical reality of man. The appeal to immediacy, to the genius of the moment, to the significance of the "experience," cannot withstand the claim of human existence to continuity and unity of self-understanding. The experience of art must not be sidetracked into the uncommittedness of the aesthetic awareness. (86-87)

Gadamer then adds a succinct restatement of this point, only in a more positive way: "Art is knowledge and the experience of the work of art is a sharing of this knowledge" (87). Through the concept of play Gadamer tries to show how this can be so. The implication of Gadamer's examination of aesthetics goes far beyond the field of art, however. It also has some important ramifications for the field of history, and for the event of understanding in general. Indeed, Gadamer's own discussion of aesthetic theory leads him into a consideration of the hermeneutical dimension of the human sciences and then into an exploration of hermeneutics, or the event of understanding, in general. In each case, the basic motifs brought out in the concept of play are central to his argument.

The Model of Play

The central feature of play, in Gadamer's understanding, is its ability to absorb into itself those who play. That is, play can fulfill its purpose only if the players lose themselves in the play (92, 95-96). This means, in the first place, that the essence of play is located not in the consciousness of the players but in the movement of play itself. If the players are self-conscious about their participation in the play, the purpose of play is frustrated; for a distance remains between the players and their activity, a distance that keeps the play from being play in the full sense. To be sure, there is a certain lightheartedness in play; it is not serious in the same sense as one's work or the life-and-death issues that one sometimes faces. Yet this lightheartedness is not the same as an aloofness from the play. Genuine play absorbs the players into the structure of its movement and hence shapes their consciousness in its movement. In so doing, it reaches presentation through the players. Thus, the players are not the subjects of play, though the play cannot become actual without them. One can say that, when players play, they are played by the game. Moreover, the essence of the game is located in the movement of the game rather than in some substrate underlying the game (93, 97, 105). Play is found nowhere but in the play itself. The activity of play presents a structure of back and forth movement that, in the case of mere playing, has no end. It does not move toward a goal outside of itself but exists for the sake of the playing itself. This sort of play Gadamer compares to the "play" that exists in nature, the back and forth movement whose purpose is its own activity (94). But even in the case of a game, which presents tasks that are other than the endless to and fro movement of "primordial play," it is the movement within the game, the enactment of its structure, that is its essence. Moreover, the game, like play, absorbs the players into itself (97).

Now this understanding of play implies that the meaning or purpose of play is "pure self-presentation" (94, 97). That is, it seeks nothing other than the presentation to itself of the structure of its to and fro movement. In play or a game, the real concern is not the presentation of itself to onlookers but simply its coming to be through its enactment by the players. Furthermore, each enactment is an "original," that is, not a copy of what once was but in each case a coming to be of the play or game in its own reality. It is, in one sense, the play or game that was played before, since there is the same essential structure. On the other hand, it is also a new and original play or game, since it is enacted anew and in its own unique way according to the present movement of the players.

Play and Art

Gadamer argues that the nature of play provides a clue to "the ontology of the work of art." That is, an examination of art in the light thrown on it by the model of play uncovers its essence in a way that moves us beyond the pitfalls of a subjectivist aesthetic. For it enables us to see that art, like play, is also the re-presentation of something that absorbs us into itself. Unlike play, however, it is not mere self-presentation but a presentation for others (98-99). Hence the audience or viewer is an essential part of the work of art.

Gadamer initially articulates the similarity between play and art by turning to the dramatic play. A drama fulfills its purpose when the players lose themselves in it. And its essence is located in the structure of its movement, which re-presents something to the audience. This focus on the onlookers means that the players in a drama are not the actors but the members of the audience. They are the ones who become absorbed in the movement of the play. To be sure, the actors too can become absorbed in the play; but this involvement happens to the degree that they are on-lookers as well as actors. In a dramatic play, then, an attentive viewer is carried away into the self-forgetfulness that accompanies absorption in the structure of play. Moreover, such absorption leads one out of the world of everyday existence and into the world of action being re-presented (111). Involvement in dramatic action does not end at this point, how-ever, for the experience of self-forgetfulness is a prelude to reconciliation with oneself through a recognition of the truth of the dramatic action (112-13). That is to say, even though the action of the play carries us away from ourselves and our world for a time, it does so in order to enable us to see the world and ourselves afresh and in our true being. Dramatic action can produce this insight because, like art in general, it is a transformation into structure that intends to reveal the truth of things.

> Transformation means that something is suddenly and as a whole something else, that this other transformed thing that it has be-come is its true being, in comparison with which its earlier being is nothing. When we find someone transformed we mean pre-cisely this, that he has become, as it were, another person. There cannot here be any transition of gradual change leading from one to the other, since the one is the denial of the other. Thus the trans-formation into a structure means that what existed no longer ex-ists. But also that what now exists, what represents itself in the play of art, is what is lasting and true. (100)

What existed previously and are no more because of transformation are the players and their world. But if a play takes our world and ourselves from us, it also gives it all back to us as a new world, now seen in its true being. "The world of the work of art, in which play expresses itself fully in the unity of its course, is in fact a wholly transformed world. By means of it everyone recognizes that that is how things are" (101-102). Such recognition is far more than the acknowledgment of something we already know. Rather, it is the emergence of something "from all the chance and variable circumstances that condition it," so that we can recognize it. That is, there is "an illumination" of something previously hidden (102).

This disclosive "transformation into structure" depends on the en-actment of the play in the present. The reality of a play consists of its re-presentation through enactment, even if the "enactment" takes place only in the act of reading a play. And, of course, each enactment is a new in-terpretation of the play; even a poor or erroneous interpretation is at least faithful to it inasmuch as it is a reenactment of it (109). On the other hand, the terms *poor* or *erroneous* indicate that there is a standard for judging interpretations. That standard is the structure of the play itself. Since, on the one hand, that structure is meant to be reenacted in new interpretations, there is no one eternally valid interpretation or original enactment that must be copied (109-10). On the other hand, since it is a perduring structure, it does provide boundaries within which each reenactment should occur. Every interpretation is therefore subject to a criterion of right re-presentation (106).

Gadamer also extends these insights to other art forms, such as sculpture, painting, and architecture. In these cases, as well, play provides a clue to the transformation into structure that is the artistic event and that occurs when the player is engaged in the play of that structure.

Play and Understanding

The concept of play also provides a clue to the nature of the hermeneutical phenomenon in general, whether in the work of the human sciences or in communication between individuals. "Many aspects of the dialogue between men," Gadamer notes, "point to the common structure of understanding and playing: risking a word or 'keeping it to oneself,' provoking a word from the other person and receiving an answer from him or giving an answer oneself."[34] In the case of understanding between persons, then, there is also a certain loss of self that is prelude to the reception of a richer self than existed before.

> In speaking with each other we constantly pass over into the thought world of the other person; we engage him, and he engages us. So we adapt ourselves to each other in a preliminary way until the game of giving and taking—the real dialogue—begins. It cannot be denied that in an actual dialogue of this kind something of the character of accident, favor, and surprise—and in the end, of buoyancy, indeed, of elevation—that belongs to the nature of the game is present. And surely the elevation of the dialogue will not be experienced as a loss of self-possession, but rather as an enrichment of our self, but without us thereby becoming aware of ourselves.[35]

This last sentence is Gadamer's response to those who, in the contemporary scientific, methodical spirit, resist the giving up of the autonomous self-possession that regards the world as its project and therefore

---

[34]Gadamer, "On the Problem of Self-Understanding," in *Philosophical Hermeneutics*, 56.

[35]Ibid., 57.

subject to its manipulation and control. The event of understanding, on the contrary, calls for the willingness to lose oneself in pursuit of the subject matter, to be absorbed in the back and forth movement of play in the dialogue. Nevertheless, this loss of self is not the self's destruction; it is the self's enrichment through what is disclosed in the play of dialogue. "When one enters into dialogue with another person and then is carried along further by the dialogue, it is no longer the will of the individual person, holding itself back or exposing itself, that is determinative. Rather, the law of the subject matter is at issue in the dialogue and elicits statement and counterstatement and in the end plays them into each other. Hence, when a dialogue has succeeded, one is subsequently fulfilled by it, as we say."[36]

The play that takes place in a dialogue, or in any event of understanding, is not a phenomenon that exists in its own isolated sphere. On the contrary, the play of conversation with others—whether face to face, through writings, or through the tradition mediated to us in language— takes place in the flow of tradition. Indeed, tradition provides the context in which conversation is possible, for it gives us the world that conversation presupposes and to which it points. When we converse, we are not simply using language as a tool with which we can express our thoughts and point to a world otherwise existing for us apart from language. Instead, language is the medium through which our thoughts are constituted and shaped and by which the world is opened to us. Language functions in this manner because it carries with it a tradition—a world of things, categories, attitudes, hopes, and so on—that becomes ours when we learn the language. Hence, through language and what it carries the past is made effective for us in the present, primarily at a preconscious level. The play of conversation, therefore, takes place in a context profoundly shaped by what Gadamer calls the "effective-history" of the past. The subject matter that absorbs us in dialogue is something with which we are already related in some way through the operation of effective-history.

This important realization does not mean, however, that dialogue is hemmed in by tradition. Tradition and its effective impact on the present are necessary presuppositions for dialogue, and dialogue can never fully leave its tradition behind. Yet dialogue has the freedom of play in its absorption in the subject matter. That is, each dialogue is its own original reenactment or interpretation of the subject matter, so that one can never

---

[36]Ibid., 66.

say in advance where the play of dialogue will lead. New insight is possible and does occur because the event of understanding is a play that comes to be in its own original way in the present. It also occurs with a view to the future possibilities that arise out of this play in the present. This fusion of past and present, with an eye to the future, like the metaphoric association of similarity in dissimilarity, has the power to generate new insights. And since this possibility resides in the play that engages the self in the self-forgetful back and forth movement of a dialogue centering on the subject matter, such insight is not, in the first place, an autonomous work of the subject but the experience of being grasped in a fresh way by the subject matter, which comes to presentation in a unique way in this particular event of understanding.

The Fusion of Horizons

At other points in *Truth and Method,* Gadamer speaks of this play with the subject matter, which results in new understanding, in terms of a "fusion of horizons." He uses the term *horizon* to indicate that we are historically located in a situation that defines the scope of what we can see: "The horizon is the range of vision that includes everything that can be seen from a particular vantage point" (269). The concept of horizon, therefore, has reference to our subjective points of view, but it includes much more. For the horizon also has reference to the historical situatedness of individuals, and hence to the prejudgments of which they are not aware. It refers, that is to say, not only to what is seen at any particular moment but also to what could be seen in a particular historical situation. To have broad horizons is to have a large perspective on things, a perspective that enables one to stand back from what is near and place it in relation to other things. On the other hand, to have narrow horizons is to lack perspective and thus to overestimate what is close at hand. Of course, the limits of what could be seen cannot be precisely defined; the ability to do so would require a transcendence of the historical situation. Still, the concept of horizon is useful as a reminder of our historicity and as a way of illumining how we can and do operate within its limits.

There is another reason we cannot precisely define the limits of a horizon: namely, horizons are not fixed realities. Rather, a horizon moves as individuals move from one place to another. They are open and can grow (or perhaps shrink). Our horizons, then, are movable and open and are consequently able to fuse with other horizons that can broaden our perspective. Such fusion is what occurs in our encounter with the past. Again, this fusion of horizons can occur because all horizons, whether of the present or past, are mobile. In fact, the horizon of the present comes out of the past and includes a past horizon in the form of tradition, even if those in the present are wholly unaware of this fact. Yet there are parts of the past from which we do become alienated to some degree. And any overcoming of this alienation through a new understanding of that lost past involves a fusion of horizons. That is, by relating the past to our own thinking so that we can express its meaning in our own speech, "we regain the concepts of an historical past in such a way that they also include our own comprehension of them" (337; cf. 272-73, 358). Now this observation decidedly does not mean that we quickly assimilate the past to our mode of thought. To do so short-circuits the process of fusion by collapsing the horizon of the past into the present. A genuine fusion of horizons, therefore, calls for a recognition of the otherness of the past (see 272). Nevertheless, this recognition cannot take the form of a transposition of ourselves into the past, as if we could leave our own skins. Instead, it must take the form of relating ourselves to what has come from the past by allowing ourselves to be questioned by it and therefore to enter the play of question and answer in an effort to understand the question lying behind its answer. For to understand the question as a genuine question is to open ourselves to the potential claim of the past on our lives. As a result, the recognition of the otherness of a past text is a step along the way to relating it to ourselves; that is, it is a prelude to the fusion of horizons, which enlarges our own horizon.

As with the concept of play, one is not only engaged in following the movement of question and answer, one is also engaged in new interpretations and the emergence of new meanings. For if understanding involves relating past and present, a new present means new relationships and hence new meaning. Gadamer explains this idea by bringing application into the process of understanding. That is, all true understanding involves application, not as a moment after understanding, but as a moment within the event of understanding itself (see 274-78). This fact can be illustrated by the way understanding operates in the realm of law. Laws are formulated in relation to certain situations. Yet they can remain applicable in changed situations. On the one hand, every new application seeks to be faithful to the law; on the other hand, every new application gives new meaning to the law, even when it succeeds in being faithful. So it is in understanding something from the past.

> No text and no book speaks if it does not speak the language that reaches the other person. Thus interpretation must find the right language if it really wants to make the text speak. There cannot, therefore, be any one interpretation that is correct "in itself," precisely because every interpretation is concerned with the text it-

self. The historical life of a tradition depends on constantly new assimilation and interpretation. An interpretation that was correct "in itself" would be a foolish ideal that failed to take account of the nature of tradition. Every interpretation has to adapt itself to the hermeneutical situation to which it belongs. (358)

This is an essentially metaphoric process, since it involves a recognition of identity-in-difference. That is, the fusion of horizons entails viewing the past in terms of forms from the present and vice versa. In this way, there is an increase in knowledge through the bringing together of different horizons or positions that mutually illumine each other.

Implications for Imagination

Even though Gadamer does not bring imagination into his discussion of play or, for the most part, into his general discussion of hermeneutics,[37] the earlier analysis of imagination gives reasons for regarding the activity of play as thoroughly imaginative. For the dynamic at the heart of "seeing as," which survives the critique of the limitations of the ocular metaphor, is also the central dynamic in play. That is, the loss of self in play comes through the absorption of the self in its back and forth movement; and this loss, in turn, is made possible through *taking* the movement *as* a significant structure, that is, a structural movement that is capable of being taken as a meaningful activity, which one can take part in and is worth entering into. It would, perhaps, be possible to describe this activity in terms of "seeing as," but the nature of play uncovers the limitations of this metaphor, while also saving its central insight. For one of the important dimensions of play is its ability to transcend the subjectivity of the players by taking up and transforming their subjectivity. When one plays, one is not merely engaged in viewing things a certain way. Rather, one's whole self is engaged in the movement of play, so that not only one's sight but also all one's senses, as well as one's pattern of action, are taken into the structure of play and therefore shaped by it. Hence this involvement includes one's sight and one's conscious awareness, while taking in much more besides. One does not simply play. One is played. Yet the movement of play still depends on the openness of the players to its dynamic structure, that is, their ability to take it as a movement that invites and elicits their participation.

Such a construal may not be wholly within the conscious awareness of the player; it may not be in the player's consciousness at all. Never-

---

[37] An exception is "The Universality of the Hermeneutical Problem," in *Philosophical Hermeneutics*, 12.

theless, the enactment of play depends at some level on this openness, this ability to take the play as something. This construal, this "taking as" that includes conscious awareness while transcending it, is the dynamic at the heart of both the image of "seeing as" and the activity of play. For the reason for using the image of "seeing as" to define imagination is not this image's association with sight, or even with conscious awareness, but its representation of the activity of construing things as meaningful. The concept of play has made apparent that such construals need not be limited to the conscious activity of the mind. It is an activity that goes on every moment, whether we are aware of it or not.

One brief mention of imagination by Gadamer gives some support to this connection between imagination and play.[38] After insisting that the meaning of statements depends on the questions to which they are (either explicitly or implicitly) answers, he asserts that methods alone cannot give us the questions. For the uncovering of questions, one needs imagination. "It is imagination [*Phantasie*] that is the decisive function of the scholar. Imagination naturally has a hermeneutical function and serves the sense for what is questionable. It serves the ability to explore real, productive questions."[39] In other words, imagination is our capacity to be open to the play of the dialogue with a text, so that one can enter into its questions and move with it in its response to the questions. One can press this role of imagination even further in light of Gadamer's statement that questions, too, have a background, namely, whatever has motivated them. Thus, openness to statements requires openness to what motivates the questions. This movement corresponds to a movement in the reverse direction, a movement to the statement. And such a back and forth movement, in light of the play in which one is engaged in the present, elicits new questions with new motivations and new responses. Again, we see imagination as openness to the movement of play, by which we take it as something meaningful and are taken into it in order to reenact it in a unique way in the present.

This description of imagination is in accord with Gadamer's articulation of the hermeneutical phenomenon in terms of "understanding as" (81-82). That is, any understanding is an understanding of something as something. Thus, "understanding as" is the dynamic at the heart of the play of dialogue. The parallel between "understanding as," "taking as," and "seeing as" is clear, which provides strong support for my interpretation of imagination as the dynamic power in the movement of play.

---

[38]Cf. Gadamer, "Semantics and Hermeneutics," 88-89.

[39]Gadamer, "Universality of the Hermeneutical Problem," 12.

In sum, imagination is the power of "taking as" that enables one to be open to the play of dialogue (including the "dialogue with ourselves" that is thought), whether this is a dialogue with a contemporary, a text, a tradition, or whatever. I prefer "taking as" to "understanding as" because the former more directly suggests the holistic nature of imagination. Since it emphasizes the active nature of our imaginative encounter with the world, it also underscores the fact that understanding includes a facility, an ability to do something. Imagination could also be defined as attunement to the movement of play, by which we are taken into its movement.[40] In either case, this form of the imagination must be understood as something that is not located primarily in the subjectivity of the individual, though the subject is certainly included. The primary locus of imagination is the relationship between the understanding subjects and that which is to be understood. This relationship, which originates in the prereflective play by which we are initially taken into a structure of meanings, is the presupposition for all conscious imaginative activity of the subject.

The notion that we already dwell in a prereflective way in a world of relationships, of things and people that take us into a play with them, so that we take them as meaningful for ourselves in some way, suggests that the play of understanding is the essence of human life. If so, the play of dialogue, and imagination as its dynamic power, is present in all of life. This formulation is another way of bringing out the historicity of human life, a way that highlights the relationship between historicity and understanding and thus of historicity and imagination. In this case, however, imagination does not appear to be so much a power of construction as an openness to what the play of dialogue can uncover for us in our historically shaped present.

Prejudgment and Imagination

To say that we already live, in a prereflective way, in a world of relationships is to say that our language gives us a tradition that situates us in our world. Thus, Gadamer states that "language is not only an object in our hands, it is the reservoir of tradition and the medium in and through which we exist and perceive our world."[41] In other words, we come to our world and experience it through certain "prejudices" (or prejudg-

---

[40]Cf. Winter, *Liberating Creation*, 110.

[41]Gadamer, "On the Scope and Function of Hermeneutical Reflection," in *Philosophical Hermeneutics*, 29.

ments) that our tradition has given us. Now prejudgment is usually decried as destructive; and the Enlightenment saw itself as the emancipation from all such shackles. However, although prejudgments can function destructively (and the Enlightenment has rightly given rise to a methodological consciousness by which we seek to overcome destructive prejudgments), the fact is that the categorical rejection of prejudgment is unjustifiable. Gadamer states: "Prejudices are not necessarily unjustified and erroneous, so that they inevitably distort the truth. In fact, the historicity of our existence entails that prejudices, in the literal sense of the word, constitute the initial directedness of our whole ability to experience. Prejudices are biases of our openness to the world. They are simply conditions whereby we experience something—whereby what we encounter says something to us."[42] Thus, we require prejudgments. To put it in other terms, the play of dialogue with an other depends on the prior movement of play between ourselves and the tradition that our language brings to us. For our language gives us a wealth of knowledge that is presupposed in any dialogue and "provides an initial schematization for all our possibilities of knowing."[43] The imaginative play that every new dialogue brings into being, then, depends on the imaginative play of the dialogue with our heritage, which is already under way in a largely prereflective way. Every new dialogue is hence a discontinuous experience that rests on an encompassing experience of continuity.[44]

Creative imagination thus has its roots in the everyday activity of imagination, receiving its direction from the latter, even while going beyond and transforming it. That is, as in metaphor, its realization of the new arises out of a novel extension of the old into new areas. It must be stressed that dependence on tradition, on the everyday forms of understanding, does not entail an inability to uncover new insights. On the contrary, as Gadamer notes:

> We welcome just that guest who promises something new to our curiosity. But how do we know the guest whom we admit is one who has something new to say to us? Is not our expectation and our readiness to hear the new also necessarily determined by the

---

[42]Gadamer, "Universality of the Hermeneutical Problem," 9.

[43]Ibid., 13, 15.

[44]To put this point in other words: every understanding, even though it may be new and therefore discontinuous with prior understandings, depends on a preunderstanding through which our relationship with the subject matter becomes possible.

old that has already taken possession of us? . . . Like every image, however, this one too is misleading. The nature of the hermeneutical experience is not that something is outside and desires admission. Rather, we are possessed by something and precisely by means of it we are opened up for the new, the different, the true.

Such new insights can grasp us, since experience does not always fit predetermined forms of thought. Instead, it sometimes reorganizes our understanding while it is itself changed in the exchange between past and present.

> There is always a world already interpreted, already organized in its basic relations, into which experience steps as something new, upsetting what has led our expectations and undergoing reorganization itself in the upheaval. Misunderstanding and strangeness are not the first factors, so that avoiding misunderstanding can be regarded as the specific task of hermeneutics. Just the reverse is the case. Only the support of familiar and common understanding makes possible the venture into the alien, the lifting up of something out of the alien, and thus the broadening and enrichment of our own experience of the world.[45]

This power of experience is not an indication that experience is, after all, proto- or extralinguistic. Rather, it indicates that the power of language is open to the world. Language, rather than being a rigid system that is closed in on itself, limiting the possibilities of our experience, is a universal reality in that it is "all-encompassing," reaching out to include the entirety of our experience of the world.[46] In this light, Gadamer rightly argues that language is a "game of interpretation" in which we are all "it" and in which we are all engaged every day.[47]

Through this linguistic interpretation we understand and therefore comport ourselves in a certain way. Who and what we are, then, is decisively shaped by this activity of understanding. Indeed, understanding is so basic that it constitutes our being (230-31). Since understanding is more than our conscious judgments about things and consists largely of our prereflective relationship with the world, Gadamer can also say, "It is not so much our judgments as it is our prejudices that constitute our

---

[45]Gadamer, "Universality of the Hermeneutical Problem," 9, 15.

[46]Cf. Gadamer, "Scope and Function of Hermeneutical Reflection," 25; and idem, "Man and Language," in *Philosophical Hermeneutics*, 67.

[47]Gadamer, "Scope and Function of Hermeneutical Reflection," 32.

being."[48] Whether we speak in terms of understanding or of prejudices, however, everything points to language as the medium through which we engage in the back and forth movement of this play. Consequently, imagination, too, has a linguistic dimension, for its power of attunement is the linguistic and metaphoric power of "taking as."

This, of course, is a conclusion already reached in the discussion of imagination and metaphor. However, this exploration of Gadamer's notion of play has also led to some important conclusions that the conjunction of metaphor and imagination did not make apparent. These conclusions may be briefly summarized as follows: (1) imagination is a form of openness that leads to the absorption of the self into the movement of a dialogue that has the subject matter as its central focus; (2) what imagination uncovers in this way is not something in addition to tradition but tradition itself in its meaning for the present; (3) the re-presentation or disclosure of the truth of things, which is unique in each new situation, emerges from the past and requires the context of tradition; and (4) imagination is therefore not primarily located in personal subjectivity but in the relationship between persons and the subject matter. In short, the model of play has the virtue of underscoring imagination's location in our historicity and in the transsubjective nature of human life and understanding. It also has the virtue of opening up the question of the relationship between imagination and disclosure.

• Imagination and Disclosure •

If imagination is in fact the dynamic at the heart of play, then the operation of imagination should not be described in a one-sidedly constructivist way. On the contrary, imagination emerges out of the interplay of tradition, subject matter, and subjectivity. It is, then, a complex reality containing both receptive and constructive dimensions. Thus, an understanding of our ultimate environment does not rest on the constructions of an essentially autonomous subject but emerges in the course of imaginative play. Moreover, it proves itself, or fails, in the continuing movement of play. In other words, the interplay of tradition, subject matter, and subjectivity engages the imagination in such a way as to open us up to, or to disclose, certain possibilities for life-in-the-world. And these disclosures are given support, or rendered questionable, through their concrete actualizations in life.

If imagination is a part of the play of understanding, tradition is essential to the imagination. That is, the past shapes the imagination far

---

[48]Gadamer, "Universality of the Hermeneutical Problem," 9.

more profoundly than we can ever consciously measure. Hence, any effort to bring all our imaginatively shaped assumptions to light, so that we
can self-consciously refashion them according to some newly developed
points of view, is doomed to failure. Any suggestion that we can, and
therefore should, do so is a futile protest against the reality of our historicity, for it fails to appreciate the far-reaching implications of the fact that
our prejudgments constitute us more than our judgments.[49] We take for
granted much that tradition has given us, and only because of this can we
function humanly and humanely in the world. That is to say, we cannot
avoid taking many things on "authority," so that we can get on with the
business of living productively.

A rehabilitation of the concept of authority is thus in order. Of course,
this cannot be done by trying to reassert the authority of tradition simply
because it is tradition. The Enlightenment rightly challenged such views
by insisting on the power of reflection to disclose the inauthenticity of
some traditional notions and practices. However, authority's real value
for human life becomes apparent when we realize that its essence is not
the exercise of arbitrary power over people's minds but acceptance by
people who recognize its superior knowledge and insight. Gadamer
makes this point by juxtaposing two different views of reflection.

> Tradition is no proof and validation of something, in any case not
> where validation is demanded by reflection. But the point is this:
> where does reflection demand it? Everywhere? I would object to
> such an answer on the grounds of the finitude of human existence
> and the essential particularity of reflection. The real question is
> whether one sees the function of reflection as bringing something
> to awareness in order to confront what is in fact accepted with other
> possibilities—so that one can either throw it out or reject the other
> possibilities and accept what the tradition *de facto* is presenting—
> or whether bringing something to awareness *always dissolves what
> one has previously accepted.*[50]

The problem with the latter view of the nature of reflection is that it depends on a dogmatic rejection of tradition just because it is tradition, a
dogmatism that has no more justification than the reverse procedure. In
short, the role of reflection, including the conscious, creative activity of
the imagination, is to critique and test certain parts of our tradition, not
to reconstruct our world from the ground up. The latter attempt fails to

---

[49]Cf. ibid.

[50]Gadamer, "Scope and Function of Hermeneutical Reflection," 34.

appreciate the implications of human finitude and of the limited powers of human thought.

To be sure, the fact that reflection has the power to open up new possibilities, which we may choose over a traditional practice or point of view, means that tradition is not a prison from which there is no escape. But the previous argument about the relationship between tradition and thought would also indicate that the new is not wholly free from tradition; it does not arise ex nihilo. Again, the interplay of tradition, subject matter, and subjectivity means that new knowledge and insight are dependent on the tradition in at least two ways: (1) the tradition points one in a certain direction, so that one's questions also move more or less in this direction and the answers one formulates correspond to this direction; (2) new knowledge and insight are the result of novel syntheses between what tradition has bequeathed and what one now experiences or between various threads of tradition that were hitherto separated. Both forms of the relationship between tradition and new knowledge and insight indicate the metaphoric nature of the growth of knowledge. Even in the "hard sciences," which depend on precise observation and measurement, the questions one chooses to ask and the sorts of things one deems important to quantify and record are dependent on the history of one's discipline.

The metaphoric nature of the growth of knowledge is implicitly suggested by Gadamer's argument that the structure of a language grows through "the continuing growth of expressions into new realms of application."[51] This growth in language is coincident with a growth in knowledge and insight, since the creation of new linguistic configurations through metaphoric combinations leads to new understanding of our world and since coming to terms with new experience requires new extensions of language.[52] The important point to stress here, however, is not simply this act of transference, but the ability of language to illumine through extension into new realms of application. In other words, terms and images are chosen and become important, not because of the subject's free and autonomous activity of construction, but because of their power to open up dimensions of human life, to act disclosively. Admittedly, new syntheses are a constructive work of individuals, yet they are also guided by the ability of the newly applied terms and images to enable a greater attunement to the subject matter. Furthermore, our judgment of

---

[51]Gadamer, "Semantics and Hermeneutics," 85.

[52]Cf. Gadamer, "Scope and Function of Hermeneutical Reflection," 35.

their ability to do so is itself shaped, though not fully determined, by how our tradition has brought us into relationship with the subject matter. Such judgments are also guided by how well the new insight and knowledge cohere with present experience and future expectations. Yet experiences and expectations are themselves bound to tradition in some way.

Once again, one can adequately understand the emergence of new knowledge and insight only by placing them in the context of an interplay between tradition, subject matter, and subjectivity. To isolate any one of these elements is to falsify the nature of the imagination and to misunderstand the relationship between humans and their world. The complex interplay between reflective judgment and tradition, as one focuses on a particular subject matter, indicates that one cannot deal with the issue of the justifiability of a practice or point of view by making a simple appeal to critical rationality or tradition alone. Reflection and self-awareness are necessary and confront us as constant demands if we are to avoid traditionalism or authoritarianism.[53] Yet the critical work of reflection cannot assume an ahistorical, nontraditional standpoint from which to engage in its critical testing of tradition. Rather, reflection finds space to operate within the play of dialogue, as that dialogue occurs within and depends on the ongoing life of tradition. That is to say, new insight emerges as a result of the creative, metaphoric extensions produced by genuine dialogue, through which the disclosive power of tradition is uncovered.

Such insight becomes the basis for the critique of other aspects of tradition that are brought into the light of reflection. In this way, there is the possibility of genuine, even radical criticism within a particular tradition. For a new insight that is generated through the disclosive power of a tradition can become the basis for a far-reaching critique of prior understandings of the same tradition. Moreover, since there are a number of possible traditions that can make a claim on us, criticism of a tradition may be rooted in the disclosive power of another tradition. That is to say, if in the play of dialogue we find one tradition more compelling in its disclosive power than others, the one that proves more fruitful will provide a basis for the criticism of other traditions. Of course, even in the case of being grasped by one tradition rather than others, we do not experience the power of a tradition from a tradition-free vantage point. The emergence of new insight, the acceptance of a particular tradition, and the reflective criticism of tradition all take place within the ongoing life of tradition and never outside it. Thus, even though criticism is necessary

---

[53]Cf. ibid., 38.

to keep the authority of tradition from becoming ossified and authoritarian, such criticism requires some sort of traditional framework as the supportive context within which its critical evaluations can occur.[54]

An important implication of these considerations is that the linguisticality of human life does not, in itself at any rate, warrant the notion that our world is essentially of human construction. Instead, it is just as reasonable to suggest that language discloses our world to us by making available ways of being that are rooted in the nature of the self-world relation. We indeed have no access to the self-world relation outside of language. But, as I have been arguing in various ways, the ability of language to be open to the world, on one side, and to bring us into relationship with that world in ways that we find more or less adequate and justifiable, on the other side, provides some reason for regarding language as a medium for human life, through which life's possibilities are disclosed to us, rather than as a tool, through which we construct or reconstruct a world.

The close connection here between disclosure and the justifiability of possible ways of being is not fortuitous, for disclosure is a matter not of immediate insight but of the solidifying of a discovery through a history of experiences tending to confirm the fruitfulness of the discovery. An initial sense of the fittingness of a possible way-of-being-in-the-world is, of course, necessary for one to take it seriously. Yet its disclosive power does not fully emerge until it is embodied in the life of an individual or, more important, a community.[55] Moreover, even the initial sense of the fittingness of a possible form of life may not be a conceptual matter. Instead, the form of life may be, and often is, proposed at the level of cultural expression, which appeals as much to the affective and volitional dimensions of the person as to the cognitive dimension, and at the level of patterns of action, which can elicit praxis that only later undergoes the scrutiny of conceptual thematization. In fact, there is no reason to assume that conceptual creations and interpretations of possible ways of being have any sort of priority over patterns of action and cultural expressions. On the contrary, the position that I have been developing is more compatible with the view that cultural expressions and patterns of action, which are closer to the prejudgments or initial forms of relationship to the world that are expressed in a language and the tradition it embodies, have a certain priority over conceptual the-

---

[54]Cf. ibid., 41-42.

[55]For a discussion that operates along these lines in a consideration of the resurrection, see Peter Selby, *Look for the Living: The Corporate Nature of Resurrection Faith* (Philadelphia: Fortress Press, 1976).

matizations. It is thus a mistake to think of disclosure in primarily conceptual terms, just as it is wrong to limit it to brief ecstatic moments of insight. In this light, it is possible to speak of being grasped by the disclosive power of a tradition even before reflecting on it in any conscious way.

As already noted, we cannot deny that a moment of ekstasis is involved, in the sense of "standing outside of oneself" in order to envision life in a new way. This sort of experience is an important aspect of the creative activity of the imagination. That is, the experience of transcending what now is, in an envisioning of what might be, is an act of taking the world as something more than one has experienced so far. It is therefore an act of creative imagination to the degree that it moves beyond the usual ways of taking the world. Such a moment of ekstasis, to the degree that one experiences it as disclosive, also involves action according to the new construal of the world and so the embodiment of it in concrete patterns of life. If this proves fruitful for life, its disclosive power receives confirmation and is extended even further as its implications are more fully realized.

We must view issues of truth and intelligibility in this light. That is, we must ask and answer such questions in a way that is congruent with this understanding of the disclosive power of a proposed way-of-being-in-the-world. To do so involves the realization that we are not dealing with something that is subject to proof or verification, in the positivist sense of these terms. Nevertheless, these matters are not left to the whims of arbitrary choice, either. For there is an intermediate area between these two extremes in which most of life is lived and most of its important questions answered. In this area the reasonableness or justifiability of proposals is what is at stake, and the mode of argumentation is more akin to persuasion than proof. A key feature of this approach is its sensitivity to the fact that what counts as reasonable can be determined only in the situation that one has in view.

McClendon and Smith argue for the importance of taking into consideration the contextual nature of formulating criteria of reasonableness and examine the justification of religious convictions, especially Christian and Jewish religious convictions, in this light. They note that the justification of any convictional stance cannot find neutral ground on which to build an argument. Nevertheless, there do seem to be some broadly shared "loci of justification," that is, general categories that are thought by most people to be important elements in any justification of a convictional stance. These categories include such concerns as "truth, consistency, eudaimonia, satisfaction, and righteousness." This prevalent agreement can be deceptive, however, since the meaning of each of these terms is open to dispute and determined for each person by the convictional stance assumed. Furthermore, the list of important categories varies from stance to stance. Still, such categories are useful, since they serve as "points of reflection, criticism, debate, and correction"—even across convictional lines.[56]

An important implication of this approach to justification is that the determination of what sorts of considerations are important and are therefore brought into play can be made only in the situation of a convictional stance. Thus, for a Christian or Jew who wishes to affirm that God led Israel from Egypt, a variety of issues comes into play. Among them are the nature of the historical events to which appeal is made, the persuasiveness of the interpretation of these events, and the appropriateness of the confessing individual's affective and performative response.[57] Moreover, such considerations are often interrelated. For example, the affirmation of God's involvement in Israel's liberation from Egypt can reasonably be made only by a person or community whose life stance is thoroughly shaped by a commitment to faith in that God, for the very meaning of this confession emerges in the context of lives that are shaped by it.[58] Also, a lack of congruence between such a confession and the confessor's stance in life leads to serious doubts about the genuineness of the confession.[59] Hence, the effort to justify a set of religious convictions must take into consideration a wide variety of factors, and which factors are important cannot be determined apart from the convictions themselves.

In light of the complexities involved in justifying religious convictions, and given the fact that such convictions, though they may be reasonable, are not necessarily based in the first instance on conceptual articulations of that reasonableness, it is evident that the effort to provide justifications for a way of being—that is, apologetics—is essentially an ad hoc enterprise.[60] That is, as questions arise, it is important to deal with them, yet to try to offer an overall justification that anticipates all possible questions is to presume to have a knowledge of every aspect of one's own way of being and of future issues that far exceeds human limits.

---

[56]James W. McClendon, Jr., and James M. Smith, *Understanding Religious Convictions* (Notre Dame IN: University of Notre Dame Press, 1975) 163.

[57]See ibid., 59-78.

[58]See ibid., 67.

[59]See ibid., 74-78.

[60]Cf. George A. Lindbeck, *The Nature of Doctrine: Religion and Theology in a Postliberal Age* (Philadelphia: Westminster Press, 1984) 129-34.

Another dimension of the issue of justification, which is apparent in the dialogical and intersubjective nature of one's life in tradition, is its communal nature. That is, one engages in the tasks of critical reflection and of making judgments about the disclosive power or truth of a tradition within the context of a conversation with others. As we engage in dialogue with others, we gain new insights or check insights we think we have. Hence truth is something we discover through conversation and test through the critiques of others. This is not to say that truth is merely that on which all or most can agree, a lowest-common-denominator approach to truth. It is to insist that our insights and that on which they are based must be open to public scrutiny and must be able to account for themselves in the public arena.

An important aspect of such a dialogical approach to the question of truth is its openness to the perspectives of others who have a different experience of the way a tradition impinges on them. Thus, through dialogue we come to understand the perspectives of those who find oppressive a tradition, or an understanding of a tradition, that we had thought to be fruitful. Or, conversely, we may discover that others find fruitful a tradition, or an understanding of a tradition, that we had dismissed or ignored. In this way, the critical possibilities of new insight are grounded in a wide conversation that is open to a diversity of perspectives.

The implications for the relationship between rationality and imagination are far-reaching. They indicate, on the one hand, that rationality is shaped by our imaginative construals. On the other hand, our imaginative construals are in some ways subject to standards of reasonableness that cannot be manipulated at will. The answer to this seeming paradox may reside in the way in which both are ultimately related to ways-of-being-in-the-world. Through imaginative construals of human life, we shape our rational operations. And the fruitfulness of these operations helps to determine the authenticity of such construals. Now the determination of the fruitfulness of an idea or project involves issues of internal and external coherence. That is, any position will be tested for its ability to hold together consistently. It will also be measured against other ideas that one holds as true and projects that one regards as important for human life. In addition, it will be judged in terms of its fit with experience.[61] Such determinations involve rational operations, so that in

---

[61]Of course, when it comes to an encompassing set of convictions, such as a set of religious convictions, one may not hold other comparable ideas against which to test such convictions. Still, one can test its internal coherence and, to some degree, its fit with experience—even though such tests will certainly be less than objective, in the positivist sense.

these ways rational considerations test the work of imagination, even while imagination shapes them. This mutual relationship between imagination and rationality, deriving from their relationship to life in the world, is implied in Mary Hesse's description of rationality: "Rationality consists just in the continuous adaptation of our language to our continually expanding world, and metaphor is one of the chief means by which this is accomplished."[62]

• Conclusion •

Summing up, the imagination is the power of "seeing as," the power by which we see things through meaningful forms, according to Mary Warnock. Without denying the sound intuition at the heart of this proposal, this chapter has tried to articulate the definition further and to modify it in some important respects. In the first place, Ricoeur's discussion of metaphor and imagination makes clear the metaphoric nature of the imagination's work and thereby illumines the imagination's ability to generate new insight through bringing near what has been far apart. By associating imagination with metaphor, Ricoeur's treatment also suggests that the inventive power of imagination needs to be conjoined with its power of discovery. That is, imagination's syntheses not merely are creative projections but harbor the power to disclose, at both cognitive and affective levels, the world and possible ways-of-being-in-the-world. Although the discussions of both Warnock and Ricoeur are quite helpful, they suffer from an exclusive use of the ocular metaphor. It is above all Gadamer's articulation of the model of play that moves us beyond this limitation and at the same time locates the imagination solidly in our sociohistorical context. In light of Gadamer's discussion of the play of dialogue, through which understanding emerges, the imagination appears as the power of openness to the back and forth movement of dialogue. Through the imagination we are attuned to dialogue in a way that allows the new to appear through novel syntheses. These various threads can be woven together in a functional description of the imagination: the imagination is the corporate and personal power of taking things in terms of meaningful forms, forms which are embedded in and mediated to us through the history shaping us (tradition), which disclose, shape, and are shaped by living experience and which give rise to, guide, and are reformed by reflective thought.

What has this analysis of imagination established? One thing we can confidently say that it has not established is the notion that imagination

---

[62]Quoted by Ricoeur in *Rule of Metaphor*, 243.

is an epistemological grounding for human knowledge. Thus, we cannot appeal to the imagination as a foundation for knowledge of an objective world. But neither can we appeal to it as a foundation for a subjective projection of the world. For, while we have no basis for viewing the imagination as a mirror of the external world, we also lack a basis for taking it as an essentially constructive power located in the human subject. On the contrary, this analysis of imagination has suggested that it is located somewhere in the interplay among persons, on one hand, and between persons and the world, on the other.

That is to say, the work of the imagination takes place in the ongoing stream of tradition. Although it can and often does transform tradition to some extent, through its power of metaphoric synthesis, it can never completely transcend tradition. Not only does tradition provide the "debris" that imagination uses in its constructive synthesis, but also tradition has already shaped the imagination in a profound way. Even in its flights of fancy, the imagination does not escape this fact. Now this observation does not provide a basis for approving or disapproving the work of the imagination. It merely reminds us that the freedom of the imagination is a finite freedom, a fact that any consideration of the importance of imagination for theology must take seriously.

One must also take seriously imagination's orientation toward the world. That is, imagination's "images" are not a substitute for the world of experience but a way of mediating the world to us. Such a connection with the world may, of course, be suspended in flights of fancy. However, in cases where one is ultimately concerned with life in the world, there must finally be a focus not on imagination and its constructive powers but on possible ways-of-being-in-the-world. In short, in such cases imagination is the power of attunement to the play of give and take among persons and the world. It is the power that opens us to the dialogue between persons in the context of a third party to the dialogue (such as a community or nature).[63] Through this power we are able to extend the dialogue and therefore uncover something new. Always, however, the continuing and open-ended play of conversation is the context for imagination's creative work. And its work is not purely constructive but con-

---

[63]This is H. Richard Niebuhr's insightful understanding of a dialogue. A conversation between two isolated individuals, if it were possible, would be a duologue. In fact, however, conversations take place in a context—seen as nature, society, nation, God, etc.—and are therefore dialogues. Cf. his *Responsible Self: An Essay in Christian Moral Philosophy* (New York: Harper & Row, 1978) 69-89.

structive in and through its ability to be open to the power of the dialogue to disclose possible ways-of-being-in-the-world.

This understanding suggests that an adequate appreciation of the role of imagination in any sphere of human life requires that we attend to the nature of the dialogue in which it is operative. In some dialogues, the imagination's constructive powers may indeed come to the forefront. For example, games giving free rein to fantasy are not concerned about the fit between imagination's constructions and one's experience in the world. In other dialogues, imagination may be so much in the background that its presence tends to go unnoticed. For example, certain scientific conversations have this character. Most dialogues, however, fall somewhere between such extremes. The question of the truth of what one uncovers in each case cannot be decided by whether the imagination is operative. Rather, the disclosive power of imaginative construals, their ability to open up fruitful ways-of-being-in-the-world, is a measure of their truth. That is, as seen above, the issue of truth is an issue of justifiability rather than of the origin of a construal of the world. To speak in this way is to assert that truth is neither a mirroring of things in themselves nor a subjective projection of the world. It is rather the uncovering of ways-of-being-in-the-world that reside in the relationship between self and world, and not in either one alone. This approach also asserts that such uncovering takes place in the continuing dialogue that tradition, or the past as it makes itself felt in the present, makes possible.

The upshot of this approach is that a consideration of the implications of imagination for Christian theology can be adequate only if it takes its cue from the nature of the Christian dialogue. It is not required to take at face value whatever Christians have to say about themselves. But one must attend to the nature of the dialogue taking place within the Christian tradition if one hopes to say something worthwhile about the imaginative nature of Christian thought. Thus, the next chapter will focus on the place of imagination in the life of Christian faith. In this way I hope to lay the groundwork for a proposal about the role of imagination in Christian systematic theology.

IMAGINATION AND FAITH

In view of the important role of imagination in human life, it is clear that faith must take account of its own imaginative nature. Yet the precise nature of the play of imagination in the realm of Christian faith is dependent on the kind of conversation in which faith is engaged. The purpose of this chapter, then, is to clarify the kind of conversation that takes place in this sphere and hence how the imagination comes into play. The central thrust of my argument is that, in light of the nature of the play of imagination and of the self-understanding of faith, there is no warrant for supposing that faith should or could take itself to be about the business of affirming concepts that are essentially human constructs, created by ourselves for the purpose of projecting a framework of meaning. Rather, Christian faith arises out of the disclosive power of the expressions of faith that are found in the Bible and in the rest of Christian tradition.

At the outset it is important to stress that this analysis of Christian faith is in fact an analysis of *Christian* faith. Thus, it is not an effort to define or describe faith in general. Rather, even the most abstract and general descriptions are part of an analysis of the concrete reality of Christian faith and therefore depend on the existence and expression of that faith. This fact is underscored by the order of this chapter. That is, it begins with an analysis of the origin and shaping of faith within the ongoing play of the Christian tradition. This discussion provides a basis for an examination of the authority of the Bible within Christian life and thought and for an exploration of the distinctive role of the imagination within the life of faith.

• Faith and Christian Tradition •

If the imagination's operation in Christian faith is to be in harmony with the general operation of imagination, it cannot be a heteronomous event. Furthermore, if something is imposed from without, apart from the willing response of the person, the result is not a disclosure of the power of Christian faith to make life whole but coercion without insight and therefore without the free responsiveness of the person's imagination, will, and intellect. In such a case, the essence of faith is lacking. On the other hand, if we are not ready to accept the autonomous operation of the imagination posited by Kaufman, we are left with a third alternative, a theonomous relation between the imagination and tradition.[1] Here there is a resonance between the imaginative understanding of the individual and the articulation in Christian tradition of the ultimate framework of life, a resonance rooted in the noncoercive power of the Christian tradition to lead us to acknowledge it as a faithful and true witness to the way things are. In this way, the Christian tradition's ultimate foundation, the biblical witness, becomes a revelatory authority for Christian life.

The process of coming to recognize the revelatory power, and hence the authority, of the biblical witness, in a nonheteronomous and nonautonomous way, is provocatively examined by Paul Ricoeur in a number of essays. This examination of the relationships among faith, imagination, and the Christian tradition will therefore begin with an analysis (and adaptation) of his treatments of issues relevant to this question. We will then be in a better position to consider the basis and nature of the authority of the Bible in the life and thought of the Christian.

Imagination and the
Nonviolent Appeal of Revelation

In order to articulate an understanding of revelation that avoids the pitfalls of heteronomy and autonomy, Paul Ricoeur turns to the various "originary expressions of revelation," which reveal God in ways that are appropriate to their forms. That is to say, revelation cannot be properly understood if one considers only one of the forms in which it comes to expression. The usual tendency has been to assume such a univocal understanding by taking the prophetic model of revelation as primary and subsuming all other originary expressions under it. If one refuses this approach, however, and takes a closer look at the variety of expressions in the Bible, it becomes clear that revelation is not so easily reduced to a single concept. For the Bible contains several different kinds of originary expressions, each of which has a different sort of revelatory disclosure to offer.

Prophetic expressions provide "the original nucleus of the traditional idea of revelation," for here the prophet acts as a messenger for God. "The prophet presents himself as not speaking in his own name, but in the name

---

[1]Cf. Paul Tillich, *Systematic Theology*, 3 vols. (Chicago: University of Chicago Press, 1951-1963) 1:85-86, 147-50.

of another, in the name of Yahweh. So here the idea of revelation appears as identified with the idea of a double author of speech and writing. Revelation is the speech of another behind the speech of the prophet."[2] This characteristic is clearly a key aspect of any adequate understanding of revelation, since it underscores the fact that revelation arises outside of us and can—and often does—stand over against us. However, Ricoeur rightly notes that an understanding of revelation that rests only on prophetic discourse risks "imprisoning the idea of revelation in too narrow a concept, the concept of a speech of another." This narrowing down of the idea of revelation results from separating prophetic discourse from its context, especially the essential context provided by Israel's narratives; and it results in an intimate connection between revelation and "inspiration conceived as one voice behind another" (76).[3] As a result, revelation tends to be identified with the idea that Scripture has been dictated by God. Moreover, since there is "an almost invincible association between the idea of prophecy and that of an unveiling of the future," the content of revelation is "assimilated to a design in the sense of a plan that would give a goal to the unfolding of history" (76-77).

This narrowing of revelation into a single concept that becomes heteronomous in its application can be avoided if we keep in mind that there are other modes of discourse in the Bible, among them the narratives that provide the context for prophetic oracles.[4] In the case of narratives, the narrator or author falls into the background, often disappearing altogether, leaving the narration itself to be considered. Within the biblical narratives, God is not present as one who addresses us in the first person. Rather, God is spoken of in the third person. "Yahweh is designated in the third person as the ultimate actant—to use the category of A. J. Greimas—that is, he is one of the personages signified by the narration itself and intervenes among the other actants of the goings on. It is not a

---

[2]Paul Ricoeur, "Toward a Hermeneutic of the Idea of Revelation," in *Essays on Biblical Interpretation*, ed. Lewis Mudge (Philadelphia: Fortress Press, 1980) 75. Subsequent citations are noted in the text and refer to this edition. Cf. idem, "Naming God," *Union Seminary Quarterly Review* 34 (1979): 220.

[3]Cf. Ricoeur, "Naming God," 220: "It is easy to understand how, through forgetting the narrative genre and the other genres where God is also named, a certain hypostasis of the prophetic genre could have led to identifying revelation and inspiration and to the entire 'subjectivization' of the naming of God."

[4]Ricoeur's essay entitled "Naming God," which makes many of the same points as his essay "Idea of Revelation," notes that the narrative naming of God has a primary place among the various forms. See especially p. 220.

double narrator, a double subject of the word that we need to think about, but a double actant and consequently a double object of the story" (78).

Hence we are led "to meditate on the character of the events recounted," which has important implications for revelation.

> The idea of revelation then appears as connected to the very character of these events. What is noteworthy about them is that they do not simply occur and then pass away. They mark an epoch and engender history. . . . These events found an epoch because they have the twofold characteristic of both founding a community and of delivering it from a great danger, which, moreover, may take diverse forms. In such instances, to speak of revelation is to qualify the events in question as transcendent in relation to the ordinary course of history. The whole faith of Israel and of the early church is tied up here in the confession of the transcendent character of such nuclear founding and instituting events. (78)

As a result, the primary locus of "the imprint, mark, or trace" of God is not speech but history (since these narratives are ultimately rooted in historical events); and the question of inspiration is not a primary concern but arises only "after the fact" in second-order reflection on the narration of the story. In such reflective moments the problematic of inspiration has its place, yet it is only through an analogical transfer of prophetic categories that the narrator may be said to be speaking in the name of God (80). In other words, the narrative mode of discourse should not be absorbed into the prophetic, and will not be if properly understood—even in the question of the source and authenticity of the narrator's insight into the events.

The relationship between prophetic and narrative modes of discourse is marked by tension as well as analogy, for prophetic utterance frequently pronounces a threat to the continued existence of the community and hence undercuts the security deriving from the founding events that are related by narrative. Thus, these two modes of discourse set up a dialectic of founding and disorientation that cannot be resolved in a rational synthesis. Rather, we are left with "a double confession, never completely appeased; a double confession that only hope can hold together" (81).[5] Now in view of the gulf between these founding events and the prophetic announcement of the destruction of the old and creation of the new, this hope must not take the form of a "Stoic idea of providence" or a "teleological representation of the course of history," which gives each

---

[5]Cf. ibid., 220-21.

form of discourse its place in a tidy system. Ricoeur argues that this danger of identifying revelation with a divinely decreed design can be avoided if we attend to the fact that "there are at least three other modes of biblical religious discourse that cannot be inscribed within this polarity of narration and prophecy" (81).

One of these three modes of discourse is the prescriptive, the "practical dimension" of revelation. It expresses the will of God for the conduct of human life. If one thinks of God's will primarily in terms of an abstract imperative, much like Kant's categorical imperative, it is impossible to prevent a heteronomous understanding. However, the Hebraic understanding of Torah was rooted in and organically connected to the founding events of Israel's life. Thus, "the memory of deliverance qualifies the instruction in an intimate way" (83).[6] The divine commands are given to a redeemed people and are not merely imposed from without. This feature can be seen even more clearly when we recognize that the relationship between Israel and God is broader and more concrete than the idea of commanding and obeying. That is, the law "is part of the covenant between God and Israel: The idea of the Covenant designates a whole complex of relations, running from the most fearful and meticulous obedience to the Law to casuistic interpretations, to intelligent mediation, to pondering in the heart, to the veneration of the joyous soul. . . . The well-known Kantian respect for the law, in this regard, would only be one modality of what the Covenant signifies, and perhaps not the most significant one" (83).

Within the space provided for a variety of ethical feelings, the law displays a "historical dynamism" in that the teaching of Torah is marked by an alternation between the proliferation of casuistic rules and the concentration on the central matters of the law. The unchanging direction of this dynamism is toward holiness and perfection (84). This direction toward holiness and perfection is at the heart of the law and makes its claim on our wills. Here, then, is the locus of the "ethical dimension of revelation." Here, too, we can see how the law is something other than a heteronomous reality, since it is an appeal for perfection that is directed to the will in light of an encompassing relationship with God. The implication for the idea of revelation is that it is historical in more than one sense. "If we continue to speak of revelation as historical, it is not only in the sense that the trace of God may be read in the founding events of the past or in a coming conclusion to history, but in the sense that it orients

---

[6]Cf. ibid., 221.

the history of our practical actions and engenders the dynamics of our institutions" (85).

Wisdom constitutes still another mode of originary discourse, though it also "surpasses every literary genre" (85). Here we seem to have little more than practical advice on the art of living well. But it is in fact much more, for its thrust is "a reflection on existence that aims at the individual behind the people of the Covenant, and through him, every human being" (85).[7] Hence wisdom discourse goes beyond the covenant framework and points to the situation of every individual by taking human "limit-situations" as its theme. These limit-situations raise fundamental questions about life, for they are "those situations—including solitude, the fault, suffering, and death—where the misery and the grandeur of human beings confront each other" (85-86). Ricoeur continues: "Hebraic wisdom interprets these situations as the annihilation of humans and the incomprehensibility of God—as the silence and absence of God. If the question of retribution is so acute here, it is so to the extent that the discordance between justice and happiness, so cruelly emphasized by the triumph of the wicked, brings to light the overwhelming question of the sense or nonsense of existence" (86).

This basic question is answered in wisdom neither by showing how suffering may be avoided nor by providing its rationale and thereby justifying the ways of God but by placing "suffering into a meaningful context by producing the active quality of suffering" (86). For Ricoeur, Job provides the "best example of wisdom." We find that Job ultimately has to repent for supposing that existence makes no sense—not, however, because he receives an answer to why he has suffered but because in his encounter with God he discovers "an unsuspected meaning which cannot be transcribed by speech or logos a human being may have at his disposal" (87). If we can speak of God's design for the world in this connection, then, we can speak only of a design hidden from human eyes. Yet, by finding the possibility of hope in spite of the situation, a hope resting on the God who gives existence a meaning that we cannot capture in our human systems of thought, Job finally "conjoins cosmos and ethos" through "the pathos of actively assumed suffering" (86). Thus, when Job is grasped by the realization that his suffering has not severed him from the God who provides an unsuspected meaning for his life and repents of presuming to know more than a mere mortal can, his suffering receives a new quality through which and only through which this sur-

---

[7]Cf. ibid., 221-22.

prising and still-secret meaning comes to expression. For this new quality is the new attitude of hope in spite of one's situation, a hope rooted in the surprising presence of God rather than in a system of meaning that can be derived from the situation.

How does this mode of discourse affect our understanding of revelation? In the first place, it clearly presents a different viewpoint than the prophetic, for the sage in no way claims that "his speech is the speech of another" (87). Nevertheless, "he does know that wisdom precedes him and that in a way it is through participation in wisdom that someone may be said to be wise" (88). Thus, the sages do not presume to be operating autonomously. Rather, their wisdom comes from their relation to a reality preceding and encompassing them. Moreover, since wisdom belongs with God, this participation in wisdom "is not to be distinguished from intimacy with God." In brief, the sage uncovers a divine reality through attending to wisdom, just as the prophet discloses God's will through inspiration.

The fifth mode of discourse noted by Ricoeur is the hymnic. In this case, as we see especially in the Psalms, the worshiper addresses God in the second person in order to praise, to make requests of, or to thank God. The relationship with God that such forms of address disclose is, of course, dependent on God's work in nature and history. Nevertheless, the lyric genre is not simply a repetition of the narrative's story in a different mode. For the act of praise, supplication, or thanksgiving "elevates the story and turns it into an invocation" (88-89). Hence this particular modality of our relation to God cannot be reduced to either the narrative's speech about God in the third person or to the prophetic proclamation of God's word in the first person. The nature of revelation in this case also cannot be reduced to either of these modes.

> If we were to say in what sense the Psalter may be said to be revealed, it certainly would not be so in the sense that its praise, supplication, and thanksgiving were placed in their disparate author's mouths by God, but in the sense that the sentiments expressed there are formed by and conform to their object. Thanksgiving, supplication, and celebration are all engendered by what these movements of the heart allow to exist and, in that manner, to become manifest. . . . The word forms our feeling in the process of expressing it. And revelation is this very formation of our feelings that transcends their everyday, ordinary modalities. (90)

On the basis of his analysis of the various originary modes of discourse in the Bible, Ricoeur reaches four important conclusions. First, "the analysis of religious discourse ought not to begin with the level of theological assertions." Rather, theological language, since it is propositional, is "a second degree discourse which is not conceivable without the incorporation of concepts borrowed from speculative philosophy." Thus, in order to reach the level at which faith first becomes articulated, where faith has its origin, it is necessary to "give priority to those modalities of discourse that are most originary within the language of a community of faith" (90).

The second conclusion is that the originary forms of discourse that express the community's faith are inextricably connected to this faith. They are much more than the means to express ideas that exist independently of these modes of discourse. In Ricoeur's words, "The confession of faith expressed in the biblical documents is directly modulated by the forms of discourse wherein it is expressed" (90). This modulation arises from a "mutual accomodation [*Sic*]" between the confession of faith and the structure of discourse.

> Each of the forms of discourse . . . encompasses a particular style of confession of faith where God is named in an original fashion. This is why we miss what is unique about biblical faith if we take categories such as narrative, oracle, commandment, and so on, as rhetorical devices that are alien to the content they transmit. What is admirable, on the contrary, is that structure and kerygma accomodate [*Sic*]each other in each form of narration. It is within this mutual accomodation [*Sic*] of the form and the confession of faith that the naming of God diversifies itself.[8]

A proper understanding of the biblical act of naming God thus can come about only if one takes into account "the interplay between story and prophecy, history and legislation, legislation and wisdom, and finally wisdom and lyricism" (92).[9]

Likewise, an understanding of revelation that appreciates the importance of these originary modes of discourse will not "be formulated in a uniform and monotonous fashion which we presuppose when we speak of the biblical revelation." Ricoeur's third conclusion, then, is that the concept of revelation needs to be "polysemic and polyphonic." It is not true that the various modes of discourse simply lead to heterogeneous notions of revelation. On the contrary, there is an analogical bond between the different forms of discourse, so that the different meanings that they give to the concept of revelation are also related in an analogical fashion. Such a relationship derives from a single reference term, namely,

---

[8]Ibid., 220.

[9]Ibid., 221.

prophetic discourse; for there we find the basic meaning of revelation: a message "about God's name and in God's name" (92). As we have seen, although this definition provides a point to which other originary modes of discourse can be referred, it does not adequately define what transpires through these other forms—hence the need for a concept of revelation that can include more than the idea of a "double divine and human author."

Ricoeur's final conclusion is that the revealed God does not become subject to our control, not even conceptually. That is, the revealed God remains hidden. "In none of its modalities may revelation be included in and dominated by knowledge. In this regard the idea of something secret is the limit-idea of revelation. The idea of revelation is a twofold idea. The God who reveals himself is a hidden God and hidden things belong to him" (93). Thus, no one and no institution can claim to have revelation in its possession, for it is not the kind of thing that can be possessed.

Understood in these terms, revelation is not a heteronomous imposition of something that is purely external to the individual. On the contrary, revelation's claim is a "nonviolent appeal," since its originary modes of discourse appeal to us at the level of some fundamental human experiences where truth is "spoken of in terms of manifestation rather than verification"—that is, a level of living experience that is prior to the objectifying forms of thought that give rise to questions of verification (95-96). This is not a prelinguistic experience, for it, too, comes to expression and is given shape through language (cf. 96, 90).[10] Still, language here opens us to some "cardinal experiences" that "can enter into resonance or consonance with the modes of revelation brought to language by the most primitive expressions of the faith of Israel and of early Christianity" (96). By means of this resonance the biblical modes of discourse draw us into acknowledging their revelatory power.

Ricoeur further articulates the nature of this nonviolent appeal by analyzing it under the category of poetics, which he believes has traits that are homologous to the biblical revelation. That is, poetic discourse also has a revelatory function. To show this feature, Ricoeur introduces three "preparatory concepts" and the idea of split reference.

The first preparatory concept relates to the act of writing. When something is written, it breaks free from the situation of oral discourse, since it is no longer tied to the time and place of the author and the intended audience. Hence writing is a form of communication that "is immediately

---

[10]Cf. ibid., 216.

autonomous with regard to its author's intention" (99). The reader, then, is called on to consider and interpret the issue of the text rather than "the finite intentional horizon of the author." The issue of the text also goes beyond the horizon of the original audience.

The concept of a work is the second preliminary idea introduced by Ricoeur. A work is the result of the shaping of discourse according to "the operation of literary genres such as narration, fiction, the essay, etc." (99). As a result, each work has a certain style, or unique configuration, which can also be described as a "verbal icon," a rule for the production of images (100).[11]

The third preparatory concept is that of "the world of the text." With respect to this world, Ricoeur states:

> What is finally to be understood in a text is not the author or his presumed intention, nor is it the immanent structure or structures of the text, but rather the sort of world intended beyond the text as its reference. In this regard, the alternative "either the intention or the structure" is vain. For the reference of the text is what I call the issue of the text or the world of the text. The world of the text designates the reference of the work of discourse, not what is said, but about what it is said. Hence the issue of the text is the object of hermeneutics. And the issue of the text is the world the text unfolds before itself. (100)

To understand Ricoeur's point about the world in front of the text, it is necessary to grasp his view of the referential function of poetic texts. Such texts do not refer in the sense that ordinary or scientific discourse refers. While some have taken this fact to mean that poetic texts do not refer at all, but merely celebrate their own language, Ricoeur insists that "this suspension or abolition of a referential function . . . is . . . the negative condition for the liberating of a more primitive, more originary referential function" (101). This more primitive referential function is the text's ability to redescribe reality through its fictive language. In Aristotelian terminology, "the mythos is the way to true mimesis, which is not slavish imitation, or a copy, or mirror-image, but a transposition or metamorphosis—or, as I suggest, a redescription" (102). Such redescription opens up the possibility for a particular way of "participation-in or belonging-to an order of things which precedes our capacity to oppose our-

---

[11]Cf. Ricoeur, *The Rule of Metaphor: Multidisciplinary Studies of the Creation of Meaning in Language,* trans. Robert Czerny et al. (Toronto: University of Toronto Press, 1981) 207-15.

selves to things taken as objects opposed to a subject" (101). And such a referential function can properly be described as revelatory because here truth is manifestation, that is, "letting what shows itself be." According to Ricoeur, what shows itself is "a proposed world, a world I may inhabit and wherein I can project my ownmost possibilities" (102).[12] Moreover, this world is usually hidden from us because of our everyday preoccupations, which submerge us in an environment filled with objects that we seek to dominate. The manifestation that occurs through poetic texts, then, is much like the emergence of Atlantis from its watery depths.

Ricoeur's use of poetic language in order "to set off the horizon of significance" where the Word of God may be heard is not an attempt to identify biblical revelation with poetic revelation. Rather, he sees an analogy between these forms of revelation that illumines the way the biblical texts operate (103). That is, they operate according to the function of split reference and thereby propose a world that we may inhabit. What this means for revelation in the biblical sense is briefly summarized by Ricoeur. "This areligious sense of revelation helps us to restore the concept of biblical revelation to its full dignity. It delivers us from psychologizing interpretations of the inspiration of the scriptures in the sense of an insufflation of their words into the writer's ears. If the Bible may be said to be revealed this must refer to what it says, to the new being it unfolds before us. Revelation, in short, is a feature of the biblical world proposed by the text" (104). In part this similarity between areligious and biblical revelation does not amount to an identity, because the latter has a specific feature that is lacking in the former—that is, its ultimate referent is God.

The fact that the Bible's originary modes of discourse speak of God gives them a religious character that cannot be fully subsumed under the category of poetic texts. The reference to God serves to qualify them as texts that speak of something beyond our control or ability to grasp conceptually. Each mode of discourse points in its partial way to this one referent; and in this way a circulation of meaning between these modes of discourse is begun, a meaning that never quite reaches its goal, since God remains "a vanishing point and an index of incompleteness" for these texts (104).[13] Furthermore, the fact that these texts speak of God's relation to

---

[12]Cf. Ricoeur, "Naming God," 219.

[13]Cf. ibid., 222-23, where Ricoeur notes that the form of Jesus' parabolic discourse also expresses the fact that God eludes us. Its limit-expressions are indications that this language transgresses all usual boundaries in the direction of naming the unnameable: God. He also argues, on the other hand, that religious

the world means that the possible ways of belonging to or participating in a world that they propose have a fundamental significance for all dimensions of life. For they provide schemas or models (that is, "procedures and methods for providing images") by which we can name God, and as a result, they are the basis for a life that is thoroughly shaped by their construal of the world.[14] Again, we see that Ricoeur in no way wants to identify biblical texts with literary texts. There is a homology between them but not an identity.

Ricoeur's treatment of the similarities between biblical and poetic texts presupposes a refusal to accept the pretensions of consciousness to posit itself, a pretension that was examined in some detail in the previous chapter. Thus, in allowing a poetic or biblical text to propose a possible world to us, a world that may in fact lay claim to us, one must be willing to let go of any illusions of autonomy. The notion that the self founds itself, and therefore is that from which every rule of validity is derived, makes the subject "the supreme 'presupposition.' " However, the willingness to attend to the issue of a text, as articulated by Ricoeur, involves a very different sort of presupposition. He describes this presupposition in the context of a discussion of Christian proclamation.

> Listening to Christian preaching also stands in the order of presuppositions, but in a sense where presupposition is no longer self-founding, the beginning of the self from and by the self, but rather the assumption of an antecedent meaning that has always preceded me. Listening excludes founding oneself. The movement toward listening requires, therefore, . . . letting go. . . . It requires giving up (*dessaisissement*) the human self in its will to mastery, sufficiency, and autonomy. The Gospel saying "whoever would save his life will lose it," applies to this giving up.[15]

This giving up of self is no violation of the human subject, since we already belong to "an experience that bears us" before our reflection be-

---

language involves more than merely limit-expressions, for it includes models, which are marked as religious models through their conjunction with limit-expressions.

[14]Cf. ibid., 225-27. It should be noted that these models, since they speak of God, who is beyond naming, are qualified by the limit-expressions that continually relativize them. The limit-expressions, then, make these models dynamic by inverting them "into an opposed image." For example, God is understood through the models of father, mother, spouse, brother, etc. and not through any one of these in isolation. See especially p. 226.

[15]Ibid., 219.

gins. Thus, every effort to justify or ground anything "is always preceded by a relation that already carries it" (107).[16]

If the consciousness does not posit itself, then it cannot set itself up as the standard of meaning. Rather, it receives meaning from the world of the text. That is, the issue of the text provides a possible way of understanding oneself and hence of expanding one's horizons. Ricoeur calls this step the "act of understanding oneself before the text." Such an understanding is quite different than trimming the text to suit a supposedly autonomous consciousness. "To understand oneself before the text is not to impose one's own finite capacity of understanding on it, but to expose oneself to receive from it a larger self which would be the proposed way of existing that most appropriately responds to the proposed world of the text" (108).

Ricoeur has still one more category to introduce before he has finished his analysis of what it means to give oneself up in reading the biblical text, that is, the category of testimony (cf. 110). Here one meets a concept that is wholly repugnant to a would-be autonomous consciousness, for it denotes one's dependence on external events and the "signs of the absolute" that appear in them. From the perspective of Christian faith, on the other hand, this is its virtue, since it brings into play the dimension of historical contingency that is lacking in the "deliberately nonhistorical and transhistorical" concept of the "world" (109). That is, the idea of testimony is to be understood as the account of an experience of the divine and hence as the attestation of the divine through events, acts, and persons. Such attestation or testimony differs from Kantian-type symbols and from examples in that the act of testimony does not become effaced before that to which it refers (as Kantian symbols and examples do). For Ricoeur the role of testimony is necessary because the existence of unjustifiable evil in the world "does not allow us the leisure to grant our veneration to the sublimity of the moral order" (111). If we are going to be able to affirm some order or value for the world, then, it will only be because there are persons, acts, and events "that attest that the unjustifiable is overcome here and now." For only thus will the ideas, ideals, and ways of being depicted by the symbol come to be seen as possessing reality. At one point Ricoeur succinctly brings together the various threads that belong to a "hermeneutic of testimony."

---

[16]This insight Ricoeur attributes to his reading of Gadamer's *Truth and Method*. He also notes that, through the concept of belonging to, he finally moved beyond Husserlian idealism. See pp. 106-107.

Testimony better than either an example or a symbol places reflection before the paradox which the pretension of consciousness makes a scandal of, I mean that a moment of history is invested with an absolute character. This paradox ceases to be a scandal as soon as the wholly internal movement of letting go, of abandoning the claim to found consciousness accepts being led by and ruled by the interpretation of external signs which the absolute gives of itself. And the hermeneutic of testimony consists wholly in the convergence of these two movements, these two exegeses: the exegesis of self and the exegesis of external signs. (111-12)[17]

Ricoeur also compares the structure and function of historical testimony to Kant's understanding of "aesthetic ideas," as presented in *Critique of Judgment*. Kant argued that the imagination has the power to present ideas of reason for which we can find no adequate concept. Through the presentation of such ideas, we are stimulated to think about them and to try to conceptualize them. However, since these ideas cannot be adequately grasped through concepts, we are stimulated to think further. So it is with historical testimony. It presents an originary affirmation through which the self's consciousness is determined, yet does so in such a way that we can never exhaust its meaning with our concepts. Hence historical testimony continually gives rise to further thought (116).

This comparison to Kantian "aesthetic ideas" suggests the degree to which imagination is central to the operation of revelation. For these ideas belong initially to the realm of the imagination, and only later to the realm of thought. So, too, historical testimony appeals to "an imagination that opens itself" before it appeals to "a will that submits." In this way, revelation engenders a nonheteronomous dependence.

What are the poem of the Exodus and the poem of the Resurrection . . . addressed to if not to our imagination rather than our obedience? And what is the historical testimony that our reflection would like to internalize addressed to if not to our imagination? If to understand oneself is to understand oneself in front of the text, must we not say that the reader's understanding is suspended, derealized, made potential just as the world itself is metamorphosed by the poem? If this is true, we must say that the imagination is that part of ourselves that responds to the text as a Poem, and that alone can encounter revelation no longer as an unacceptable pretension, but a nonviolent appeal. (117)

---

[17]For a further discussion of testimony, see Ricoeur, "The Hermeneutics of Testimony," in *Essays on Biblical Interpretation*, 119-54.

In sum, the Bible becomes revelatory when the proposed world in front of the biblical texts leads one to take the world in which one lives and acts concretely as appropriately redescribed by this proposed world, that is, when the biblical texts engage and lead the imagination.[18] This appeal to the imagination does not come in a single form but in the various modes belonging to the types of literature found in the Bible. Thus, the prophetic, narrative, legal, wisdom, and hymnic genres, in their own distinctive ways, propose a world that has God as its ultimate referent. When, through their appeal to the imagination, these texts exercise a disclosive power, the God who is indirectly presented in them becomes manifest or revealed. In accordance with the nature of the biblical testimony, such manifestation is taken to be a self-manifestation of God, who has acted to leave a trace or mark of the divine nature in history. Revelation, then, is mediated through history and the texts that carry the testimony to that history. These texts become revelatory for one today when, through their disclosive power, they engage the imagination, so that one takes the proposed world to be appropriately redescribed by them; that is, when one's life is understood to realize its ownmost possibilities in this world that is everywhere and always referred to God as its ground and goal.

The existence of the various genres stands as a reminder of the inability of any human form of speech, even the biblical forms of testimony, to express adequately the reality of God, and of the fact that revelation appeals to various dimensions of human life that cannot be encompassed within a single genre. Revelation, then, is not a monovalent concept but a complex symbol conveying the richness of God's self-manifestation in and through the biblical witness. The several genres together initiate a circulation of meaning among themselves through their common reference to God as the ultimate horizon of the world they propose. This circulation is the interplay of differences and similarities among the texts, through which the meaning of the biblical testimony emerges. Yet this interplay does not remain wholly within the text, since it refers to the world in front of the text. This trajectory of meaning beyond the text potentially brings it into contact with our horizon, so that, through a fusion of horizons, our world is transformed through the redescriptive power of the text and faith arises.[19]

---

[18]Cf. David Tracy's discussion of "realized experience" in the *Analogical Imagination: Christian Theology and the Culture of Pluralism* (New York: Crossroad, 1981) 107-15, 193-202.

[19]Since this redescription has its effect through a fusion of horizons, it involves

Narrative, Symbol, and Metaphor

As already demonstrated, the appeal to the imagination comes in various modalities, according to the diverse modes of discourse found in the Bible. In each case the text provides ways of redescribing reality that engage and lead our own imaginative construal of how things really are. Yet, although each mode must be respected and included in our understanding of revelation, Ricoeur does give priority to the narrative mode when speaking of the text's power to redescribe the world.[20] This is because the biblical narratives relate those events that have founded the community of faith and are therefore "transcendent in relation to the ordinary history" (78). Consequently, the other modes of discourse depend on this one.

Ricoeur relates the redescriptive power of narrative to the redescriptive power of metaphors. Like metaphors, narratives have the potential of creating semantic innovations through the work of synthesis. In the case of narratives, this synthesis is the result of the story's plot. "By means of the plot, goals, causes, and chance are brought together within the temporal unity of a whole and complete action. It is this synthesis of the heterogeneous that brings narrative close to metaphor. In both cases, the new thing—the as yet unsaid, the unwritten—springs up in language. Here a living metaphor, that is, a new pertinence in the predication, there a feigned plot, that is, a new congruence in the organization of the events."[21]

The new congruence of the plot " 'grasps together' and integrates into one whole and complete story multiple and scattered events," thereby providing a redescription of reality that invites us to make it our own.[22] That is, a fictional narrative, through the configuration of its plot, provides a mimesis of everyday life; but this mimesis is a redescription rather than a mere

---

more than an adoption of the "biblical world." The model of the fusion of horizons highlights the interplay between the proposed world in front of the text and the world we have hitherto inhabited. For a more detailed discussion of the nature of the appeal of the text and its connection to the fusion of horizons, see the following discussions of narrative, symbol, and metaphor and of the function and authority of the Bible.

[20]Cf. Ricoeur, "Naming God," 220: "The whole of contemporary exegesis has made us attentive to the primacy of the narrative structure in the biblical writings. . . . The naming of God is thus first of all a narrative naming."

[21]Ricoeur, *Time and Narrative*, vol. 1, trans. Kathleen McLaughlin and David Pellauer (Chicago: University of Chicago Press, 1984) ix.

[22]Ibid., 10-11.

imitation, so that the mimetic power of narrative is able to reconfigure our everyday living. In this way, argues Ricoeur, narrative structures our temporal lives in a manner that makes them human. "Time becomes human to the extent that it is articulated through a narrative mode, and narrative attains its full meaning when it becomes a condition of temporal existence." Such articulation of human life occurs through an intersection of the world of the narrative and the world of real action, an intersection that Ricoeur likens to Gadamer's idea of a fusion of horizons.[23]

This work of narrative is intrinsically connected to the fact that human life is given a meaningful structure through symbolic forms. "If, in fact, human action can be narrated, it is because it is always already articulated by signs, rules, and norms. It is always already symbolically mediated."[24] By *symbolic forms* Ricoeur means "cultural processes that articulate experience," which means that symbols are not merely mental realities that guide action but are "a meaning incorporated into action and decipherable from it by other actors in the social interplay." In other words, symbols provide "the rules of meaning" by which actions are understood within a social matrix.[25] Thus, the composition of narratives rearticulates a preunderstanding of human life, which is shaped by symbolic forms.[26]

For Ricoeur this fact seems to mean a logical priority of symbols over narratives. That is, narratives depend on symbols for their possibility. However, given the historicity of human life and hence the mediation of experience through meaningful patterns that emerge through the history of life in the world, one could also argue the reverse: symbols emerge only out of our history together in the world and the reenactments and stories to which it gives rise. The approach developed in this essay is more in

---

[23]Ibid., xi, 45, 52 (quotation), 71, 77-78. Cf. George Stroup, *The Promise of Narrative Theology: The Recovery of the Gospel in the Church* (Atlanta: John Knox Press, 1981) 164-69, 194. Stroup argues that the result of this fusion is a new narrative that informs the identity of the believer, a narrative that is identical with neither the narratives in the text nor the former narrative of one's personal life.

[24]Ricoeur, *Time and Narrative*, 57.

[25]Ibid., 58. This emphasis on the central role of symbols does not take away from the crucial role of metaphoric process. Rather, symbols also operate metaphorically in that their "literal" meaning gives rise to a figurative transfer of meaning. Cf. Ricoeur, *Interpretation Theory: Discourse and the Surplus of Meaning* (Fort Worth TX: Texas Christian University Press, 1976) 55; and Gibson Winter, *Liberating Creation* (New York: Crossroad, 1981) 34.

[26]Cf. Ricoeur, *Time and Narrative*, 54.

harmony with the latter position. Yet it is necessary to add that a meaningful history mediated through reenacted and told narratives is already symbolic at the moment of narration and reenactment. At the primordial level, then, narrative and symbol emerge together and call for each other. Nevertheless, the historicity of life suggests a logical priority for the narratives through which meaningful patterns come to be discerned and expressed in symbols. On the other hand, with respect to the biblical narratives, there can be no question that they were preceded by and dependent on a number of symbols (although they also generated new symbols).

Biblical narratives take up and bring into play a large number of symbols, such as God, creation, sin, salvation, Kingdom of God, and Messiah. Without the preunderstanding that such symbols provided, the events to which the narratives witness could not have carried the meanings that they did.[27] On the other hand, the symbols by which people came to understand these revelatory events were not entirely adequate to the events. For example, Peter's confession that Jesus is the Messiah initially kept him from seeing some important facets of Jesus' unique identity (Matt. 16). It was only after the particular life history of Jesus could assume a greater place in the disciples' thought, and could therefore be joined with the confession of his messiahship in a way that was aware of both the identity and difference between Jesus and the Messiah—that is, in a genuinely metaphoric way—that the meaning of the symbol of Messiah could become truly fruitful for faith. Through the metaphoric bringing near of the different realities of events and prior symbols, in other words, these symbols are broken open in a new way. Consequently, their meaning for the Christian faith can be understood only within the context provided by the narratives of the faith and the interplay between these narratives and the other originary modes of expression in the Bible.

Not only do prior symbols become a part of a new context in the biblical witness, new symbols also emerge out of its originary modes of discourse. For example, the symbol of the cross has emerged and become central because of the fate of Jesus. To be sure, its symbolic potential is rooted not only in the life history of Jesus but also in the already-existing practice of crucifixion, so that it was already a symbol that was available in that culture. Still, it emerged as a central symbol heavily weighted with meaning through the nature of Jesus' fate and its impact on his followers.

Within the ongoing stream of Christian tradition, new symbols continue to emerge, and old symbols become more central or more periph-

---

[27]Cf. Tillich, *Systematic Theology*, 1:137-44.

eral. For example, Paul Tillich points to the different sorts of symbols that have played a central role in theology's evaluation of its sources through the centuries.

> While the norm for the early Greek church was the liberation of fi-
> nite man from death and error by the incarnation of immortal life
> and eternal truth, for the Roman church it was salvation from guilt
> and disruption by the actual and sacramental sacrifice of the God-
> man. For modern Protestantism it was the picture of the "synop-
> tic" Jesus, representing the personal and social ideal of human ex-
> istence; and for recent Protestantism it has been the prophetic
> message of the Kingdom of God in the Old and New Testaments.[28]

For Tillich himself the central symbol was the new being in Christ. More recently, some have found the symbol of liberation from physical and spiritual bondage to be of pivotal significance. The list could easily go on, but the important point is that the effective-history of the biblical text leads to ever-new actualizations of the text's meaning and hence to ever-new configurations of symbols.

It is important to keep in mind that symbols are ambiguous and re-quire interpretation in action and thought.[29] That is, symbols possess more meaning than any interpretation can articulate (they are multivalent), so that their precise meaning for a situation becomes evident only through an act of living interpretation. Furthermore, symbols are limited in that they conceal even as they reveal, for any symbolic form excludes some possibilities while opening up others. These two characteristics of sym-bols have important implications. The latter characteristic points to the need for openness to a number of symbolizations of God, the human, and the world, so that no single symbol will become so dominant that its con-cealment becomes an oppressive distortion. The danger of distortion also has implications for the ambiguous nature of symbols, since their ambi-guity means that even a potentially disclosive symbol can be used in a way that oppresses and destroys people. The issue of how one interprets a symbol is therefore basic. The narratives in which the symbols are embedded provide essential clues for interpretation, as does the living experience within which symbols are concretely interpreted.[30] Further-

---

[28]Ibid., 48.

[29]Cf. Winter, *Liberating Creation*, 71-80; and Ricoeur, *Interpretation Theory*, 45-69.

[30]Further discussion of the criteria arising from the text and from living expe-rience can be found in the next chapter.

more, the interplay between text and contemporary horizon gives rise to metaphors that provide clues to the interpretation of symbols. That is, metaphors within the biblical text and metaphors arising out of the appropriation of these texts throughout history provide guides to our understanding of the symbolic configurations to which the fusion of horizons gives birth.[31]

• The Function and Authority of the Bible •

The ability of the originary modes of biblical discourse to engender faith, through their testimony to the trace of God in history, is the basis for the Bible's authority in the community of faith. It also provides an insight into the nature of that authority. When one in whom faith has arisen reads the biblical text, the imaginative production of meaning that is at work in the text (that is, its redescription of the world) guides the further operation of the imagination of the believer.[32] That is to say, the text leads us to take the world as being the sort of world that it discloses.

This trajectory of the imagination, moving from text to one's life in the present, is another way of speaking about what Gadamer calls the fusion of horizons. The virtue of the metaphor of a fusion of horizons is that it underscores the dialectical nature of this process. Also, the notion of ho-

---

[31]Metaphors can assume this role because they exploit differences between meanings within a language. Symbols, on the other hand, are more directly rooted in the forces at play in the world and mediate these forces to us in a meaningful way through their structure. Symbols are also linguistic, but they structure life in the world through their rootedness in the interplay between life and world. In contrast, metaphors provide structure through their redescriptive power, which arises out of a figurative interpretation of literally contradictory statements. Cf. Winter, *Liberating Creation*, 37: "Symbols are more than metaphoric events. Symbols reach down into the depths of life. The symbolization of the family gathers the impulses of sexuality, loyalty, care, and love in a surface meaning of interpersonal community. Surface meaning refers to accessibility rather than superficiality of meaning. Religious symbolization gathers depths of disruption and hope, trust and commitment, cosmic order and chaos, into patterns of meaning. In this respect, symbols disclose the archetypical directionalities within life and cosmos. Thus, there is a surface and depth to the symbol which is of a different order from the duality of everyday and higher order meaning [the duality that is characteristic of metaphors]." Cf. also Ricoeur, *Interpretation Theory*, 57-69.

[32]Cf. Ricoeur, "The Bible and the Imagination," in *The Bible as a Document of the University* (Chico CA: Scholars Press, 1981) 50.

rizon contains within it the essential factor of history or tradition. It is tempting, when one has in view the formation of the imagination by the mythos of the biblical text, to suppose that the imaginative understanding of the world in terms of "the world in front of the text" involves the placing of our lives and their many components *within* the textual world. However, such an operation, if it were really possible, would not lead to an expansion of our horizons. Rather, it would be the collapsing of our horizon into the horizon of the text. Of course, part of the point of Gadamer's discussion of a fusion of horizons and of the necessity and hermeneutical productivity of prejudgments is to insist that it is really not possible to surrender our own horizon in favor of another, not even the horizon of the biblical text. The upshot of this point is that the horizons that enter into fusion are mutually illuminating. Admittedly, because faith has been engendered through the witness of the biblical text, the Bible has a certain priority as the bearer of the unsurpassably authentic revelation of God and of human life before God. That is, it makes a claim on us and definitively shapes our lives. Yet our understanding of that claim arises out of the interplay between the text and our present situation, so that the prejudgment inherent in the latter already gives us certain perspectives, certain questions, from which to view the subject matter of the text.

These perspectives, as Gadamer has argued, can be hermeneutically fruitful and not just distortive. The text can indeed transform and correct our initial predispositions. But it does not accomplish this by leading us to ignore them, as if they could simply be left aside. Instead, it engages us in the play of dialogue, meeting us in our situation and moving us along in the interplay between the horizons of the text and the interpreter. The text moves us from where we were through the event of dialogue with the text, so that the outlook we come to assume will be one that has moved through and been affected by this dialogical interplay. In other words, the imaginative construal that is guided by the text will carry the trace of the dialogue through which that construal came into existence and will do so in at least two respects. First, even when the text's horizon corrects and purifies our understanding, that correction is inevitably shaped to some extent by what was in need of correction. This is another way of making the point that questions help to determine the nature of the answer. Second, the horizon of the present frequently sheds new light on the past and thereby discloses new meanings and truths. In both cases, it is a mistake to speak in terms of merely subsuming the present under the horizon of the text.

Again, I want to underscore the fact that our present horizon is genuinely productive of meaning in the fusion of horizons. Just as the metaphoric interaction of semantic fields gives rise to a new meaning that has the power to affect the original meaning of both semantic fields, the bringing together of horizons has the ability to illumine each horizon. Does this interaction endanger the priority that I have affirmed for the biblical text? It certainly could. That is, our current predispositions could in fact overshadow the text and hence prove distortive rather than hermeneutically fruitful. However, this possibility in itself is no reason to avoid the challenge. Indeed, we cannot avoid it, even if we wished. Rather, it is a reason to engage in conversation with others as we engage in dialogue with the text. In this way, our struggle over the question of the authenticity of our understanding can take place in a public forum that helps to check and correct our own struggles.

Such a conversation with others needs to include the traditions that have interpreted the Bible down through the centuries. Indeed, this interpretation, or "effective-history," of the text has already had an impact on the believer prior to explicitly conscious acts of interpretation. For the text influences us through its continuing effect in the tradition or traditions that touch the believer. Through this effective-history the meaning of the text has been enriched (and sometimes distorted), so that our own understanding has been enhanced (or distorted) by it. Furthermore, conscious attention to this history can further enhance our understanding by uncovering new insights or by revealing distortions of the text.[33]

In the play between the believer and the biblical text, there is an authority accorded to the Bible that goes far beyond that of a literary text in general. Krister Stendahl has rightly insisted that the church, and to some degree our culture as a whole, takes the Bible as something other and more than another piece of literature.[34] The above exploration of Ricoeur's outlook already reveals two dimensions of the Bible's appeal to the imagination that makes the biblical text unique among poetic texts. First, its ultimate referent is God, so that the world it discloses is a world whose meaning is derived from its relation to God. Through this reference to God

---

[33]I have predominantly used the image of a fusion of horizons here. However, the image of play, in which the structure of play becomes uniquely actualized in each event of playing, could be used with equal fruitfulness. The point that Gadamer underscores is both the continuing identity of the play and the new transformation into structure that takes place each time people engage in the play. It is this dialectic of identity and transformation that I have been articulating in the elaboration of the mutual illumination that takes place in the fusion of horizons.

[34]Krister Stendahl, "The Bible as a Classic and the Bible as Holy Scripture," *Journal of Biblical Literature* 103 (1984): 3-10.

the Bible appeals to our imaginative understanding of the ultimate framework of life. To respond to its appeal, then, is to have one's life thoroughly reshaped by the proposed world in front of the text, for its claim reaches to the most basic human orientations and values. Second, this world is not a world that anyone could discover, regardless of his or her place in history, but is a world that is disclosed through testimonies to the trace of God in history. Hence, a response to the Bible's appeal includes affirmations about the nature and meaning of concrete historical events, which is quite different from the appropriate response to other poetic texts.

A third dimension to the authority of the Bible, which Ricoeur does not discuss, is essential to an adequate understanding of this issue: namely, the dimension provided by the community of faith, through which the effective-history of the Bible as a testimony of faith continues. This dimension is important because the response of faith, when confronted by the Bible's appeal and claim, is related to the fact that the Bible is kept alive as a testimony of faith within the life and witness of the church. The Bible does not come to people as an ancient document that has long since been handed over to antiquarians as a relic of what some very credulous people once believed. On the contrary, it has a history as the normative document of communities of faith that existed and continue to exist. Within those communities it has generated traditions through which its meaning has been actualized in various ways. And this effective-history of the text, both within and without the institutional churches, is an important aspect of contemporary responses to the text.

In the first place, the fact that the text has a continuing effect in history, especially but not solely within the institutional churches, means that the proposed world and way of being corresponding to that world do not meet us as mere ideas. Instead, they are something that has already been made concrete within our world, albeit in an imperfect and frequently distorted way. As a result, the appeal to our imaginative understanding comes through both reading the text and experiencing its effect in those who have responded to the Bible's testimony. Such a view of the text means, furthermore, that one's response is not the act of an isolated individual but is connected with one's relationship with a community (or perhaps communities) of faith. In other words, the community's act of taking the world as a reality corresponding to the biblical text's disclosures can help to elicit the same response on the part of an individual. For within the context of the community, there is the potential for a mutually confirming circle of ideas, beliefs, and experiences that lead one from a tentative consideration of the biblical world to a life-determining commitment and conviction.[35] In these cases, the disclosure of the biblical world goes beyond the *idea* of its fittingness to an *experience* of its fittingness.

Another implication of the communal context of faith relates to our understanding of the meaning of the text. Because one reads the text within the context of a particular tradition that has actualized the text in certain ways, one already has an initial sense of the text's meaning that is derived from its effective-history within that tradition. The imaginative understanding of faith, then, while it is the individual's own act, is inescapably and essentially social as well—both in the implicit and explicit understandings of faith and in one's coming to faith. In both cases, the Bible mediates an unsurpassable revelation through the power of its testimony, within the context of a community of faith, to disclose a world that engages and leads our imaginations and therefore also our thinking and acting. As a result, the believer accepts the Bible as an authoritative testimony to the nature of God's relation to the world and hence to the ultimate nature of the world. One is not thereby required to read the Bible in a literalist, fundamentalist fashion. The metaphoricity of our reading of the Bible should guard against such an approach. Moreover, the tradition of historical criticism has made some fundamental alterations in our horizon and the text's horizon that cannot be ignored. Also, that which, within the biblical text, lays claim to the imagination has to do with the nature of the relationship between God and the world rather than with empirical data that are somehow beyond detection through usual ave-

---

[35]I do not intend to argue that everyone who comes to faith does so through a process of explicit reflection on such matters, only that the rise of faith is connected in some way to a sense of the fittingness of the biblical witness (a fittingness that becomes evident within the context of the living experience of a concrete community). The idea of a mutually confirming circle of ideas, beliefs, and experiences is drawn from Peter Selby's discussion of the rationality of faith in the resurrection of Jesus. He argues that the resurrection was taken in the early church, and should be taken now, as part of a cluster of ideas and beliefs that come together in the transformative praxis of the church. On this basis, he develops an argument for the rationality of faith in the resurrection. While I am not concerning myself here with the resurrection as such, Selby's argument has parallels with my own and is helpful for determining the important role of the community in the individual's act of faith. Cf. his *Look for the Living: The Corporate Nature of Resurrection Faith* (Philadelphia: Fortress Press, 1976), 120-25, 131-42. Cf. also Stroup's examination of the individual's integration into a community and its identity, making fruitful use of Augustine, Barth, Schutz, and Gadamer (*Promise of Narrative Theology*, especially 170-98.)

nues of investigation. Thus, the re-presentation of our world in terms provided by the fusion of our horizon with the biblical horizon becomes the ultimate framework within which our lives are set and therefore provides a context within which to place and understand our lives, instead of providing new empirical information about them.[36]

The power of the biblical text to engage our imaginations and thereby shape our lives in a way that we find fitting—that is, in a manner that is fruitful, in the sense of displaying a congruence between ideas, beliefs, and living experience—also provides a basis for investigating the rationality or justifiability of faith. For the question of whether it is reasonable to believe is, at its base, a question of the power of faith. We cannot say that faith guarantees success in our efforts to reach goals we have set for ourselves. But we can affirm that we come to faith through the conviction that the One in whom we believe has the power to bring faith to its goal; and there is a sense in which that power makes itself felt even now.[37] The question of faith's justifiability, then, must center on the issue of faith's power.

This approach is consistent with Ricoeur's insistence that poetic texts operate at a level where truth is manifestation rather than verification. For this approach takes into account the fact that we are concerned here with belonging to or participating in a proposed world where we can realize our deepest possibilities for living. To claim that such a world is true or authentic is to assert that there is a resonance between the disclosures of the text and the living experience to which it opens us. From this perspective, to ask about the justifiability of faith is not to ask for a verification of its talk about God. Rather, God is indirectly presented through the text's world as the One who grounds and determines the world we are invited to inhabit; and the justifiability of Christian affirmations about God, arising as they do from one's participation in this world, is thus tied to the issue of the consonance between the biblical world and human experience. In other words, the power of the biblical testimony to open up experiences that we find essential to our lives as humans is at the heart of our faith and central to our treatment of questions about faith's rea-

---

[36]David Tracy's and Paul Ricoeur's discussions of religious language as limit-language that corresponds to limit-experiences are apparently attempts to articulate the fact that faith's affirmations concern life's ultimate ground and framework, not limited regions of human life in themselves. To the degree that this is indeed their point, I am in agreement with them.

[37]Cf. Gerhard Ebeling, *The Nature of Faith,* trans. Ronald Gregor Smith (Philadelphia: Fortress Press, 1961) 137, 169-70.

sonableness.[38] This power leads us beyond the point of tentatively taking the world in terms of the biblical testimony to the practical conviction that the biblical testimony is true, that it discloses the reality of the world to which we belong and in which we find and express our most authentic possibilities.

• Faith and Imagination •

Throughout this examination of imagination and Christian faith, the distinctiveness of the play of imagination in the sphere of faith has made itself felt. However, at the risk of some redundancy, I now wish to focus especially on what this examination has shown us about the nature of faith and of the imagination's distinctive role in the life of faith.

The distinctive nature of imagination's operation in the sphere of Christian faith is indicated by that with which this faith is concerned: the ultimate horizon of existence. That is, whereas the more usual operation of the understanding has to do with discrete parts of the environment, which are construed in terms of the larger context to which they belong, in the arena of faith the understanding focuses on the ultimate context for life, beyond which there is no larger framework to give this context its significance.

John Hick has pointed out that our recognition and explanation of things are usually two different activities.[39] The first is an answer to the question *what*, and the second to the question *why*. For example, we recognize a red object as a book. When called on to explain this phenomenon, we make appeal to the larger context of the book, in which there are other recognizable items, situations, and so forth, in order to clarify what we mean. Thus, we allude at the very least to language and writing, along with the processes of printing and publication. We may also refer to even more encompassing contexts such as a culture's literary tradition and the entire civilization within which that tradition lives. In short, we recognize and interpret the significance of things in terms of the context in which they are embedded, that is, by relating them to other things that

---

[38]The biblical text, however, does not provide us with a framework for a comprehensive apologetic. For not only is the issue of consonance between text and experience multifaceted, but the particular issues and questions that arise at any time determine the way in which one deals with the harmony between text and experience. For further discussion of this point, see chapters 3 and 5.

[39]John Hick, *Faith and Knowledge: A Modern Introduction to the Problem of Religious Knowledge* (Ithaca NY: Cornell University Press, 1957) 116.

we recognize as having a certain significance for us. As the last chapter has shown, this is at root an imaginative act, since it is a matter of taking both that which is being recognized and its context in terms of meaningful forms that give them a certain significance. Otherwise stated, understanding comes from an openness to the interplay of context, subject matter under consideration, and self, an interplay by which the significance of the subject matter is laid open for us.

Now in the case of faith, which is an interpretation of the whole, the distinction between recognition and explanation disappears. Here it is not possible to explain the significance of the subject matter by appealing to its larger context. Thus, every explanation of this whole can "only consist in a perception of its significance." On the other hand, every recognition of the significance of the whole is also an explanation of that whole.[40] As a result, the imagination has a unique function at this point, as Kaufman has rightly noted. For it not only takes discrete parts of the environment as significant but adds to that imaginative construal an imaginative grasp of the whole as the ultimate context in which everything finds its place. Since the whole lacks a larger framework in terms of which it can be explained, it is understood in terms of whatever finite realities are deemed to be its appropriate analogues. As Kaufman has argued, even the idea of the whole is itself such an analogue; for we never experience the totality of things as a whole, but we do experience finite realities as wholes and are therefore able to use this experience in our understanding of life's ultimate environment.

Hick also argues that the concept of a total framework for life is dependent on at least two prior concepts: those of nature and of a human world of interacting subjects. The concept of a human world rests on, and is interpenetrated by, the concept of nature. That is, a human world is a world in which we perceive certain actions and reactions as being necessary or appropriate, but this evaluation requires a context of nature in which such actions can occur. Furthermore, the concept of a total theistic framework for life requires both the natural and human worlds as the sphere within which we live in the presence of God, who, in turn, is mediated to us through this world. "Entering into conscious relation with God consists in large part in adopting a particular style and manner of acting towards our natural and social environments. For God summons men to serve him in the world, and in terms of the life of the world."[41]

---

[40]Ibid. Hick goes on to note that, although inseparable in practice, these two activities can be distinguished for the sake of analysis.

[41]Ibid., 121-23, 129.

As with all forms of understanding and praxis, therefore, faith involves an imaginative attunement to the play of human life in the world. Yet, in the sphere of faith this attunement has its own distinctive character, since it is an attunement to the ultimate context of human life. The latter is no different from all understanding in that it, too, is a taking of something as something. On the other hand, it is different in that it is a taking of the whole as the ultimate context for everything and hence as a reality that cannot be related to anything beyond itself. In short, the religious understanding of the world is concerned not with this or that part of life in isolation but with "the uniquely total situation constituted by our experience as a whole and in all its aspects, up to the present moment."

Not only can this whole not be related to anything beyond itself, it is never experienced by us as a whole. To have an experience of the totality of things as a whole, we would have to be able to step outside of this totality. Thus, we would have to find a larger context within which to place the whole of things. This impossible situation indicates the indirectness of our experience of the whole, which brings the distinctive nature of the role of the imagination in faith into prominence at this point. For here we are not merely taking an isolable part of our experience as something significant; we are taking something that we never experience as such as something significant—indeed, as something of absolutely decisive significance for human life. On the one hand, then, we take our various experiences as part of an encompassing whole that is never directly encountered and use them as clues to the significance of the whole. On the other hand, we take this encompassing whole as possessing a certain kind of significance for ourselves and our world.

Christian faith, however, is not content to think merely in terms of a totality of things, or even of life as lived in the presence of God. Such concerns are a part of the sphere of faith, to be sure, but they receive their characteristic stamp from something that belongs to its essence, namely, the conviction that God has effected the reconciliation of the estranged world with Godself in the person of Jesus the Christ. Until we come to the point of recognizing this element of trust in Christian faith, we have failed to penetrate to the heart of the matter. That is, it belongs to the essential nature of Christian faith that it takes itself as sheer gift, as something granted by the gracious action of the God who is both Creator and Redeemer, and never as something by which we dispose of our world in whatever way we deem beneficial. Hence the perspective of faith provides an angle of vision from which the receptive dimension of imagination comes clearly into view, just as an understanding of imagination in terms of attunement helps to bring the gift character of faith into view.

This dimension of Christian faith can be underscored by examining the four chief characteristics of faith described by Gerhard Ebeling. These characteristics help to illumine the nature of faith as an event of trust that provides an understanding of the ultimate environment of life. The first characteristic of Christian faith that Ebeling explores is the fact that its ground is Jesus Christ.[42] Everything that the Christian faith has to say, and the variety of subjects with which it is concerned, all has its unity in the referral of everything to Jesus Christ as the one in whom the Christian trusts and, therefore, on whom the Christian's faith is grounded. This concentration on Jesus Christ is so complete that the confession of Jesus as the ground of faith becomes also a confession of Jesus as the ground of existence. In line with this understanding of Jesus' significance, Christians affirm the unity between Jesus and God. In other words, faith in Jesus is no addition to faith in God, as if another object of faith were now added to the Old Testament understanding of faith as faith in God. Rather, faith in Jesus is faith in God as the One who has addressed us in this person and so calls us to faith in this person.

That individuals are called to respond, and therefore to bear responsibility for themselves before God and others, is the second feature of faith delineated by Ebeling. He does not intend in this way to diminish the importance of the social context of human life. On the contrary, he recognizes that human life is essentially historical and linguistic, and so social.[43] Still, in the context of our socially constituted lives, there is an inescapable element of individual responsibility. This responsibility becomes apparent when God addresses us in the person of Jesus Christ. When the Christian tradition becomes a bearer of God's Word to us, we discover in it not primarily information about God, the world, or ourselves but the communication of Godself to us, that is, the discovery that we are loved by God. The reference here to tradition and to personal communication underscores both the corporate and personal nature of faith. It is inescapably dependent on history, that is, the continuing life of tradition, for "it comes into being, and continues its being, when it is handed on, in tradition."[44]

The third chief characteristic of faith is its expressive nature, that is, its need to express itself and to give account of itself in language.[45] Here

[42]Gerhard Ebeling, *Dogmatik des christlichen Glaubens*, vol. 1, *Prolegomena, Erster Teil, Der Glaube an Gott den Schöpfer der Welt* (Tübingen: J. C. B. Mohr, 1979) 82.

[43]Ibid., 82-83, 101-102, 104.

[44]Ebeling, *Nature of Faith*, 25.

[45]Ebeling, *Dogmatik*, 83-84.

we encounter a circle between faith and expressions of faith. On the one side, faith expresses itself; on the other, faith arises out of expressions of faith. This is rooted in the fact that Christian faith is essentially an understanding of something, an understanding that arises out of being addressed by the Word of God. Since this address comes to us as an event that transforms our existence, it at the same time determines our relation to, and hence our understanding of, the world, the self, and God. In other words, it has to do with the whole of the reality with which we deal.[46] The expression of faith's understanding thus involves an effort to explore and say something about the significance of every aspect of life as it relates to faith. In this sense Kaufman is right to argue that faith involves a construal of the world. Yet there is also this major difference between his view and the one presented here: whereas he argues that a construction/reconstruction of the world is a logically preliminary activity in relation to faith (whereby faith partially receives its structure), I emphasize the need to relate faith and the world in a dialectical process that has no single point of departure.[47] The latter approach rests on the conviction that the Word addressing the believer has its origin in God and has an essential relation to the whole of life.

The fourth characteristic of faith highlighted by Ebeling is its soteriological relevance.[48] That is, faith as attachment to Jesus Christ as the ground of existence entails a decisive change in one's life, a transformation from death to life. Faith, in other words, is an eschatological reality, determining one's existence anew and effecting a fundamental change from all forms of life that lack this central determining factor. This change can be described by various metaphors: a change from being lost to being found, from life in sin to life in grace, from darkness to light, from death to life. These and many other metaphors have been used to describe the

---

[46]Ebeling, *Nature of Faith*, 164-65.

[47]Kaufman also notes the need to reformulate this construction of the world after a concept of God has been constructed. Still, he begins with constructing a world, on the basis of which one constructs a concept of God, and this is a decisively different move than the one proposed here. Cf. also Julian Hartt, *Theological Method and Imagination* (New York: Seabury Press, 1977) 13: "Weaving everything together into a concrete interpretation of life and world requires an extraordinary effort of the human spirit. A concrete interpretation cannot be simply excogitated; it is not like a theory or an hypothesis. It is an actual course of life designed and projected to tie life and world together as an offering to God."

[48]Ebeling, *Dogmatik*, 84.

new life that now hangs on the promise of God disclosed in the resurrection of the crucified Jesus.

In this light, the word *trust* seems somewhat too mild a way of describing faith. It is a trust that attaches itself to something that penetrates to the center of human existence, a trust that hangs on a promise that determines the whole of existence. It is a unique kind of trust because it is trust in the God who redeems in love. As such, it is a trust that decisively determines one's existence, to the degree that it has taken hold of one. It is indeed a "fundamental trust." However, as Christian faith, it is not merely trust in the ultimate coherence and goodness of life but trust in the God who brings life from the dead. It can and does, then, face the often overwhelming fact of death and contradiction in life with an assurance that is rooted in this life-giving God, who has triumphed and will triumph over the forces of chaos and destruction. At this point, faith and its expression become doxological, but it is a doxology that arises from and returns to life in the world. It is a faith that knows God's negation of the forces of negation and acts accordingly.

It is difficult to see how this sort of faith could be reconciled with an understanding of imagination as essentially constructive. To treat our understanding of God as essentially a human construct that has its origin in our need to create an ultimate environment for ourselves is to destroy the possibility of taking seriously that God is in fact a God of the resurrection. In other words, it significantly vitiates, if it does not destroy, the understanding of grace as God's work, since even God is our own work.[49] To be sure, *God* is a human symbol. That is not the issue. The issue is whether this symbol mediates something more than our own efforts to make ourselves at home in the universe. And, if so, what that something more is.

If we now inquire what significance these considerations hold for Kaufman's view that the imagination's role in the sphere of faith is es-

---

[49]Cf. Hartt, *Theological Method and Imagination*, 17: "If God is now a mere idea, or if religion rests on such a metaphysical illusion, then God must always have been a mere idea, and the pious must always have been deceived. If the pious were prepared to admit this they would surely abandon the prayer of petition." Kaufman indeed does not call God a "mere idea." Yet one would have difficulty petitioning a God we have constructed and would hardly find assurance of this God's grace any more convincing than assurance of this God's ability to help in time of need. At best, it could be an assurance of the ultimately humane nature of our world. This may be no small thing, but it is not faith in the God who brings life from death.

sentially constructive, we can make two general points: such a view is not in line with the general operation of imagination in human life in the world, and it is not in harmony with the nature of the central affirmations of the Christian faith. It is necessary to add that this in no way demonstrates the reality of what faith affirms. It merely shows that the claim that faith and theology are imaginative enterprises does not in itself warrant the conclusion that they are essentially constructive in nature. The question of the truth of faith must be dealt with later, in terms of the disclosive power of faith's expressions.[50]

As we have seen in the previous chapter, the understanding of imagination as essentially constructive is contrary to a healthy appreciation of the historicity of human life. For our imaginations are shaped and given direction by our embeddedness in a living tradition. Moreover, this tradition is, in essence, a continuing dialogue that takes place within the context of the world, which is metaphorically disclosed to us through the give-and-take of the dialogue. The importance of the imagination is that it opens us to the movement of this give-and-take and thereby enables us to be attuned to the significance of things. The metaphoricity of this process means that it is not locked into a repetition of the past but, through openness to new experiences, can lead to new discoveries and insights. The upshot of this is that the uncovering of the new is not an essentially constructive work but emerges from imagination's openness to the interplay between past and present, as well as to the interplay among persons and traditions that takes place within the dialectic of past and present. Thus, the essence of imagination, at least insofar as it concerns our efforts to live appropriately in our world, is the bringing together of invention and discovery.

In terms of the linguisticality of human life, imagination is openness to the power of language to disclose the realities with which our lives are in play. In this light, it is natural to suggest the possibility that faith is the result of attunement to the power of the language of faith to open up the ultimate horizon of life. Hence a thinking believer would not be an autonomous subject engaged in the activity of constructing and reconstructing the world and God. Rather, the thinking believer is one whose imagination has been engaged by the language of faith and who is now following its lead in order to thematize explicitly its significance as that emerges in living experience. In this view, the recognition of the imaginative character of faith is a recognition that faith entails taking the world

---

[50]Cf. Ebeling, *Nature of Faith*, 129-31.

in terms of faith's expressions. Faith arises when one is captured by the disclosive power of faith's language. It is not the result of the subject's more or less autonomous construction of symbols and concepts basic to human life.

It is apparent that, given the operation of imagination in this way, the effort to turn matters of "faith" into material for the constructive activity of the subject reveals that these are not truly central matters of faith for the one who wishes to act in so autonomous a fashion. Instead, they have become peripheral concepts that one can push around and rearrange in order to express whatever is really at the heart of one's understanding of life in the world. In line with the suggestion in chapter 1 that Kaufman has found a new revelatory center for his life and thought, it is reasonable to suggest that the central matters of his understanding are rooted in that new revelatory center and are no more matters for deliberate construction/reconstruction than was God in the mind of Thomas Aquinas. For example, Kaufman does not seem to feel a need for constructing and reconstructing at least the heart of what constitutes humanization (he does argue that we must construct a picture of the human, but in line with what we know to be humanizing!). There is apparently something that he takes to be clear and self-evident here, since he believes that it can guide our constructive work. If humanization were itself the result of construction rather than a self-evident starting point, we would require an even more fundamental principle than the idea of humanization to guide this construction.[51]

If it is in accord with the nature of imagination that faith can be imaginative and yet grounded in a disclosure of truth, it is also in accord with faith that imagination can be attuned to the ground of faith. Christian faith entails self-abandonment to the God who addresses us in Jesus Christ. What we have seen about the nature of the imagination shows that this position does not violate the imagination but is in harmony with its function in all perception and cognition.

---

[51]I do not mean to suggest that Kaufman ever maintains that a full picture of the human is self-evident to all. He notes, on the contrary, that different sociocultural contexts lead to different assessments of the human. Moreover, he argues that the history of Jesus leading to the cross can be valuable in constructing a picture of the human. Nevertheless, we construct this picture in accordance with what we take to be humanizing. Since Kaufman never explains how we decide what is humanizing, and since he argues that our insight into what is humanizing guides our use of traditional materials in the construction of a picture of the human (as well as pictures of God and the world), he does seem to assume that something here is self-evident and is therefore able to guide our construction (as opposed to being the object of construction).

The reality affirmed by faith is accepted with a practical certitude that brings the whole person, including the full powers of his or her imaginative attunement to the world, under its sway. Thus, one who has this faith and wishes to think through its meaning for life, that is, who wishes to do theology as one who has been grasped by the Christian faith, does not, at the point where he or she wishes to engage in such critical thought, suddenly step outside the sphere of faith in order to construct/reconstruct it according to some specifications that are basically derived from another tradition.[52] And it would certainly be cynical to suggest that only unthinking persons have this sort of faith; whereas those who think have put themselves into a position to construct/reconstruct the symbols and concepts of faith, so that they can then give this new construction to unthinking believers for their edification.

The believer, when following the lead of the Christian tradition, does not necessarily fail to recognize the imaginative nature of faith. The issue is not whether faith is imaginative but what the imagination is and how it operates, that is, whether faith is a construction of the subject's imaginative inventions or the result of an imaginative attunement to the disclosive power of the Christian tradition. If the latter is the case, the issues become how faith arises and whether it is justifiable.

• Implications for the
Concept of Revelation •

The rise of faith out of the disclosive power of the imaginative, metaphoric interplay of past and present has important implications for the concept of revelation. Although a number of them have already been suggested at various points, a more systematic presentation of them in combination with a few other points is in order. It is beyond the scope of this work to provide a complete development of a doctrine of revelation, yet a few remarks should serve to indicate the direction in which this approach would move in developing such a concept.

---

[52]I do not say that other traditions cannot or do not enrich our insight. If it is right to speak of understanding in terms of a fusion of horizons, then they certainly do. Moreover, being engaged by the Christian tradition is in some ways similar to, yet ultimately different from, placing ourselves in the biblical world. The fusion of horizons is a metaphoric process taking place between horizons, whereas the notion of placing ourselves in the biblical world, so that we see things through its supposedly unchanging formal structures (cf. Lindbeck), lacks sufficient awareness of this metaphoricity (even if we do try to focus on the forms of the biblical view of things instead of its content).

In some ways, this approach supports Kaufman's criticisms of the doctrine of revelation found in some earlier theologies, that is, those theologies that treat revelation as an unassailable ground for knowledge of and talk about God.[53] If disclosure must prove itself authentic and is thus open to debate about its justifiability, it also follows that claims about revelation must be open to critical analysis, discussion, and evaluation. Although revelation itself is not susceptible to judgment according to deeper and more basic perspectives and principles, reasonable discourse, which enables sober judgments to be made, still is possible. Thus, there is a sense in which, as Kaufman argues, a claim about divine revelation is a conclusion.[54] On the other hand, it cannot avoid being a conclusion based on criteria that are not wholly independent of what is taken to be revelatory, so that it is not merely a conclusion but a premise as well. The circularity of this process is essentially the same as the circularity of the experience and justification of any disclosure, even though in this case it is the disclosure of a very different order of reality.

So far this discussion has taken an approach that may seem simply to identify revelation and disclosure. This is not its intention. Rather, the presupposition informing these ruminations is that there is an intimate connection between them; namely, revelation is mediated through the disclosive power of the Christian tradition, particularly as it is rooted in its biblical source. The warrant for this view is found in the connection between that tradition and the rise of Christian faith, for the rise of faith in the living and lifegiving God of the biblical texts is itself an experience of divine self-manifestation or revelation. That is to say, at the level of the originary expressions and experiences of faith, revelation is not a doctrine formulated by theologians to be fed to the faithful but is an experience of the power of the biblical texts to point in their various ways to God, who is not just the ultimate Source, Sustainer, and Goal of life but is also the One who renews life through the very event of disclosure itself. That is, this God is manifested as prevenient and hence as the ultimate ontological source of the revelatory encounter.[55] This affirmation of faith is the

---

[53]The claim that revelation is self-authenticating often amounts to an effort to find an incorrigible foundation for statements about God (although it may be susceptible to some other explanation).

[54]Kaufman, *An Essay on Theological Method* (Missoula MT: Scholars Press, 1975) 3.

[55]Cf. Ronald F. Thiemann, *Revelation and Theology: The Gospel as Narrated Promise* (Notre Dame IN: University of Notre Dame Press, 1985) especially 1-7.

premise that theology must then critically examine to exhibit its meaning, explore its implications, and demonstrate its justifiability or its unreasonableness.[56] Such examinations and explorations cannot result in a logically neutral conclusion that revelation has in fact occurred, yet they can provide justification for faith's self-understanding and reach a conclusion in this "soft" sense (just as they may also reach the opposite conclusion).

In light of the connection between revelation and disclosure, it is clear that imagination is at the heart of the revelatory encounter. Just as the imagination is that power through which we are attuned to the metaphoric, disclosive play of tradition and present situation, it is also the power through which a disclosure becomes the opening of a possible way-of-being-in-the-world that is defined by one's relationship to this God. In short, one experiences a revelatory encounter with God when one takes the God to whom the biblical texts point to be the transcendent reality that grounds, limits, and defines one's world. The involvement of the imagination means that such a revelation does not occur without the constructive engagement of our creative capacities. On the other hand, this constructive engagement occurs within the process of our imaginative *attunement* to the ongoing play of tradition and present situation, so that construction works hand in hand with, and is dependent on, the receptive powers of the imagination. Thus, with Kaufman, this outlook affirms that it is through the "work of the human imagination that God—ultimate reality understood as active and beneficent, as 'gracious'—makes himself known."[57] However, Kaufman means by this comment something quite different than I do, since he tends to focus almost exclusively on imagination's constructive power.

The employment of the concept of revelation in this context is warranted because faith and theology take this disclosure to be the self-manifestation of that which is ultimate—God. As such, it provides the intelligible center for life, while illuminating all facets of existence.[58] Thus,

---

[56]For a more detailed discussion of the role of theology, see the next chapter.

[57]Kaufman, *Essay on Theological Method*, 68.

[58]This understanding of revelation is very close to the view articulated by the early Kaufman in his *Systematic Theology*. It differs from his discussion of revelation in that, whereas Kaufman tends to emphasize the founding events and to regard the texts as a source for reconstructing them, this approach stresses the disclosive power of the texts that mediate the revelatory encounter. Also, this view of revelation allows for more attention to the critical examination of claims that a divine revelation has occurred, for, even though revelation serves as a point of

revelation serves as the basis for the community of faith's self-understanding and its judgments of appropriate forms of life. In this sense it
serves as a "final" revelation. In view of the nature of the imaginative grasp
of any disclosure, it is clear that revelation's intelligibility, that is, its internal consistency and its fit with our general understanding of the world,
becomes apparent only through the fusion of the biblical horizon with our
own. Hence the revelatory event does not give us a timeless grasp of a
system of truths, even about God. Rather, its nature and significance
emerge only in the event itself. The continuity of any present revelatory
encounter with earlier encounters is provided by the fact that it is an encounter with the God to whom these texts and traditions point. But any
attempt to understand and describe the nature of this God is dependent
on forms available in one's present situation, which brings us to the other
side of the dialectic. That is to say, the newness of this encounter resides
in the fact that it occurs within the metaphoric play of past and present.
In other words, its intelligibility is not separable from the way in which it
throws light on the rest of existence *and* the way in which the rest of existence throws light on it.

The claim that revelation illumines the rest of existence should not be
understood to mean that it provides a foundation for the creation of a logical system in which all aspects of life can find a place. All efforts to find
such a total framework of meaning founder on the experiences of finitude, contradiction, and evil. The illumination provided by revelation,
then, is of a different sort, namely, the illumination provided by an orientation with which to face life's uncertainties and negative experiences.
As Ricoeur notes in relation to Job, the meaning provided by revelation
grows out of the pathos of actively assumed suffering, not out of an ability to understand all aspects of life from a transcendent point of view.

The fact that revelation is mediated through the disclosive power of
the various genres in the Bible points to some other important implications. As Ricoeur insists, one important consequence is the dissolution of
a "uniform and monotonous" concept of revelation (92). For *revelation*, a
term drawn from the prophetic experience of receiving a communication
from God that is to be announced to others, is used analogically to refer

---

departure for Christian faith and life, it is open to critical scrutiny. To be sure,
there are not some more intelligible or more fundamental perspectives that provide a foundation demonstrating the truth of a revelation, yet the approach to
justification discussed in chapters 3 and 5 can deal with such issues in a non-
foundationalist way. Cf. also H. Richard Niebuhr, *The Meaning of Revelation* (New
York: Macmillan, 1941) 68.

to a disclosure of the ultimate mystery that occurs in various ways in the different genres. Thus, the idea of a double speaker, God and the prophet, is not appropriate in other genres, such as narrative, wisdom, hymn, and law. In such types of literature revelation is mediated through and modulated by the illuminative power of the narratives and wisdom sayings, the lyrical pathos of the hymn, and the prescriptive force of the commandment (92-93). Each genre points in its own way to the hidden God, who "circulates among all these modes of discourse, but escapes each one of them," who serves as their "vanishing point" (96). Revelation, therefore, transpires when these various forms of discourse disclose a possible world in which God is the ultimate reality and when this disclosure becomes the occasion for taking such a world as the one in which our most authentic possibilities are realized, not just through our own efforts but through the empowering presence of the ultimate mystery. Furthermore, God remains a mystery because the interplay of these various genres resists the creation of a total system of thought or of a picture of God, thereby disclosing God as a "vanishing point" rather than as an object standing before us. In short, revelation enables the community of faith to name God, not in the sense of possessing God or even a picture of God (which could be used to check to see how well statements about God correspond to the reality), but in the sense of confessing the mystery that circumscribes and relates graciously to the life of the community and the world.

As noted above, the appeal of revelation is to the imagination. It does not take the form of a heteronomous imposition by an external authority but of a nonviolent appeal to which one is invited to respond. Thus, it does not provide the community of faith with a weapon that it can use to enforce assent. On the other hand, the revelatory event must justify itself in the possibilities for life it unveils and in critical examinations of its claims. In this context, the community of faith may be able to present a persuasive case for the reality of its confession. However, the other possibility must also be held open: its claims may be shown to be improbable or surpassed by some other disclosure or revelation. It should also be clear that this understanding of revelation in no way denies the possibility of revelation in other traditions. It merely affirms that the community of faith lives on the basis of a revelatory encounter with the ultimate mystery as mediated through the disclosive power of the biblical texts and the traditions growing out of them. Consequently, this encounter will definitively shape its understanding of God, the world, and itself, not through adding to the store of empirical knowledge about ourselves and our world, but through placing these realities within an understanding of the mystery that constitutes their ultimate horizon.

• Conclusion •

We have discovered in this examination of faith and imagination that Kaufman is certainly right to insist on the imaginative character of faith. Paul Ricoeur's explorations of the relationship between Christian faith and the Bible underscore this fact and yet suggest a different approach than the one Kaufman has proposed. Central to Ricoeur's proposal is the insistence that consciousness must let go of all pretensions to found itself. For the awareness that consciousness is historically constituted and mediated opens one to the possibility of discovering one's world and one's self through poetic texts. The Bible is such a poetic text. Yet it is also more. In the first place, it is a text that has God as its ultimate referent. And, second, it is a text that contains testimony to the trace of God in history. Because consciousness is not self-positing, but is historically constituted, biblical texts and their testimony do not first have to submit to criteria grounded in our own consciousness before then can function authoritatively. Rather, their power to act disclosively leads to their authoritative function in communities of faith.

The conjunction of the disclosive power of texts speaking about God and a community of faith gives the Bible an authority that is different in quality than the authority of poetic texts in general. Because of the continuing power of the biblical witness to engender faith within the ongoing community of the church—a community that has the potential of providing a context in which the disclosive power of the Christian tradition can become concretely manifest—the church accords a unique role to the Bible. The Bible fulfills this role when the intersection between community and text brings about a new re-presentation of the biblical witness.

Faith's apprehensions depend on the power of the imagination to use finite realities to come to an understanding of the whole. Even the idea of a whole is an imaginative extension of our (imaginatively shaped) experience of finite wholes. However, this exploration of faith and imagination has also made it evident that the conclusions that Kaufman draws from this fact do not necessarily follow. As in the operation of the imagination in our understanding of entities within our world, the imagination's work in the sphere of faith takes place within the historical stream of tradition and is intimately shaped by tradition. In this light, I have argued that it is a mistake to treat the imagination as if its role were essentially to construct and reconstruct the images by which faith is shaped. Rather, the imagination attunes us to what is disclosed through faith's traditions. A tradition's disclosive power, then, is what shapes the imagination and gives rise to faith.

This understanding of the relationship between imagination and faith is in harmony with Christian faith's self-understanding, for Christian faith affirms that God has taken the initiative to come to us in Jesus the Christ. The supposition that such a faith could simply affirm images or concepts whose origin is essentially human constructive powers, without any reason to suppose that these images or concepts actually reveal a God who transcends our thought and who has acted on our behalf, runs directly contrary to the essence of faith. Thus both the nature of the work of imagination and the essence of faith suggest the inadequacy of Kaufman's approach.

As this examination of faith and imagination has made clear, re-presentations of the biblical witness need not always be in the form of reflective thought. On the other hand, they must eventually enter the sphere of reflection, since part of human life is the intellectual clarification and criticism of our thoughts, feelings, and actions. This chapter provides ample testimony to such a need. When faith becomes reflective and critical, theology is born. What is theology? and how is it related to faith? These questions must now occupy us in the next chapter.

IMAGINATION AND THEOLOGY

When one comes to faith, the richness of the metaphoric language of faith engages and leads the imagination. Yet, although this richness has a profound formative power, it calls for further clarification and critical analysis of its significance for Christian life and thought. Theology has arisen as an attempt to provide such clarity and critical insight. Because of its relationship to faith, the nature of the theological task is determined by its dependence on the prior reality of faith. That is, it is a derivative, critical, second-order reflection on the language and experiences of faith. Furthermore, since theology is also involved in its own way in the play of dialogue between biblical text and contemporary situation, it, too, depends on the work of imagination and not only on rational operations. In this chapter I explore the major implications of theology's derivative and imaginative character for its self-understanding and operation.

First, I explore what it means to describe theology as a second-order enterprise. The relationship between theological conceptualization and criticism, on one side, and the metaphoric language of faith, on the other, is at the heart of this examination. Second, I attend to the sources of theology, the nature of which becomes evident through an examination of the implications of Gadamer's model of the fusion of horizons. This model is also at the heart of the next section, which examines the working canon that any theology is compelled to use in its evaluation of its sources. The exploration of criteria of adequacy to the situation, in the following section of the chapter, presupposes this model as well. This section focuses especially on how Kaufman's criteria for theology can still fit into the theological enterprise as I have described it. Finally, I suggest some of the implications of this understanding of theology for the way in which it deals with the question of truth (that is, apologetics).

• Theology as a Second-Order Enterprise •

Theology operates at a different level of discourse than the originary affirmations of faith; for, whereas the latter are expressions of our primordial participation in a network of relations, the former operates in terms of conceptual distinctions that are the result of a reflective activity that differentiates the subject from the world. That is, the subject, in reflection, approaches the world as an object of thought standing over against the subject. Although the fact that human life is initially rooted in a world does not destroy the validity of such reflection, it does have some basic implications for the conceptual forms of thought to which reflection gives rise; for reflection is inevitably shaped by and in some ways dependent on our more primordial participation in a world of meaning.

Conceptual thought is not therefore reducible to poetic/metaphoric thought. There remains an irreducible difference rooted in the fact that conceptual thought operates through a system of semantic intersignifications that makes possible a greater precision of conceptual meaning than is present in metaphoric language.[1] Conceptual thought is, in Philip Wheelwright's term, "steno-language" in that it operates according to agreed upon meanings that are articulated through verbal definitions. Concepts thus do not guarantee better knowledge of the world. Rather, they are ways of providing specific meanings and thereby making possible certain forms of human activity and interaction.[2] As a result, conceptual discourse does manage to open up some undeniably important dimensions of human life. For example, it makes possible the forms of rationality we know as science and technology, which are clearly possibilities for human life that we could not now suppress, even if we were so inclined. Furthermore, some aspects of social life, such as the formulation of laws, require steno-discourse. Concepts, then, are univocal, or at least a more controlled form of multivalency than one finds in metaphoric language. And, because of this quality, they are a necessary aspect of human life.

This ability to provide greater specificity of meaning makes the conceptualizations of theology important, for the iconicity of metaphor and

---

[1]Cf. Paul Ricoeur, *The Rule of Metaphor: Multidisciplinary Studies of the Creation of Meaning in Language,* trans. Robert Czerny et al. (Toronto: University of Toronto Press, 1977) 257-313., esp. 289-95.

[2]See Philip Wheelwright, *The Burning Fountain: A Study in the Language of Symbolism* (Gloucester MA: Peter Smith, 1982) 15-17; and idem, *Metaphor and Reality* (Bloomington: Indiana University Press, 1962) 37-38.

symbol expresses meanings that call for interpretation. That is to say, the originary language of faith expresses meanings in which the faithful participate and that are richer than any interpretation can articulate; yet this language calls for an interpretive articulation in order to provide the faithful with clearer, critical insights into its implications for their lives in the world. This is essential, since, among other things, clarifying the meaning of the language of Christian faith makes possible a critique of distortions and oppressive appropriations of that language. Even though such interpretations cannot be adequate or exhaustive, therefore, they perform an essential service to the church. Ricoeur locates the necessity of this "transposition from . . . 'figurative modes' to 'conceptual modes' of expression" in the dynamism of figurative speech.

> This dynamism is the primary condition for any move from figurative expression to conceptual expression. The process of interpretation is not something superimposed from the outside on a self-contained expression; it is motivated by the symbolic expression itself which gives rise to thought. It belongs to the essence of a figurative expression to stand for something else, to call for a new speechact which would paraphrase the first one without exhausting its meaningful resources.[3]

In short, theology must try to provide an interpretive clarification and criticism of the language of faith, yet always remain aware that it cannot provide an exhaustive or final interpretation.

The role of Christian theology, then, is to be a second-order critical reflection on the significance and coherence of the Christian faith, as it has emerged through and finds continued expression in the originary language of faith. Theology depends on this originary language in at least two ways. First, faith's primary expressions provide the object of theology's reflections. Theology does not have its own independent avenue to the realities of faith, since it is an interpretive enterprise. This qualification means, too, that theology has no direct access to God, as if it could bypass the indirectness of faith's language. Theology must therefore respect the fact that it has to do with a God who is mediated through revelatory language and the events to which that language testifies. In other words, theology cannot presume to transcend this indirectness through a grasp of God *in se*. Christian faith affirms that we know God as God acts for us in revelatory events and testimony. While it is right to insist that faith rests on the assurance that God's action for us is an expression of

---

[3]Ricoeur, "Biblical Hermeneutics," *Semeia* 4 (1975): 129.

God's true being, and not some mask that God assumes in relation to us, this statement cannot be turned into a claim that we have a knowledge of God's inner reality as it exists in itself. Not only does revelation have a doubly indirect quality, through event and testimony, but also an ability to know the divine life from within would entail a complete abrogation of our finite, socially and historically shaped understanding.

Second, theology depends on faith's originary expressions in that the rationality of the former is partially determined by the latter. This conclusion is the upshot of the claim that human rationality always operates in conjunction with an imaginative construal of the nature of things. Thus, some of the conceptual distinctions with which theology operates, as well as many of the rules guiding its reflection, are rooted in faith's imaginative understanding. On the other hand, the fact that theology operates within a particular construal of the world does not mean that it should exercise a wholly unique logic. Such an idea is precluded by the many connections between faith's expressions and expressions belonging to other areas of discourse.[4] Furthermore, the claim that there is a fit between faith's affirmations and living experience has implications for the issue of faith and rationality. It means that the various forms of discourse that express the nature and meaning of our experience of the world must be taken into account by theology in its effort to explore and exhibit this fit. This is not to say that theology must simply accept what other forms of discourse claim. But if theology is to challenge a contemporary point of view, it must do so in a way appropriate to the form of discourse in which the challenge is being made.[5]

This last point can be illustrated through the debate between "Christian realism" and liberation theology. Reinhold Niebuhr's articulation of Christian realism depended both on his understanding of the biblical doctrine of sin and on an interpretation of our human experience of that sinfulness within society.[6] On the other hand, liberation theology's insistence on the possibility and necessity of transformative praxis, which

---

[4]Cf. Patrick Sherry, *Religion, Truth, and Language-Games* (London: Macmillan, 1977) 55-57.

[5]In spite of his questionable use of the phrase "ordinary human experience," I take this to be the genuine insight in Ricoeur's argument that theology's task is "to coordinate the experience articulated by the Biblical text with human experience at large and as a whole" ("Biblical Hermeneutics," 130-31).

[6]See, e.g., R. Niebuhr, *Moral Man and Immoral Society: A Study in Ethics and Politics* (New York: Charles Scribner's Sons, 1932).

is not bound by the ostensible probity of "realism," rests on a different understanding of the biblical view of sin and redemption and on a contrary assessment of what is shown by human experience.[7] In both cases there is an attempt to deal with the experience of the fallible and fallen human will, which requires attention to the ways in which this will has its effect. Although each brings theological principles to bear on the consideration of living experience, each is also forced to consider other forms of discourse about human life, such as political science and sociology.

Theology's interpretation of the Christian faith at the conceptual level serves at least three purposes. In the first place, it helps to articulate, in an intellectually responsible way, the implications of the gospel for how we are to act and think in our contemporary situation. That is, theology has the task of clarifying how faith impinges on the context in which the community of faith finds itself. Its interpretive activity, then, is a re-presentation of the language of faith in terms appropriate to a specific context. In this way, meaning that is implicit or sensed in an inchoate or general way in faith's originary language is made explicit and precise. Furthermore, the language and actions of the community of faith are thereby tested against faith's originary language. On the other hand, such specification of meaning is at the same time a narrowing down of the hermeneutical richness of faith's symbols and metaphors. Thus, theology never replaces the language of faith and must continually return to this originary language to reexamine its old interpretations and to uncover new meanings.

If theology is concerned about the correlation between the affirmations of Christian faith and the contemporary situation, it must also attend to how these affirmations affect human beings in the situation. Thus, theology's second function is to test, in a critical way, the language and actions of the community of faith to see how they affect human life. To be sure, theology has no neutral vantage point from which to test the church's influence on human well-being. Its understanding of what is human and humane is, after all, dependent on its own originary, disclosive language. Yet it is still possible to engage in a critical reflection on such matters to see if the living experience arising out of the church's confessions and actions prove fruitful for human life or are experienced as distortive and oppressive. How this might happen raises a host of issues that are treated in the discussion of the criteria of theology.

---

[7]See, e.g., Matthew Lamb, *Solidarity with Victims: Toward a Theology of Social Transformation* (New York: Crossroad, 1982).

The third purpose served by theology is the exploration of the internal coherence of faith's affirmations. This function does not imply that theology should try to fit the affirmations of faith into a logically tight system, or that the Christian faith is an isolable system of symbols that we can treat as a whole that is neatly separable from life.[8] On the contrary, we must leave room for tension and paradox and for the inextricable intertwining of Christian faith and life. Nevertheless, it is necessary to deal with the question of whether faith can reasonably claim that the tensions and paradoxes to which it gives rise can be accepted without requiring a sacrifice of the intellect. That is to say, even though we cannot expect to find an overarching system into which the Christian faith's originary expressions will neatly fit, we can hope to trace out the affirmations of Christian faith in order to catch a glimpse of how they hold together in their relation to one another and to living experience. This is a never-ending task, yet one we cannot avoid.

Even though theology is a second-order operation, it does not follow that it can have no impact on the originary level of faith. To be sure, theology cannot serve as the ground for faith and has no neutral place to stand from which it can give faith its essential content. Still, theology's reflection on the originary expressions of faith can reveal distortions in the way these expressions have been brought into play in the church and in Scripture. To the degree it can do this and can appeal to resources within the language of faith for the correction of such distortions, theology can indeed help to shape even the primordial language of faith. In other words, even as a second-order enterprise theology can test Scripture and tradition in light of faith's most authentic understanding.[9] However, this understanding of theology stands opposed to Kaufman's claim that theology gives faith its basic understanding of the world and God. Theology can make its contribution to faith's primordial language only by feeding back into the reality out of which it initially came—the reality of faith.

In this understanding of theology, the theological enterprise clearly presupposes the imaginative construal of faith. On the other hand, theology calls for some imaginative construals of its own. While oriented and shaped by faith's initial act of imagination, theology must do more than

---

[8]Cf. George A. Lindbeck, *The Nature of Doctrine: Religion and Theology in a Postliberal Age* (Philadelphia: Westminster Press, 1984) 115.

[9]How this critical function can take place within the approach I am articulating should become clearer as I deal with the sources, norm, and criteria of theology and with the issue of how theology can deal with the truth question.

engage in logically precise explanations and extensions of faith's language. For the logical operation of theology is conjoined with an imaginative grasp of how that language is internally connected and how it relates to various areas of life. That is to say, such connections and implications are not entailed by an inexorable logic. As a result, different perspectives can bring out different sorts of connections and implications, or different ordering principles for theology. Such connections and implications are already present in faith's initial apprehensions, yet theology is engaged in a reflection that extends and may even try to correct such apprehensions.[10] To do this, it must become attuned to the significant questions and the dialogue that they put in motion. That is, the task of theology calls for a sensitivity to the interplay between biblical testimony and the present situation, through which we take the gospel as possessing a certain meaning for life and thus take life as having a certain meaning.[11] The reflective activity of theology needs this imaginative grasp

---

[10]See David Kelsey, *The Uses of Scripture in Recent Theology* (Philadelphia: Fortress Press, 1975) 158-81, where he notes that different ways of using Scripture in theology depend on different imaginative discrimens that are rooted in a community's understanding of how Scripture relates to its life.

[11]This position has some important similarities to the one outlined by George Lindbeck in *Nature of Doctrine*, 113-24. Lindbeck maintains that dogmatic or systematic theology has the task of describing everything in terms of its religion, "and doing this by means of religiously shaped second-order concepts." Because of "their comprehensiveness, reflexivity, and complexity," religions call for "thick description," that is, description of their behaviors, institutions, and processes in terms of the meaningful contexts they provide. This thick description is thus the exhibition of "the full range of the interpretive medium" embodied in a religion. Lindbeck continues: "Because this range in the case of religion is potentially all-encompassing, description has a creative aspect. There is, indeed, no more demanding exercise of the inventive and imaginative powers than to explore how a language, culture, or religion may be employed to give meaning to new domains of thought, reality, and action. Theological description can be a highly constructive enterprise" (p. 115). While I agree with Lindbeck about the imaginative character of this task and about the priority of the "cultural-linguistic" matrix for human life, I disagree with his largely nondialectical way of treating the relationship between the cultural-linguistic framework and living experience. To be sure, he does at one point acknowledge a dialectical relationship between experience and religion (p. 33). Yet his overall treatment of the issue still moves in one direction: from religion to experience. In light of the dialectical play of dialogue and its relationship to living experience, through which dialogue is open to disclosures of the new, there is reason to doubt that the priority of the cultural-linguistic matrix can

in order to find its bearings. Imagination, then, is pivotal for the actual work of theology and not just for faith.

• The Sources of Theology •

In light of earlier arguments about the importance of the effective-history of interpretations of the Bible and about the production of meaning in the fusion of horizons, it is clear that, in this view, the Bible cannot be the only source for theology. Certainly, the Bible serves as the basic and unsurpassable source for theology, because of its central role in giving rise to and shaping faith through its testimony to God's action in history. Nevertheless, there are also other sources for theology.

The traditions that emerge from the effective-history of the Bible are among the other sources, for their concrete and particular actualizations of the meaning of the biblical testimony inevitably influence the way in which we retrieve the message of the Bible for our own situation. For this reason, Paul Tillich rightly states that the "biblicist" ideal of leaping over two thousand years of church history in order to uncover the pure meaning of the gospel without the accretions of tradition is impossible to realize. On the contrary, "every person who encounters a biblical text is guided in his religious understanding of it by the understanding of all previous generations."[12] The description of the act of understanding in terms of the concepts of a fusion of horizons and of the effective-history of the text leads inevitably to such a conclusion.[13] Moreover, this position entails a recognition that the particular denominational tradition within which a theologian operates exercises an especially formative influence. I do not say that theologians should operate with narrow denominational blinders; but the perspective from which one does theology, engages in

---

itself justify such a primarily one-directional treatment of the matter. If not, then Lindbeck's effort to distinguish form (or deep grammar) from matter (or experience) in such a way as to make the former relatively unchanging (cf. pp. 34-35 and 79-84.) and his effort to articulate the theological task through the notion of "intratextuality" (pp. 113-24) become questionable, for they depend on the general movement from interpretive scheme to experience and will therefore require significant modification if a movement in the opposite direction is allowed a significant role (as in the approach informed by the models of play and the fusion of horizons).

[12]Paul Tillich, *Systematic Theology*, 3 vols. (Chicago: University of Chicago Press, 1951-1963) 1:36.

[13]Naturally, Tillich was not explicitly using such concepts. Yet at this point his position fits well with these concepts.

ecumenical conversation, and participates in dialogue with those outside the Christian faith will be shaped by the tradition to which one belongs. A recognition of this fact leads to an acceptance of church history—or, more precisely, the traditions arising out of church history—as a source for theology.

Such a source is, to be sure, ambiguous in what it offers contemporary theology. Not all actualizations of the meaning of the biblical testimony have been authentic. Yet many have been and are consequently hermeneutically fruitful; for they enrich our understanding of the Christian faith through their particular re-presentations of the meaning of that faith. Since such re-presentations wish to be faithful to the biblical testimony, the Bible has priority even at this point. However, we are not dealing here with finding new ways to express the same meaning that one could have found simply in the Bible itself if one wished. On the contrary, in the act of re-presentation a particular meaning is embodied in a concrete actualization within a situation, and this meaning is disclosed through this actualization and only through this actualization. In other words, meaning emerges from the intersection of text and situation and not apart from it.[14] The particular meanings embodied in such a re-presentation contribute to our theology through their influence on our own horizon, insofar as a re-presentation belongs to a living tradition that helps to constitute our horizon, and through their ability to illumine the horizon of the biblical text itself. It should be obvious that such influences are both conscious and nonconscious.

Our attempts to come to a greater understanding of church history through critical methods help to bring these influences into conscious awareness. Historical approaches thereby make an essential contribution through their methodological check on our understanding of Christian traditions and hence through their ability to increase our insight into the history of Christian thought.[15] However, historical method cannot replace the fusion of horizons, which transcends such self-conscious checks on our understanding. The fusion of horizons inevitably includes a moment of application through which the text can make a claim on us—even in our initial sense of the text's meaning, a sense that guides our use of method. Methodological approaches, on the other hand, try to establish a distance between text and interpreter that leaves the latter unaffected and even in control of the former. Such methodological distanciation can

---

[14]Cf. my discussion in chapter 3 of Gadamer's model of play.

[15]Cf. Tillich, *Systematic Theology*, 1:38.

be kept from becoming a source of alienation from tradition only when it is kept within a more encompassing framework of understanding.[16]

The hermeneutical fruitfulness of Christian traditions is evident wherever one looks at the actual practice of Christian theology. Even the Reformation protest against the Roman Catholic use of tradition, in the name of the principle of *sola Scriptura*, was not an abandonment of tradition. On the contrary, the appeal to Scripture took place within a framework oriented and shaped by the tradition. For example, the Reformers' understanding of Paul was mediated through Augustine. Furthermore, their question about justification was not simply a repetition of Paul's concerns. Rather, it arose out of its time and was therefore partially shaped by the tradition out of which the Reformers came and to which they still belonged in many respects.[17]

The potential contribution of tradition can be further illustrated by an interpretive move that had far-reaching consequences for medieval theology, namely, Thomas Aquinas's understanding of Exodus 3:14. This passage, in which God is named "I am," had been understood as an expression of God's eternity, at least since the time of Augustine. Thomas was shaped by this tradition in his understanding of the passage. On the other hand, he reshaped this tradition through his reflection on what it means to affirm God's eternity in this way. His conclusion was that the designation of God as "I am" means that God is not God because of a divine essence in which God participates. Instead, God's existence is God's essence.[18] In light of current historical-critical exegesis, Thomas's interpretation was painfully wide of the mark (as was Augustine's). Yet, in spite of this undeniable fact, some still argue that there is a dimension of the biblical message that is properly brought to expression, or re-presented, in Thomas's exposition: that is, God is God in virtue of, and only in virtue of, God's free act of being.[19]

Now Thomas's own expression of this truth is not simply a repetition of the biblical message about God's freedom vis-à-vis the world. It is,

---

[16]Cf. my discussion in chapter 3 of Gadamer's models of play and a fusion of horizons. Cf. also Paul Ricoeur's discussion of the schema guess-explanation-understanding in *Interpretation Theory: Discourse and the Surplus of Meaning* (Fort Worth TX: Texas Christian University Press, 1976) 71-88.

[17]Cf. Tillich, *Systematic Theology*, 1:36-37.

[18]Thomas Aquinas, *Summa theologiae*, I, q. 3.

[19]See, e.g., Walter Kasper, *The God of Jesus Christ*, trans. Matthew J. O'Connell (New York: Crossroad, 1984) 147-57.

rather, a re-presentation utilizing philosophical concepts and distinctions current in his time, as well as biblical perspectives, and therefore could not have grown out of the ground of the Bible alone. That is, even though it may be an authentic re-presentation of the biblical testimony about God, Thomas's understanding cannot be derived directly from the biblical text. If nothing else, his distinction between essence and existence cannot be found in the Bible; yet it adds something to our understanding of the biblical message once it is brought into play. Thus, it serves as a source for theology—even if in no other way than as a mistake one wishes to correct (since a reaction cannot help but be shaped in some ways by that to which it is a reaction).

Even those who do not regard Thomas's position as a mistake cannot simply repeat his understanding, any more than he could repeat the view of Exodus 3:14. That is, his point can contribute to but cannot fully shape theology today, since his concepts are no longer ours. An example of this contribution can be seen in Walter Kasper's retrieval of Thomas at this point. Kasper argues that, by understanding Thomas's argument in terms provided by the contemporary philosophy of freedom, which stresses an active or dynamic concept of being, the Thomistic interpretation can be seen to be in harmony with the biblical affirmations about God. That is, God is absolute spirit who in transcendent freedom is there for us in love. Kasper's treatment of Thomas draws on an understanding of spirit as a reflective reality, that is, "a conscious being in-himself and for-himself" who is characterized by "freedom that goes out of itself and fulfills itself in action." Drawing out the consequences of such a starting point, which leads us to see God as absolute person, Kasper concludes that "God is the subsistent being which is freedom in love" and ties this view to the biblical affirmation that "God is love."[20] Thus, he both makes a claim for faithfulness to the biblical message and makes use of Thomas's understanding, while also re-presenting Thomas and the biblical message in a new way. The point to note here is not Kasper's material conclusion but his manner of operation. Whether or not he is right about God and about Thomas, his attempt to engage in conversation with the tradition and to remain faithful to the Bible exemplifies how Christian traditions serve as a source for theology.

Even those aspects of a tradition that we judge to be distortions of the biblical message can be useful for theology. In the first place, they can alert us to possible dead ends for our own theology. In this case, they are not

---

[20]Ibid., 150-51, 153, 155.

so much a source as signposts indicating mistaken paths. On the other hand, even distortions can harbor genuine insights, and can serve as a source for theology by opening our eyes to hidden truths. Furthermore, they inevitably become a source for theology when a theologian's own thought is shaped by a reaction to them, for if nothing else, they thereby help to shape the questions with which one's theology is occupied.

The full range of human culture also serves as a source for theology, for our culture is a constitutive part of our horizon. Furthermore, past cultures and other contemporary cultures can serve to broaden our horizon as we come to understand them. Indeed, past cultures that are connected to our own culture contribute to our horizon in ways that elude our conscious awareness, since their effective-history has an impact on our culture and therefore on our horizon. Various disciplines of thought and research can help to bring this influence to awareness, but they cannot make it fully transparent to us. Still, such disciplines are important for theology in that they increase our awareness of these influences and thereby enable us to examine them critically. As a result, we can gain greater insight into their true hermeneutical fruitfulness and into the ways they distort our understanding. Thomas's interpretation of Exodus 3:14 and Kasper's use of this interpretation, presented above, provide an illustration of one way in which culture acts as a source. That is, in the cases of Thomas and Kasper, cultural reflection provided some concepts and distinctions that were taken into their theologies. Tillich succinctly describes this and other ways in which the theologian has to do with culture. "He uses culture and religion intentionally as his means of expression, he points to them for confirmation of his statements, he fights against them as contradictions of the Christian message, and above all, he formulates the existential questions implied in them, to which his theology intends to be the answer."[21]

My only qualification of Tillich's statement has to do with the "existential questions" and theology's answers. To begin with, although existential questions are not to be denied their importance and place, it has become clear that we cannot rest content with narrowly existential and personal concerns. The concept of a fusion of horizons, in fact, takes us beyond such concerns (while including them) into the world of social relationships and realities.[22] Furthermore, the questions with which the-

---

[21]Tillich, *Systematic Theology*, 1:38.

[22]See Gadamer, "On the Problem of Self-Understanding," in *Philosophical Hermeneutics*, trans. David E. Linge (Berkeley and Los Angeles: University of California Press, 1976) 44-58.

ology deals may arise from the domain of the Christian faith as well as from culture. The Christian message may prompt questions that would not otherwise have been asked. Finally, culture's own answers to questions can make a contribution to theology, and not simply the reverse. This possibility seems to be implied by Tillich's claim that the theologian uses culture's means of expression and points to culture for confirmation of statements. It is important to remember that this view does not mean that the biblical message is denied priority in this interchange between theology and culture. Rather, it means that our interpretation of the biblical message does not take place apart from the contributions that culture makes to our understanding in general and to our understanding of the Bible in particular.[23]

This exploration of theology and culture has deliberately avoided the suggestion that "common human experience" can be a source for theology.[24] Since there is no such thing as raw experience, *"common* human experience" cannot play such a role.[25] Living experience, however, may function as a source for theology. Since experience helps to constitute our horizon, in the dialectical interplay of tradition and experience, it is inevitable that such experience will serve as a source for theological reflection. This experience cannot be assumed to be a universal, unchanging reality, as the phrase "common human experience" suggests, but is shaped by and hence inextricably tied to its horizon. Yet, as has already been argued, this fact does not necessarily imply that experience has nothing of its own to contribute. Rather, the openness of metaphor, and of language in general, to the extralinguistic world means that experience contributes to the emergence of new insight and knowledge. Experience thus will also contribute to theology's ongoing reflection and criticism.

Although the historicity of human life and understanding does not mean that experience has no contribution to make to theology, it does

---

[23]Note, for example, my discussion below of the "anthropological constants" outlined by Schillebeeckx. Here are some cultural "answers" that contribute to our understanding of redemption. Another example can be seen in the fact that contemporary understandings of the Christian's responsibility in society derive from biblical themes *and* contemporary understandings of the nature of human society. Cf. Dorothee Sölle, *Political Theology,* trans. John Shelley (Philadelphia: Fortress Press, 1974) 59-63.

[24]Contra David Tracy, *Blessed Rage for Order: The New Pluralism in Theology* (New York: Seabury Press, 1978) 43-45.

[25]Cf. Francis Schüssler Fiorenza, *Foundational Theology: Jesus and the Church* (New York: Crossroad, 1984) 296-301.

mean that there are limits to the sorts of contributions experience can make. For example, it certainly means that experience cannot serve as an *independent* arbiter of theology's affirmations, since those affirmations themselves help to shape Christian experience. Furthermore, experience cannot serve as some sort of foundation for faith and theology. On the other hand, living experience can help to disclose avenues to new insight and knowledge, as I have argued above. Also, it can help to support or call into question certain understandings of life in the world as they prove to be fruitful or distortive and oppressive. It is important to remember that such critical testing in light of experience is not a neutral examination of theology's claims. Nonetheless, it is possible to test the congruence between these claims and living experience, not only in the light of a particular interpretation, but also in light of other interpretations or even other traditions than that to which one has belonged. To be sure, this does not provide a direct and immediate verification or refutation of theological concepts, but it does provide an important, if indirect, check. In short, living experience contributes to the emergence of new insight and helps to test theology's affirmations.[26]

My discussion has already indicated that these sources do not have equal weight for theology. In particular, the Bible plays the central role, so that other sources find their proper roles through their relationship to the biblical testimony.[27] Within this framework, they do play an essential role, since they make an indispensable contribution to the fusion of horizons. Because this fusion is an effort to understand the meaning of the biblical testimony and the claim it makes on our lives, this order of priority cannot be abandoned without giving up the heart of Christian theology, understood as an expression of faith's desire to reach greater understanding.

This insistence on the central role of the Bible among the various sources must in no way be taken to mean that every part of the Bible should be given equal weight or should automatically be treated as an authority to which one is subject. On the contrary, as will become evident in the discussion of theology's material norm and criteria, the biblical testimony itself requires a critical re-presentation in light of the disclosive

---

[26]See also my discussion of the play of imagination, in chapter 3, and of theology's criteria and apologetic activity, below.

[27]Cf. Tillich, *Systematic Theology*, 1:40: "There are degrees of importance in this immense source material, corresponding with its more direct and more indirect relationship to the central event on which the Christian faith is based."

power of its own central message. Hence, the recognition of the central place of the biblical testimony is a very different thing than submission to whatever one finds in the Bible.

The use of these sources in theology clearly requires the work of imagination. The ability to sense the important questions, to discern relationships between current images and concepts and biblical symbols, metaphors, and ideas, to be sensitive to how Christian traditions articulate biblical meanings and human concerns—these and other dimensions of the use of sources in theology call for an openness to the play of dialogue between horizons, through which a creative grasp of the Christian faith becomes possible. In short, they call for imagination, as the power of openness to dialogue through which we take the Christian faith as having meaning for life today. The greater the power of creative imagination, the surer the grasp one will have of the central issues and concerns that are addressed by the Christian faith.

Much of my discussion has presupposed the ability to evaluate critically interpretations or re-presentations of the biblical message.[28] The question then arises of how such evaluations are to be made. It is clearly not possible to formulate a purely logical and conceptual form of analysis that gives a sure answer to this question, since conceptual and logical methods of analysis are preceded by an appeal to our imaginative grasp of how things are to be understood. Thus, our imaginative grasp of things is a fundamental factor, even when we raise questions about authenticity of interpretation. Nonetheless, the determination of whether an understanding is authentic can be guided by a norm that expresses the central meaning of the gospel, as that meaning has emerged in the life of the church in its effort to be faithful to the Christian faith, and by other criteria inherent in the Christian message (which also become apparent in the church's living interpretation of the Bible).

• Theology's Material Norm •

The central and definitive role of the Bible in Christian theology is reflected not only in the fact that, as the most relatively adequate witness, the Bible has a unique authority among the various sources, but also in the fact that the material norm by which the various sources are judged, including the Bible itself, is derived from the biblical testimony.[29] We do

---

[28]I include here the critical evaluation of interpretations that one finds in the Bible itself.

[29]Cf. Tillich, *Systematic Theology*, 1:50.

not have direct access to the meaning of the biblical text—its meaning emerges only through our conversation with it—so that we cannot presume to have an ahistorical and timeless grasp of its meaning. Consequently, it is only through the interplay of text and present situation, in the context of the effective-history of the text, that the meaning of the biblical witness emerges. Crucial to this emerging meaning is what emerges as central to the Bible's testimony, for the overall meaning of the biblical testimony comes to be understood and judged in terms of this center, which thus serves as the material norm for theology.

As this description of the emergence of a norm indicates, the way in which the text impinges on our current situation is determinative for what we take to be central. Both sides of this interaction are important factors in the emergence of a norm. On one side, the text bears a meaning to which the theologian seeks to be faithful. On the other side, this meaning can emerge only through our act of understanding from within a particular situation. This latter fact means that the theologian does not make a decision about the central norm for theology as an isolated individual, since the situation includes society and the Christian tradition to which the theologian belongs. In this light it is clear that the interplay between text and community is determinative in this matter.[30] The theologian's task is to be sensitive to the nature of this interplay and what is disclosed through it.[31]

Since the central norm emerges out of the interplay between text and contemporary community of faith, this norm cannot be treated as the eternally abiding center of the Bible. Other communities in other times and circumstances will discover (and have discovered) different centering norms.[32] This fact is a reflection both of the historicity of faith and theology, on one side, and of the rich pluralism of the Bible's testimony, on

---

[30]Cf. ibid., 47-52.

[31]Naturally the theologian's own subjective involvement in the response to the text by the community of faith is an important factor here. For example, it will certainly help the individual theologian to discern the nature of what is disclosed and will predispose him or her to take it as a genuine disclosure. Cf. David Tracy, *The Analogical Imagination: Christian Theology and the Culture of Pluralism* (New York: Crossroad, 1981) 248-304, especially 273: "Any Christological reinterpretation must note that the disclosive reality in a present experience of the Christ event (the experience as mediated principally through the tradition judging itself by the original apostolic and wider scriptural traditions of witness) should provide the central theological clue to new interpretations of the event."

[32]Cf. Tillich, *Systematic Theology*, 1:47-52.

the other.[33] The use of a norm in fact presupposes some sort of unity within this diversity, but it does not deny the diversity. Indeed, this very diversity requires that one use a norm to judge the relative adequacy of the various expressions of faith even within the Bible itself.

It is tempting to speak of this norm as a "canon within the canon." However, this phrase suggests a fixed standard that does not vary. In light of the movable nature of theology's norm, it is better to follow David Tracy and call it a "working canon."[34]

An appreciation of the historicity of faith and theology leads to another conclusion: one must not allow one's working canon to operate in such a way that it destroys the possibility of learning from parts of the Bible that stand in tension with this central norm. To put the point more positively, a working canon needs to be open to enrichment through other perspectives. Hence we must constantly be in dialogue with all parts of the biblical testimony and with other Christian traditions and theologians who have found a different center from which to work. In short, the emergence and use of a norm require the context of genuine conversation if a norm is to be a truly fruitful critical principle and not a source of oppressive distortions. In this way, we become more aware of our own limitations and are open to the possibility of broadening our horizons.[35] At times this openness could lead to the emergence of a new working canon, but it need not. Often it will lead to an enrichment of our understanding of the center of our theology and therefore of the Christian faith as well. Always it requires the sort of intellectual humility that will not insist that everything be wholly subject to the control of one's intellect. Such humility is based on a recognition of the limitations of one's own historical understanding (and that of one's church and tradition) and of the inexpressible wealth and mystery of the Christian faith. In brief, theology is contextual and dialogical, so that pluralism represents potential enrichment as well as tension. On the other hand, in its positive evaluation of pluralism, theology must not forget that the possibility of fundamental distortion is always present. Consequently, theology cannot avoid the critical task of judging the adequacy of various proposals and perspectives.

Once again, the imagination is intimately involved in theology's discernments at this point. Just as a sense of how the Bible is to be used as a source for theology is not determined by a given, self-evident system,

---

[33]Cf. Tracy, *Analogical Imagination*, 254-55.

[34]Cf. ibid., 290 n. 29, 254.

[35]Cf. ibid., 252.

so the sense of what constitutes the center of the biblical witness comes only through an imaginative attunement to the important questions in the conversation between text and community. There is no predetermined, logical procedure by which one uncovers the norm. The theologian, therefore, must be attuned to the conversation between the situation and the biblical message in order to uncover its significant questions and answers. Since the theologian engages in this imaginative construal as a member of society, his or her understanding is shaped and guided by society's understanding of the important questions with which life today is engaged. Furthermore, when the theologian operates as a part of a church, as is often the case, the imaginative stance that is already present in the faith of the church will guide the theologian's imagination.[36] Even if the theologian is not identified with the church, the latter remains important, since one's understanding of the Christian faith is affected by the way in which that faith comes and has come to expression.

Even though the imagination has a communal dimension, the theologian's own imaginative powers still are called into play. Although society and church provide an indispensable context and guide for the theologian, they do not absolve one from the necessity of coming to a personal grasp of the norm of theology. When the theologian makes such a construal, it may be at variance with and challenge the common understanding. Yet, if someone's understanding is so idiosyncratic that conversation with the larger community is impossible, it is highly unlikely that such an understanding conveys an authentic insight into the biblical witness. Even when society or a church is engaged in systematically distorted communication, thereby indicating that faithfulness to the Christian faith should express itself in opposition to the prevailing stance, such opposition needs to be expressed in understandable terms. In other words, the questions lying behind a distorted understanding are also crucial for an authentic understanding, if the latter is to be a genuine grasp of the meaning of the Christian faith in a concrete context. One may not wish to remain with such questions, but one will inevitably begin with them. Hence the theologian's attunement to the important questions in a situation is not an isolated achievement. Rather, it depends in large measure on what the larger community takes to be important and meaningful.

Not only is the initial emergence of theology's central norm a process involving the imagination; the use of this norm in the work of theology

---

[36]Cf. Kelsey, *Uses of Scripture*, 158-81. What Kelsey describes as the "discrimen" arising from the imaginative act of the theologian is close to what I mean here.

also requires the imagination. Again, we do not have a given, self-evident system by which we can decide how to apply the norm. This decision rests on the nature of the norm and the theologian's insight into how it relates to the various issues being addressed. Such insight rests on the ability to attune oneself to the dialogue between the norm and one's situation, so that one can take the norm as possessing a certain meaning vis-à-vis the situation. Thus, it is this power of attunement, or openness, to dialogue (that is, the imagination), rather than a formula for arriving at the authentic meaning of the norm for any particular issue, that is fundamental to the use of theology's norm.

Both in uncovering and using a norm, the theologian certainly uses rational arguments to support what he or she does. However, these rational arguments are not grounded in a prior system that one uses to reach decisions about the norm and its use. For they follow rather than precede the theologian's imaginative construal. That is to say, the theologian's initial construal of the norm and how it relates to the world is an imaginative stance that then guides how he or she uses rational considerations. If the imaginative stance is genuinely attuned to the dialogue, it should strike us as fitting and should give us a perspective that generates new insights and opens our eyes to much in the biblical text and in our living experience that fits with this stance. In large measure, then, rational arguments are ways of showing the stance's internal coherence, its faithfulness to the text, its fit with living experience, and its ability to make sense of ever larger reaches of our lives. These arguments do not constitute a logical proof of one's understanding. Nevertheless, they may prove persuasive through their ability to help others see the coherence and fittingness of one's construal. Moreover, to the extent that one's construal deals with common concerns more adequately than do others, it carries even greater weight. At any rate, rational argumentation by a theologian constitutes an effort to engage in conversation with others and to invite them to take things in terms of one's imaginative stance. It cannot legitimately be an effort to prove one's case through logically incontrovertible arguments.[37]

The stress on community and concrete context as the necessary milieu for the emergence and use of a norm indicates the importance of praxis in this entire process. That is, the emergence and use of the norm are not merely intellectual processes but processes involving the action and con-

---

[37]Cf. the discussion below of criteria of adequacy and of the truth question in theology.

crete concerns of a community. What one takes to be the norm, therefore, arises out of the intersection of the text, on one side, and the concerns and demands of living experience, on the other. We can say, not that experience and action have a self-evident meaning that is incorporated into the norm, but that the meaning of the biblical message becomes evident only in concrete situations and therefore in situations in which action is involved. The interplay of situation and text, therefore, means that praxis plays a fundamental role in the determination of the meaning of the biblical message.

• Criteria of Adequacy •

The material norm by which a theologian operates guides in the critical articulation of the meaning of the gospel for a concrete situation and helps to uncover and correct distortions. It does not operate alone, however, since there are a number of criteria of adequacy to the situation that a theologian also uses for guiding and judging theological proposals.[38] The criterion of the material norm has as its primary focus the central meaning of the *biblical message* for a particular situation. Other criteria emerge out of a concern for "relative adequacy *to the situation*,"[39] specifically, the sort of criteria Kaufman calls presence, humanization, and relativization.[40] By noting this, I do not mean to accept Kaufman's understanding of the derivation and role of such criteria. On the contrary, as is abundantly clear from previous arguments, these criteria cannot be derived from some sphere of thought and action that is external to the basic imaginative grasp of faith. Hence they are not more fundamental truths ac-

---

[38]Although Kelsey distinguishes between criteria and norms, regarding the latter as more absolute, my discussion of the material norm of theology has treated it more as a criterion—or, more exactly, as a central vision of the nature of the gospel that provides an organizing center for a constellation of criteria (the specific nature of the criteria being determined by the nature of the norm). As I have argued, even the material norm is derived and mediate (just as criteria are). Moreover, the norm works in conjunction with other criteria, such as those described here. See Kelsey, *Uses of Scripture*, 160.

[39]The phrase is David Tracy's (*Analogical Imagination*, 256).

[40]It should be noted that the concern for relative adequacy to the situation does not mean that these criteria are derived from the situation. The point is the particular focus of the criteria. Actually, it is apparent that presence, humanization, and relativization are already implied by the material norm, if the norm is in fact appropriate to the situation. However, these criteria do have a relatively distinct role to play vis-à-vis the material norm and hence deserve separate treatment.

cording to which faith and its affirmations can be constructed and reconstructed. Rather, they arise out of the originary expressions and apprehensions of faith. Nevertheless, they have some value for our critical assessments of various perspectives in the Bible and in Christian tradition and of current theological proposals.

The concern for a theology's relative adequacy to the situation does not mean that theology is compelled to accept whatever standards of evaluation and rationality are in vogue in society. There are times when theology must oppose them in the name of the gospel it is trying to relate faithfully to the context. Relevance, then, calls for opposition in such cases, not for an easy alignment with society. Keeping in mind this caveat, we should remind ourselves that theology must be expressed in terms of its context. Actually, it is more accurate to say that any theology that is a genuine expression of one's understanding, and is not merely a repetition of what has been imposed from without, is inevitably expressed in terms of its context. Such expression follows from the fact that any genuine understanding of the Christian faith is a re-presentation of it in our own language and in relation to our sociohistorical location. Still, this expression can be made more conscious and articulate through careful attention to the way in which the gospel speaks to the situation, thus making explicit what is implicit or inchoate. Therefore, one criterion that is rooted in a concern for the situation is whether a theological proposal is expressed in terms that truly address our world.[41] To do so, it must express itself in our language yet convey the meaning of the gospel for the situation. Herein lies the fundamental task and challenge of theology.

Another criterion that is primarily related to concern for adequacy to the situation is the criterion of humanization. For Kaufman, this criterion is relatively independent of the imaginative framework constructed by theology and is therefore able to provide guidance for the construction of that framework. In light of the position developed here, it is clear that the criterion of humanization cannot have such an independent status, for the decision to make humanization a central concern and what one means by this term are dependent on a prior construal of the nature of things. Nonetheless, this criterion can serve a useful purpose if it is kept within the framework provided by the imaginative construal of faith.

This emphasis on the importance of a prior framework for an appreciation and understanding of humanization should not be taken to mean that contemporary forms of thought are irrelevant to a Christian understanding

---

[41]This criterion corresponds to Kaufman's criterion of presence.

of the nature of human life. Again, the play of dialogue suggests that there is a dialectical interchange between horizons. That is to say, our understanding of the Christian view of human and humane forms of life emerges in the interplay between the biblical text, Christian traditions, and our current insights into human life. For the Christian theologian, it is important for this interplay to be a re-presentation of the biblical witness, yet it is a re-presentation that depends on contemporary forms of thought for its particular form and hence for the particular truths it discloses.

The nature of this interplay could be illustrated by the work of a number of theologians. One place it is especially evident is in an essay by Edward Schillebeeckx that discusses some "anthropological constants" and their implications for soteriology. Even though we have no preexisting definition of human nature (since humans are not predetermined beings but realize their natures through their historical actualization, so that what we will be is an open question at any given moment), Schillebeeckx argues that it is possible to delineate several anthropological constants. He describes seven constants, which "point to permanent human impulses and orientations, values and spheres of value": (1) humans both have and are bodies, which makes us an inextricable part of the physical environment; (2) human identity includes relationships with other people; (3) humans are essentially social, that is, they live within social and institutional structures; (4) human life is embedded in time and space; (5) theory and practice are intrinsically related in human existence; (6) human life has a "utopian" element, that is, hope for the future and faith in its realization; and (7) the previous six constants form an irreducible synthesis in which each affects the others. One need not adopt every detail of Schillebeeckx's exposition of anthropological constants to see that he has identified some important dimensions of human life as we know it. The significant point for my purposes here, however, is that Schillebeeckx's understanding of Christian salvation is informed by these constants. This fact is clearly evident in one summary paragraph.

> Christian salvation, in the centuries-old biblical tradition called redemption, and meant as salvation from God for men, is conceived with the whole system of coordinates in which man can really be man. This salvation—the wholeness of man—cannot just be sought in one or other of these constants, say exclusively in "ecological appeals," in an exclusive "be nice to one another," in the exclusive overthrow of an economic system (whether Marxist or capitalist), or in exclusively mystical experiences: "Alleluia, he is risen!" On the other hand, the synthesis of all this is clearly an "already now" and a "not yet." The way in which human failure and human

shortcomings are coped with must be termed a form of "libera-tion" (and perhaps its most important form). In that case that might then be the all-embracing "anthropological constant" in which Jesus wished to go before us.[42]

The importance of the anthropological constants for this description of salvation is clear. Equally clear and important is the fact that Schille-beeckx appeals to the biblical basis for a Christian definition of salvation. For example, he refers to the fact that salvation is from God and has the wholeness of human life as its goal. Furthermore, he shows an overrid-ing concern for human failures and understands liberation in a way that takes into account the flawed nature of human existence. Such themes are rooted in the biblical view of God's Kingdom as it has been defined and brought near in Jesus the Christ.

What Schillebeeckx develops in some detail Tracy sums up as "the complexities of any self" who is "at once individual, historical, social and natural." Consequently, the questions that we bring to the text must be open to disclosures relating to the full range of human life, such as the cosmos, history, society, and other persons—"especially, for the Chris-tian gospel, the outcasts, the forgotten ones, the suffering, the poor, the oppressed."[43] Any theology, therefore, that does not allow for or tends to ignore this full range of human life must be judged inadequate in light of this criterion.

The criterion of humanization, then, calls for an assessment of how well a theological proposal coheres with a tradition's disclosures of hu-man and humane forms of life and of how well it fits living experience. To be sure, our experience is not raw and unmediated, so that the as-sessment cannot take the form of a direct comparison of experience and a theology's claims about human life. Nevertheless, claims about the na-ture of human life do lead to certain forms of participation in life that may or may not prove themselves through their ability to provide a coherent understanding of life and to uncover new possibilities for life. Thus, one can assess the fittingness of an understanding of human life without hav-ing to find a neutral observation point. Admittedly, this assessment does not constitute an objective verification of a particular understanding of the human. Indeed, very different frameworks may be able to show that they are justifiable in these terms. Yet it does constitute a valuable form of test-

---

[42]Edward Schillebeeckx, *The Schillebeeckx Reader*, ed. Robert J. Schreiter (New York: Crossroad, 1984) 29-39.

[43]Tracy, *Analogical Imagination*, 256, 257.

ing the reasonableness of any proposal.[44] Thus, if a theological proposal fails to fit with living experience, this criterion counts tellingly against it.

Kaufman also makes much of the criterion of relativization but generally tends to describe its value and importance by indicating the way it serves humanization. In the approach developed here, however, relativization's value goes beyond the way it serves humanization. As a result, this criterion relativizes even humanization, for it insists that everything, even human life, is directed toward something larger than itself. From this perspective, human life becomes fully human and humane only when it is understood and lived in these terms.

Among other things, this perspective means that human life is not the only reality that makes a claim on us. For example, nature, understood as the nonhuman world, has its own claim to make, which we need to respect. Thus, an active concern for ecology is based on something more than the idea that nature is a presupposition for human life. Above all, Christian faith knows God as the ultimate point of reference for the whole of life, which radically relativizes all our projects, including our project of humanizing life. We certainly cannot say that relativization undercuts concern for humanization. On the contrary, a proper appreciation of God as both Creator and Redeemer will provide an unshakable support for humanization. However, humanization's value is rooted in its relation to God and is not an end in itself.

Theological proposals must therefore be judged by their ability to relativize human projects. Furthermore, since even our statements about God are not to be confused with God, our theological statements must be judged by their ability to relativize themselves. There is no room here for an absolutizing form of dogmatism. Whenever theological proposals assume such a character, this criterion must judge them distortive and inadequate.

As with the emergence and use of a material norm, these criteria require the context of conversation with others in order to be productively employed. In the case of each criterion, our understanding of its meaning and our insight into how to bring it into play emerge through a dialogue with Christian tradition that is open to and includes serious dialogue with others (both within and without the Christian faith). The implications of this wider conversation are perhaps most evident in the case of the criterion of humanization, for through conversation with

---

[44]For further discussion of this issue as it relates to the truth claims of theology, see the next section.

others we gain a relatively full insight into how particular understandings of the Christian faith concretely affect human life. That is, through conversation we can learn from a wide variety of situations and perspectives, including especially the perspectives of those on the underside of society or those who have been excluded from society in some way. In this way, the potential for these criteria to serve the critical function of theology is greatly enhanced.

• Theology and the Truth Question •

As the attempt to provide a critical re-presentation of faith in terms of a particular situation, theology cannot avoid the question of truth. Indeed, the question has already made itself felt at several points in this chapter. To raise this question is not to conclude that theology must be primarily apologetic. Systematic theology is by and large involved not in apologetic enterprises but in critically articulating the faith of a community at the conceptual level. However, part of the task of conceptualizing is dealing with the issue of whether one is warranted in taking such concepts seriously.

As I noted in an earlier chapter, the question of warrants for faith cannot be asked and answered in terms of verification. Rather, we are here in a realm of discourse akin to persuasion, so that one must treat this issue in terms of the justifiability of one's faith. Moreover, what is required to provide justification can be determined only in the situation where justification is needed. Still, it is possible to make some general statements about the nature of the truth question in systematic theology. In what follows I outline a general approach that is consistent with the understanding of faith and theology that has been presented here.

Although his understanding of the nature of doctrine and theology is somewhat at variance with the position I have articulated, Lindbeck does provide an insightful suggestion about how we can deal with the issue of the reasonableness of religion. His own view is rooted in an understanding of religions as systems that are very much like languages and cultures. Since they are comprehensive and exceedingly complex, they are not amenable to simple tests of their truth but, like scientific paradigms, are tested and confirmed or refuted through a long, slow process in which there are no definitive refutations or confirmations. In this light, Lindbeck concludes that in religion "intelligibility comes from skill, not theory, and credibility comes from good performance, not adherence to independently formulated criteria." He continues:

> In this perspective, the reasonableness of a religion is largely a
> function of its assimilative powers, of its ability to provide an in-

telligible interpretation in its own terms of the varied situations and realities adherents encounter. . . . Confirmation or disconfirmation occurs through an accumulation of successes or failures in making practically and cognitively coherent sense of relevant data, and the process does not conclude, in the case of religions, until the disappearance of the last communities of believers or, if the faith survives, until the end of history.[45]

This approach is much like the one that raises the question of the fittingness of a faith's construal of the world. Hence, in terms of the perspective I have been developing, it well describes one dimension of how it is possible to deal with the issue of the justifiability or reasonableness of a religion.

Lindbeck's suggestion is only partially satisfactory, however. It is curious that, even though his approach emphasizes the dependence of experience on a cultural-linguistic framework, his discussion of a religion's reasonableness focuses on making sense of "varied situations and realities adherents encounter." The approach that I have been articulating certainly recognizes the need to deal with such situations and realities. On the other hand, in the view of both Lindbeck's approach and the one presented here, a religious construal harbors a truly creative dimension vis-à-vis experience; yet this dimension is not explicitly brought into play in Lindbeck's suggestion about how to deal with the reasonableness of a religion.[46] It can be explicitly brought into play by raising the question of whether the construal of faith *discloses* possible ways of living that do in fact prove to be appropriate and fulfilling. Whether they are appropriate and fulfilling cannot be determined apart from some framework that one presupposes, so this is by no means an independent way of demonstrating the truth of a religion. Nevertheless, such an approach does provide some tests of a religion's reasonableness that can be applied within the framework.[47] In this way it is possible to invite others to see whether they, too, find the religion appropriate and fulfilling.[48]

---

[45]Lindbeck, *Nature of Doctrine*, 34-41, 131.

[46]My articulation of the nature of this creativity differs from Lindbeck's in some respects. Yet both positions are open to the creativity of language and culture, and this fact needs to be taken into account when dealing with the truth question.

[47]Cf. Fiorenza, *Foundational Theology*, 301-11, who treats this in terms of the concept of "reflective equilibrium." In its widest sense, this concept refers to the mutual interaction of the tradition and the praxis and experience it informs, an interaction mediated by "background theories," which have to do with matters

An example of this sort of approach to a religion's reasonableness is found in Diogenes Allen's book *The Reasonableness of Faith*. One issue he wrestles with is the charge that religion is merely the result of psychological projection. In response, he argues that "there are two ranges of needs which are satisfied by the gospel: those which are part of the human condition, and those which are awakened by the scriptural portrayal of God."[49] The partial satisfaction of both general human needs and needs newly awakened by the gospel, and the hope for their full satisfaction, "can lead one to adhere to religious beliefs as true."[50] Thus, although he does not use such terminology, Allen in effect suggests that faith can reasonably be justified by a religion's power to disclose regions of life that would otherwise remain hidden to us. Such faith does not depend on a comparison of experience and the Christian religion's construal of the world from the perspective of an outside, neutral observer. Rather, it de-

---

that are relevant to the subject under view and which control the way in which the tradition is brought to bear on experience and praxis. Cf. also Schillebeeckx, *Christ: The Experience of Jesus as Lord*, trans. John Bowden (New York: Crossroad, 1981) 30-64, who argues that new experiences have the ability to surprise us by contradicting our expectations. This fact shows that experience is not wholly shaped by our language and culture and provides a basis for according a certain authority to experience, especially in questions such as the justifiability of a construal of the world.

[48]To be fair, it should be noted that one could take Lindbeck to be saying something very close to what I have described as the disclosive power of a religion, when he argues that the credibility of a religion comes from "good performance" and from its capacity "to provide an intelligible interpretation in its own terms." On the other hand, Lindbeck links these concerns to the "assimilative powers" of a religion, whereas I am here emphasizing a religion's power to open up new regions of life.

[49]Diogenes Allen, *The Reasonableness of Faith: A Philosophical Essay on the Grounds for Religious Belief* (Washington D.C.: Corpus Books, 1968) 54. Needs that are part of the human condition include such things as the desire for happiness, for security, and for understanding. Needs awakened by the gospel include such things as the desire for fellowship with God, for righteousness (in distinction from mere moral goodness), and for an answer to the ultimate mystery of existence. Cf. p. 54 n. 5 and p. 56.

[50]Ibid., 56. Cf. p. 69: "A belief that has developed in the context of the Christian community is not a belief with absolutely no grounds and hence is not a blind or irrational belief. The grounds are that a man has come to have faith in response to the witness of the Christian community and in the condition of faith he finds his soul nourished."

pends on a disclosure of a possible way of being, which proves itself to be authentic through its ability to lead to a living experience that is congruent with the proposed construal of the world.

Allen does not suggest that nothing more is involved in dealing with the question of a religion's claims to truth. A believer is sometimes confronted with other issues and questions that require some sort of reasoned response if one is to continue to hold to a reasonable form of faith. Furthermore, the claims of the Christian religion involve one in other issues besides the power of the Christian faith to assimilate and disclose, for Christianity makes claims about the world as a creature, about the moral goodness of the Christian life, and about the historical person Jesus of Nazareth. Each of these areas requires rational examination and makes the Christian religion potentially vulnerable to falsification.[51] In short, the justification of religious beliefs is a complex issue that can call for more than one type of rational discourse.

The complexity of religious beliefs, and hence of exhibiting their justifiability (or lack of justifiability), is also recognized by McClendon and Smith in their book *Understanding Religious Convictions.*[52] Like Allen, they recognize a mixture of historical, affective, and performative dimensions that requires a corresponding mixture of considerations when one is dealing with the reasonableness of the Christian faith. Because of this complexity, one cannot treat the Christian religion (or any other religion) as if it were open to justification or falsification on the basis of one particular form of argument. Instead, the Christian religion comprises a broad, encompassing system, of which various parts can be affected through certain forms of examination and argument without directly affecting other parts. On the other hand, since it is an interrelated system, a change in one part is likely to affect the rest in some way.

It is clear, then, that theology cannot realistically approach the truth question with the intention of conclusively demonstrating the truth of the religion that it seeks to articulate conceptually. This limitation does not count against faith or theology, however, since the Christian faith is not only, or primarily, an answer to intellectual curiosity but is a form of life intended to heal life's brokenness, and since faith arises in response to the witness of a community of faith and to a discovery of the fittingness

---

[51]Cf. ibid., 69-76, 96-114, 64-65. We cannot say that there are clearcut standards of falsification, only that falsification would be possible in principle.

[52]James W. McClendon, Jr., and James M. Smith, *Understanding Religious Convictions* (Notre Dame IN: University of Notre Dame Press, 1975).

of the religion's construal of the world, as that construal is instantiated in a community and in the life of the individual.[53] That is to say, the disclosive power of the Christian religion's imaginative grasp of God and the world can reasonably give rise to faith, without the support of rational arguments intended to show the truth of this imaginative grasp. As problems and challenges arise, supporting arguments become necessary. Yet they do not become the primary basis for faith and are therefore not an inevitably necessary justification for faith.[54] Because of an experience of the ability of the Christian construal of the world to make sense of life and to open new regions of life that become central to one's understanding and experience, the believer can affirm the Christian faith to be true. This truth is not the truth of a correspondence between our statements and the mystery of God, as if our language about God were a mirror reflecting the divine image. Rather, it is the truth of an essential insight into God's way with the world, as this is mediated through the biblical text and the metaphors and symbols that have emerged in the history between the Bible and communities of faith.[55]

· Conclusion ·

Whereas Kaufman treats theology as a sort of presupposition for faith (in that theology provides faith with the concepts of God and the world that it should affirm), the understanding of theology developed here takes it as derivative from faith and hence dependent on and shaped by the fact that a community already confesses its faith in God in the metaphorically rich language of faith. In this respect, I take my stand with Karl Barth's point of departure rather than Kaufman's.[56]

---

[53]See Allen, *Reasonableness of Faith*, 69-76, 85-95.

[54]Cf. ibid., 72.

[55]This approach is not subject to Kaufman's strictures against the idea that our language about God is akin to language that describes an object in our environment. Indeed, it agrees with Kaufman at this point, but it does not accept the idea that such language has therefore abandoned all referential claims.

[56]Cf. Karl Barth, *Church Dogmatics*, vol. 1, pt. 1, *The Doctrine of the Word of God*, trans. G. W. Bromiley (Edinburgh: T. & T. Clark, 1975) 3-24. On the other hand, it should be clear that my approach differs significantly from Barth's in some other respects. His refusal in his methodological statements to allow a multiplicity of sources for theology and to recognize the hermeneutical productivity of our own horizon and the importance of some form of apologetics are all points at which my understanding diverges from his.

Because of its derivative and conceptual nature, theology is a second-order enterprise that strives to introduce some intellectual clarity and critical insight into the realm of faith. It thereby provides an essential service to faith, since it continues the dynamism of thought engendered by the language of faith, specifies the implications of faith for a concrete situation, and provides critical tests of the life and thought of the community of faith (including the critical evaluation of biblical and nonbiblical perspectives in light of faith's most central and authentic insights and their impact on living experience). On the other hand, theological conceptualization also represents a loss of potential meaning in comparison to faith's originary language. Consequently, theology must recognize its provisional nature and seek to listen again and again so that it can be enriched through new disclosures and through the perspective provided by others.

Another important implication of theology's dependence on faith, and the dependence of faith on the doubly indirect mediation of historical events and testimony, is that theology is not engaged in a direct description of God's nature. Rather, it deals with God as God is related to the world and as that relationship is revealed through events and the testimony of faith. I do not say that theology does not deal with the genuine reality of God; rather it deals with this reality in its relationship to us and not in itself.

To speak of theology's reflection on faith's testimony to revelatory events is already to indicate the primary source for theology: the biblical witness. In view of the productivity of meaning emerging out of the fusion of horizons, there are also other sources theology needs to take into account. In particular, the Christian traditions that have re-presented the Christian faith in various times and contexts, the wide cultural milieu in which human life is lived, and living experience play an important role in helping us to re-present the gospel in our own situation. Although they are ambiguous factors in human life, we cannot reject them as sources for theology because of the dangers that this ambiguity poses. Indeed, the Bible is also an ambiguous factor in theology. Thus, there is no escape from ambiguity; we must be willing to sin boldly and believe more boldly still.

One way to try to deal with the ambiguity of the theological enterprise is to use criteria for guiding theological reflection and evaluating its results. A central criterion is provided by the material norm of theology. Such a norm consists of the central thrust of the biblical witness, as this emerges out of the intersection of church and biblical text. It is necessary to keep in mind that any material norm is not eternal and does not encompass the full richness of the Christian faith. Hence theology must be in dialogue with other perspectives within the biblical text and among the various Christian traditions. The nature of this norm and the way in which it is brought to bear on one's context are also shaped by other criteria that are concerned about the adequacy of one's theology to the situation. In this context, Kaufman's criteria of presence, humanization, and relativization have a role to play. However, their contribution is shaped by the fact that they are also dependent on the perspective of one's faith and have no independent status. Thus, although these criteria cannot act as independent guides to the construction of concepts of God and the world, in the manner envisioned by Kaufman, they can guide and correct theological interpretations of the Christian faith.

Finally, theology's intellectual activity inevitably involves it in some apologetic concerns. Given the nature of the task of exhibiting the reasonableness of faith, theology should not try to provide a general apologetic for all times and situations. Nevertheless, it is possible to present a general description of what is involved in the Christian apologetic enterprise. Central to the enterprise is faith's disclosive and assimilative power. However, because the Christian faith also involves itself in making historical claims and is a complex reality that cannot adequately be dealt with from a single perspective, the apologetic enterprise is multiform, assuming varying forms according to the situation in which a rational examination of the Christian faith is needed.

It is clear, then, that theology is not an independent arbiter of the Christian faith. It depends on the existence and form of faith. Still, it can and does reflect critically on that faith in order to introduce greater clarity into faith's understanding and practice and to offer critiques and corrective suggestions where appropriate and necessary. Thus, it performs an essential role—as a servant of faith rather than as its master.

· C O N C L U S I O N ·

Throughout this book I have been stating my agreement with Gordon Kaufman on one essential point: faith and theology are thoroughly imaginative. This is apparently a determinative issue that should lead to widespread agreement on a number of other points. It clearly has not, however, because of a basic disagreement about the nature of the imagination. The present work has been developing the nature of that disagreement. We can now review the major dimensions of that disagreement and briefly note some of the further implications of the position I have articulated.

· Kaufman's Project ·

Kaufman himself locates his work in a historicist framework, a point with which I fundamentally agree. Early on in his work, Kaufman used the historicist understanding of human life to argue for the necessity of some sort of revelatory basis for human life and thought. That is, since we have no direct contact with things in the world and no immediate insight into the truth about life, and since we are constituted by our histories, it is inevitable that we will take some historically given point of departure as the "self-evident" basis for our fundamental orientation toward life. What we choose as such a self-evident point of departure becomes our revelation. For the Christian this point of departure is Jesus Christ and the history leading up to him.

Although he has not given up any of his claim to be operating as a theologian who recognizes the historicist nature of human life, Kaufman has introduced a major shift into his theology. He has decided that the notion of revelation has no place in the basic method of theology. Taking revelation as theology's point of departure, he argues, assumes something that is in need of justification. Moreover, the attempt to start with revelation overlooks the fact that theology is an imaginative enterprise, which means that the concepts with which it works (especially the concepts of God, the human, and the world) are human constructs through and through. That is to say, according to Kaufman theology cannot operate on the basis of a given Word of God that provides us with some insight into the mystery of reality and its transcendent ground. Rather, we build concepts or symbols of God and the world in order to provide a framework for life. This framework is intended to humanize life and to relativize our ideas and projects. The drive to humanize is important because human life is something that becomes human through our concrete action in history, so that we must construct a human and humane world. Relativization is necessary because we have a tendency to absolutize our ideas and projects and thereby to distort our lives.

Kaufman's argument implicitly rests on an understanding of the imagination as an essentially constructive power. Imagination does not receive and respond—it builds. And in the arena of faith it builds magnificent and exceedingly complex edifices within which human life can live humanly and humanely. Thus, religion and religious traditions have become for Kaufman instruments by which the subject can build a suitable environment. How it is that the subject who is involved in such complex building projects arrives at a determination of what constitutes human and humane forms of life is never clear in Kaufman's program. He seems to believe that we can reach some agreement about these issues on the basis of our experience. Yet he still denies that we have any direct experience of our world. This inconsistency could be resolved by the suggestion that Kaufman, even though he exhibits no awareness of the fact, has found a new "revelatory" center for his thought (using the idea of revelation in the way he defined it in his early thought) and that he assumes that there are many in our time who share this revelatory center. Given this as yet unexpressed assumption, the concepts and symbols of the Christian religion can become building blocks for Kaufman's constructive venture.

However, since Kaufman no longer makes reference to some such revelatory center, there is a point at which he apparently assumes that we can remove ourselves from our history far enough and long enough to construct and reconstruct our world in line with an understanding of humanization whose origin is never clear. At this point he leaves behind his historicist point of view and adopts an essentially instrumentalist approach to human life or, at any rate, to the religious dimension of human life. As a result, he appears to have removed the imagination from the ongoing stream of history (at this one point, anyway) and to have made it the foundation for religious life and thought. Furthermore, he is also led to suppose that theology can precede faith to the degree that theology can dictate to faith the symbols and concepts that faith is to make its own.[1]

• The Nature of Imagination •

In contrast to Kaufman's constructivist understanding of the imagination, I have argued for an understanding of the imagination that places it solidly in the historical nature of human life and thereby regards it as both constructive and receptive. Although he did not appreciate the historical rootedness of the imagination, Kant's treatment of the productive, or transcendental, imagination is helpful. He recognized the fact that the imagination performs an essential work of synthesis, without which human consciousness as we know it would not exist. Furthermore, the imagination is active when we subsume particulars under general categories and when we make generalizations from particulars. As a result, the imagination makes the world meaningful through the generation of forms and patterns through which we understand the world. In short, the imagination is that power through which we take the world and all it contains as possessing a certain meaning.

Mary Warnock defines imagination as the power of "seeing as," citing Ludwig Wittgenstein's discussion of this form of perception as a basis for her own development of Kant's treatment of the imagination. That is, she argues that the imagination provides meaningful forms in terms of which we see the world as having a certain significance. In some cases this form may be a mental image, but in many cases it is not. It may, for example, be a structure of ideas to which we cannot attach a particular picture. Or, as in the case of music, it could be a structure of sounds instead of a visual or intellectual structure. The claim that these forms are the means through which we understand the world rests on the conviction that our physical world does not possess a self-evident meaning that we can directly apprehend. Rather, all meaningful experience is interpreted experience, which means that even the perception of familiar parts of our environment is an imaginative act.

Warnock's understanding comes very close to that of Paul Ricoeur, who also associates the imagination with the power of "seeing as." Ricoeur notes that this power links imagination to metaphoric process, since

---

[1]Of course, as I have argued above, in fact the real faith of Kaufman apparently does not reside in these symbols and concepts that are instruments for the expression of a deeper and as yet unthematized orientation.

metaphors invite us to see one thing in terms of another. For Ricoeur, the association of imagination with metaphor clearly indicates that the imagination is not merely a constructive power, for metaphors have the power to disclose truths by combining discovery and invention. The association of metaphors and imagination also indicates the locus of imagination's creativity. New or living metaphors generate new insight by bringing together ideas that are generally never related to each other. Such metaphors have the characteristic of surprising or jolting us by suddenly juxtaposing things that we have hitherto taken to be far apart. The result is that, on a literal level of meaning, a metaphor is contradictory, so that the metaphor creates a sense of dissonance that can reach a resolution only when we move to a figurative understanding of the metaphor. As a result, we discover similarities between the two terms of the metaphor, while the differences between them are preserved. This similarity in the midst of dissimilarity makes living and enduring metaphors an inexhaustible source of new insight. They create new understanding by bringing together dissimilar things, thereby giving us a fresh, unfamiliar view of things. That is to say, metaphors disclose new meanings and new truths. Furthermore, we can never be sure how far metaphors can be pressed, that is, how much they will show us. Thus, every paraphrase of a metaphor can bring out only a part of the metaphor's meaning. Other paraphrases may also be possible and just as legitimate.

Since imagination, too, is a power of "seeing as," creative imagination can be understood as a metaphoric process generating new insight through novel combinations and new extensions of meaningful forms. That is, creativity arises through the bringing together of ideas, experiences, things, and so forth that are usually not associated with each other, that are usually thought to be dissimilar.

The imagination connects us to things in more than just an intellectual way. Ricoeur explores the implications of this fact by connecting metaphors and feeling. The world around us is not merely a realm of objects that are separated from us. It is the context, the network of relationships, within which we live and through which we become the persons we are. We have a history with the world, a history mediated through the forms by which we understand the world. The full significance of this comes to light when we think of feelings not primarily as personal emotions, such as inner experiences of joy or fear, but as our way of belonging to and participating in the world. That is to say, feelings are not just interior experiences; they shape the way we are intimately connected to persons and things around us. Now, when we understand feelings as the shape of our involvement in the world, it becomes apparent that they disclose possible ways of living in the world. In this sense of the word, feelings are not our subjective, private possessions. Rather, they have to do with the way in which we are related to the world and the way in which the world is related to us. Thus, the forms through which we understand the world, and which carry the feelings that intimately connect us to the world, are able to disclose possible ways of participating in the world.

This ability is especially evident in the higher-level forms, or symbols, through which we are related to the world. For example, the symbol of the family carries a number of feelings. These feelings disclose a possible way of belonging to and participating in a particular group. Moreover, this symbol can be applied to other groups besides one's immediate kin, and in this way it can suggest certain ways of being connected to these other groups. In the Christian faith, the symbol of the Kingdom of God also has this power. It refers, in the first place, to what God has done and will do in the world to achieve the divine purpose. It is an affirmation that God's rule will ultimately be victorious. Yet it also conveys certain modes of participation in the world that correspond to God's act. And it does so at a level that relates to our prereflective and affective involvement in the world, as well as to our rational involvement. When it seizes our imagination, then, it profoundly shapes even the most intimate dimensions of our relation to the world. This power to make a claim on our lives is rooted in the power of the imagination to make use of forms that enable us to belong to and participate in the world.

The imagination's involvement in our understanding of the world through its power of metaphoric invention and discovery is an important insight. However, the linking of metaphor and imagination to the image of "seeing as" tends to focus them too much on the subject's act of intellectual apprehension. For this reason, I prefer to define imagination as the power of "taking as," underscoring the element of individual and communal praxis in imagination.

Within the historicist framework developed in this work, it should be clear that the imagination's power of "taking as" both includes and transcends the individual's subjectivity. This dimension of the imagination can be articulated by employing Gadamer's model of play, for in play the individual is engaged in a to and fro movement that shapes the subjectivity of the participants. When we relate this model to our involvement in history, it becomes evident that the imagination is embedded in a history that shapes it profoundly. Our commerce with the world takes place through operations and forms of thought given to us by our culture. Whether we are aware of it or not, then, life is lived in a stream of tradition that is passed on from generation to generation, a transmission that takes place largely apart from our conscious awareness.[2]

Now this embeddedness in tradition at times leads to a thoughtless repetition of the past, in which case the imagination is present but not in a creative way. When we act or think in a certain way only because that is the way it has always been done, the imagination has fossilized, and we are caught in traditionalism. However, when tradition enlivens the imagination through providing forms by which we are enabled to live with insight, the imagination creatively appropriates the past for the sake of the present. Hence we can live not as slaves to the past but as heirs to the wisdom, truth, and power that the past bequeaths to life in the present. In terms of Gadamer's model of play, this creative dimension of imagination can be understood as an ever-new re-presentation of the perduring form of a structure of play. On the one hand, the play is new and unique in that it is a re-presentation in a particular time and place. On the other hand, it is the same play, since it re-presents a continuing structure, that is, the tradition(s) out of which new insight has been generated. To be sure, the result of this re-presentation can be, and often is, growth and change in a tradition. The point here is that this development belongs to the nature of tradition and does not somehow take us outside of tradition.

If the past gives shape to the imagination in a constitutive way, Kaufman's understanding of the imagination as an essentially constructive power, by which we step outside of our social and historical context far enough and long enough to reconstruct it to our liking, is too one-sided. Such a view does not adequately appreciate the degree to which the imagination is at play within the stream of tradition. It is not a power that enables us to jump out of our history.

This is not to say that we are trapped in a tradition and a way of looking at things. A living tradition is a process—that is, an ever-new interpretation and appropriation of the past— and never a mere product. Thus, our imaginative involvement in a tradition results in its growth and change as it is actualized within the ongoing movement of history, just as every new actualization of play is a transformation into a new being of the enduring structure of play. That is to say, the formation of our imagination by a tradition does not mean—it cannot mean—making our world over into an earlier one. Rather, the formation of the imagination is a result of the merging of our horizon with the horizon of the tradition. As a result,

---

[2]As this stress on transmission indicates, tradition refers not only to what is handed down but also to the process of handing down.

our horizon is broadened rather than absorbed into the horizon of the past. To put it in terms used above, the fusion of our horizon with another horizon is the bringing together of two dissimilar realities in such a way that their surprising similarities are revealed and new insight emerges.

The concept of a fusion of horizons also introduces experience as an important element in this whole process. It in no way tries to reintroduce the discredited notion of raw, unmediated experience. Rather, it leads to a consideration of the experience that a tradition and its language disclose as possible forms of human life in the world. Furthermore, the interplay of past and present horizons opens the possibility of new insight and hence new experience. And because this interplay takes place within a context that is not just our projection and is not amenable to whatever we might arbitrarily wish to make of it, this reciprocity between tradition and experience can lead to discoveries that either make the tradition appear inadequate or tend to confirm the disclosive power of the tradition. This disclosive power leads one to affirm that a tradition reveals the true nature of life and therefore bears authority.

• Imagination and Faith •

If the imagination is involved in all areas of life, it is certainly involved in faith. Indeed, it has a particularly important role to play in the sphere of faith, since faith has to do with the idea of the whole of reality, a whole that we never experience as such. Now there is an important difference between our dealings with parts of our world and our dealings with the ultimate context within which everything is placed. In the former case, what we experience is related to other parts of our world and to more encompassing frameworks of meaning, whereas in the latter case we have to do with something that cannot be referred to other realities of the same order or to more encompassing realities. Because of this difference, the imagination has a somewhat different, though not wholly unique, role to play in the sphere of faith than it has in other spheres of life. Since we cannot explain the nature of the whole by referring to its larger context, we must deal with it by drawing on symbols and ideas that are rooted in our experience of parts of our world. Thus, we understand the whole by referring to the parts that have their place within it and ultimately understand the parts in terms of the whole within which they find their fullest meaning.

Christian faith comes to an understanding of the ultimate context of life through the person of Jesus of Nazareth. In particular, it is shaped by the conviction that in him God has effected a reconciliation between the estranged world and Godself. Hence Christian faith is marked by trust in this act of reconciliation and therefore by a commitment of the self to the God who is present in Jesus the Christ. This faith emerges out of a tradition and feeds back into it. That is, it results from the expression of faith by others and itself comes to expression. It is faith in a God who brings life from the dead, and it is therefore characterized by a trust and hope that thoroughly determine the believer's existence. Such a faith is ill suited to the acceptance of humanly constructed and reconstructed concepts by which we provide ourselves with an ultimate framework for life.

The experience of coming to faith is rooted not in one's more or less autonomous efforts to provide an overall framework of meaning for life but in the fact that the Christian tradition engages and leads one's imagination. By comparing the biblical text to poetic texts, Paul Ricoeur has been able to shed some light on this process. Like fictional texts, the biblical text appeals to the imagination by proposing a possible world in which we could live and realize our inherent possibilities. The Bible presents this world in a multifaceted manner through its various genres. Since there is an intimate and indissoluble connection between the text's genres and the mode of revelation mediated through them, revelation is thus a multivalent reality that should not be reduced to the mode connected to any one genre in the Bible. Nonetheless, the various modes of revelation do have an analogical bond through their mutual similarity to the prophetic mode of discourse and its corresponding mode of revelation: that is, one person speaking in the name of another. On the other hand, among the various genres narrative has priority, since it recounts the history that founds the community of faith. As a result, the other genres are dependent on narrative to provide the context in which they are operative. Narrative structures the temporality of the community of faith, and hence of the individuals within the community, and determines and shapes the symbols and metaphors guiding the community's understanding.

The resemblance between poetic texts and the Bible should not lead to an identification of one with the other. On the contrary, there are several important respects in which the Bible differs from poetic texts in general. Ricoeur notes two of them: the biblical texts have God as their ultimate referent, and they contain testimony to the traces of God in history. Another significant difference is that the Bible functions within a community that has been shaped by the biblical witness and that itself provides a witness to the Christian faith through the texture of its life and language. Thus, the Bible functions as an authority for the Christian because of its power to continue to nurture and guide the life of the community of faith. In other words, because of the biblical text's disclosive power, which comes to expression in the community of faith, the imagination of the Christian is formed by the biblical imagination.

The shaping of the Christian's imagination by the Bible does not mean playing "ancient Bible land" by trying to remake our world into the biblical world. By the same token, it also does not mean playing sixteenth-century Protestant reformer, nineteenth-century liberal, or early twentieth-century neoorthodox. Any attempt to repeat some earlier, "more pristine" form of the Christian faith overlooks the creative, metaphoric nature of the shaping of the imagination. Again, the formation of one's imagination by the biblical text should be seen in terms of a fusion of horizons, not an absorption of our horizon into a past horizon.

Since the church seeks to be faithful to the biblical witness, the Bible has a priority in this fusion of horizons. Again, this priority does not take the form of a repetition of the biblical world. Rather, when the biblical witness sheds light on our present situation, the present situation also contributes to our understanding of the significance of the biblical witness. Thus, both horizons contribute significantly to our imagination and our understanding. In other words, we discover the significance of the tradition only within specific situations. This interaction gives rise to a history of interpretation of the Bible; and as long as this history of interpretation continues, it constitutes a living tradition within which people come to their own understanding. Tradition, then, shapes the imagination and is, in turn, shaped by the imagination. Christian faith expresses itself through living, dynamic traditions, always changing as faith is re-presented.

• Imagination and Theology •

The fact that faith arises out of a fusion of horizons has important implications for theology, understood in this context as an effort to provide conceptual clarity for the life of faith, thereby introducing some intellectual rigor to faith, and to critique the practices and beliefs (including the traditions that undergird them) of the community of faith. The model of the fusion of horizons also has some significant implications for the sources of theology. Since the Christian faith is dependent on the biblical witness, the Bible is obviously a source without parallel. Nevertheless, the believer's understanding of the Bible is mediated through Christian history and through the general culture. An explicit awareness of these factors in the shaping of faith's imagination and understanding leads to a recognition that they, too, can and must operate as sources for theology. Moreover, the fact that horizons include the living experience of people dwelling within them means that experience, too, acts as a source for theology.

Theology is interested not only in the fact that the believer's understanding emerges out of a fusion of horizons but also in the question of whether this understanding is an authentic re-presentation of the Christian faith. Although there is no neutral vantage point from which one can decide this issue, there are guides that theology can use. In the first place, theology makes such judgments in light of a material norm, or working canon, that guides our understanding of the central meaning of the biblical testimony. This norm, too, emerges out of the fusion of horizons between community and text, yet it provides a sense of the central perspective from which things can be judged. In addition to a material norm, theology works with criteria that guide its judgment of an interpretation's adequacy to the situation. The criteria that Kaufman treats as guides for constructing concepts of the world and God—humanization, relativization, and presence—find a more adequate role here. Again, within the framework I have been describing, these criteria are not independent of the perspective of Christian faith. Instead, they grow out of and are shaped by faith and, in turn, can help to judge and guide the development of faith's understanding.

Although the work of theology depends on the prior imaginative construal of faith, this does not mean that theology itself is not an imaginative enterprise. On the contrary, its view of how the sources impinge on the development of faith's understanding and its ability to be attuned to the significant questions in the interplay between the horizon of the Christian tradition and the horizon of one's situation require a healthy and creative imagination. Thus, the theological imagination arises out of, and is determined in many respects by, the imaginative grasp of faith, yet the theological imagination also has its own necessary role to play.

Within the framework developed here, faith is not simply judged by its pragmatic power to achieve the goals we have set for ourselves. Still, the pragmatic power of faith is part of the way in which one deals with the question of truth, for the ability of the Christian faith to disclose truths about our world and our selves that prove themselves concretely in our lives helps to show the justifiability of one's faith. An essential difference between this approach and a purely pragmatic one is that it does not assume that we have made our own independent decisions about the goals we wish to reach. Instead, the perspective of faith discloses the deepest truths about our lives and therefore itself determines these goals. As the fittingness of these goals becomes evident, so does the power of faith. Christian theology must also deal with other questions when it is involved in issues related to the reasonableness of Christian faith. For example, it must treat questions about the coherence of faith's affirmations and about historical events that it makes central to its claims (especially with respect to Jesus of Nazareth). Thus, the apologetic enterprise is multiple and dependent on the nature of the questions that arise in a particular situation. In this sense, it is an inevitably ad hoc enterprise.

My contention has not been that it is possible to prove that Christian faith and theology are based on a genuine revelation from God. It is not necessary to prove this assertion in order to argue that Kaufman's view of theology is inadequate and that the approach suggested here is more adequate to the imaginative character of faith and theology. My argument has been developed throughout this work, negatively in chapter 1 and positively in chapters 2 through 5. The central point that I have stressed is that a recognition of the historical nature of human life, and therefore of the imagination, leads to a significant modification of the sort of constructivist program suggested by Kaufman. Whether one wishes to or not, one will begin from and be profoundly shaped by the historical tradition out of which one lives. Only by finding a new tradition within which to stand can Kaufman turn to Christian symbols and concepts and treat them as if they were essentially building blocks for him to reshape and rearrange in an essentially reconstructive effort. If this is in fact what he has done, he could conceivably justify such a move. However, it is necessary to recognize what has happened and to deal explicitly and honestly with the historically contingent and imaginative character of the new tradition to which he now belongs. Such a recognition would call for a modification of the notion that humanization could guide the imaginative construction of images of the human, the world, and God, since even our assessment of humanization is too much shaped by the imagination to make it a fixed standard of judgment.

Such considerations do not mean that one must be a Christian. They do indicate, however, that Christian theology should not presume to be giving Christian faith the narratives, symbols, and metaphors out of which it lives. Rather, when one's imagination is engaged and led by the biblical witness and its effective-history, faith precedes theology, so that the latter is a second-order reflection on the imaginative construal of faith.

• Other Implications •

This summary restatement of my argument has already touched on some of the important implications of the imaginative nature of faith. Here I briefly deal more explicitly with these implications.

First, it is perhaps not too redundant to reiterate that Christian faith and theological reflection are inevitably contextual. I do not mean that they should become contextual; to the degree that they are one's own and are not merely a repetition of something imposed from without, they already are contextual, whether or not we are aware of the fact. Since our imaginative faith is embedded in and shaped by the context in which we and the church as a whole live, we are not in a position to choose in this matter. On the other hand, we are in a position to try to become more aware of our context and the way in which we are related to it. Thus, the contextual nature of faith and theology is both an inevitable fact and a demand. We are called to become aware of our context in order to be faithful witnesses within it. This is a challenge that we never fully meet, since our context is broader, deeper, and more a part of ourselves than we can ever completely comprehend. Nevertheless, we can make progress in bringing the context to light and in exploring its relationship to Christian faith.

Living as faithful witnesses within a specific context involves two forms of responsibility. First, it involves responsibility to the biblical message. This responsibility is different from responsibility to the situation in that it includes a commitment to be shaped by the form and content of the message. Here the ongoing Christian traditions play an important role, for they suggest new configurations, latent meanings, and potential extensions and applications of the biblical witness, thereby stimulating our imagination and insight. Some traditions (including some biblical traditions) may indeed also distort the central truths and insights of the biblical message, making necessary a critical appraisal of the various traditions. Still, tradition broadens the horizon within which we seek to understand the meaning of the Christian faith for our time and place. Second, the Christian theologian is responsible to the context. This is not to say that he or she is bound to think as others think or to do as they do. In some cases it may mean exactly the contrary. Yet the theologian cannot escape the questions, thought forms, and concerns of the situation and must be responsible through attention to the situation's demands and challenges. Furthermore, to the degree that present understanding and insight have proven compelling, they must be brought into play as the theologian reflects on the meaning of the Christian faith.

The possibility of distortion suggests a second implication of this approach to faith and theology: the need for a critique of past and present horizons. Such a critique clearly cannot be exercised from a position outside of the framework of tradition. But within that framework some room for critique is possible, for the understanding provided by the fusion of horizons helps to generate criteria that can be used in a critical appraisal of Christian tradition, one's situation, and the Bible itself. That is to say, the re-presentation of the Christian faith, which continually opens us to certain forms of experience that, in turn, have their impact on and help to shape that re-presentation and the understanding it shapes and presents, gives rise to perspectives that can be a basis for critique. This development has occurred, for example, in the case of the critique of Christian traditions by Christian feminists. The fusion of contemporary horizons with the horizon of the Christian tradition, as this fusion has been partially shaped by the experience of women and has illumined that experience, has led to a critique of the patriarchalism of Christian traditions in the name of a more authentic understanding of the Christian faith.[3]

A third implication is rooted in the feeling dimension of the imagination. If the term *feeling* refers to a certain way of belonging to and participating in the world, the work of the imagination cannot be confined to the way we think. It also has to do with experience and action. In fact, the imaginative interpretation of faith is an interpretation that is often expressed in actions and modes of belonging before it is expressed in a reflective, intellectual manner. The work of imagination, then, frequently takes the concrete shape of lived interpretation, with the result that the understanding of faith and its conceptual thematization in theology are shaped in some decisive ways by praxis.

Finally, the fact that the imagination is given form and substance through our place in society and history and through our involvement in tradition means that the understanding of faith is dependent on a community of faith. Therefore, the understanding of faith grows out of some form of conversation with others, and its nurture and growth depend on a continuation of this conversation. Through dialogue our faith and our insight into its meaning are deepened and broadened. This is true not only of dialogue within a tradition but also of dialogue between people belonging to different traditions. For, since the metaphoric richness of faith defies being captured by any one articulation, so that each perspective is always partial, ecumenical dialogue serves the enrichment of our faith. We need conversation with other perspectives in order to be confronted with different possibilities of understanding and to be constantly reminded of the fact that Christian faith contains more than any single tradition, or all traditions together, can articulate and actualize. Dialogue therefore forces us to think afresh, to keep our imaginations creatively alive, and to stretch the boundaries of our understanding and our tradition.

For those concerned about the unity of the church and of humankind as a whole, dialogue has another important value: the promotion of greater understanding among adherents of different traditions. This goal may seem at odds with that of deepening the understanding of one's own tra-

---

[3]Of course, not all feminist critiques come from within a Christian tradition. However, the point I am making has to do with critiques offered by those who maintain an explicitly Christian orientation.

dition. However, although we often experience tensions between commitment to the particularity of a tradition and commitment to ecumenism, these two orientations should not be seen as mutually exclusive alternatives. In fact they belong together. If we are not narrow or sectarian in spirit, greater clarity about our faith, as understood from within a particular tradition, can contribute to ecumenical dialogue. For it allows one to enter such dialogue with a greater sense of one's Christian identity, which enables one to contribute one's own perspective in a more articulate way. Common and divergent points of view thereby become clearer, and progress is made possible.

Progress in such matters cannot be defined merely in terms of creating a framework that brings people closer together. It must also be defined in terms of greater insight into a reality that transcends us all, for the believer lives in the trust that the language of faith, even though it is thoroughly human and all too inadequate, has its source not only in human powers of construction but in a reality that brings itself to expression in faith's confessions and reflection. "The believer experiences the living God as the source which enables and makes possible such language. Thus however human it may be, this language is not an autonomous human initiative, but derives from an authority and mandate, by virtue of reality. Man is not master of reality, but only its steward."[4] Thus, the ecumenical conversation is engaged in serious questions with far-reaching implications. We cannot, then, afford to take ecumenical conversation lightly. Neither can we allow our proper passion to lead us to absolutize our understanding and to confuse that understanding with the gospel itself. An appreciation of the significance of the imaginative venture of faith encourages us to be passionately involved, for the issues deserve our passion. At the same time, an awareness of the imaginative richness of faith will keep us from assuming that we have captured the truth, so that we will be able to enter the conversation with humility and a willingness to listen to see what we may learn.

---

[4]Edward Schillebeeckx, *Christ: The Experience of Jesus as Lord,* trans. John Bowden (New York: Crossroad, 1981) 56.

·INDEX·